# BY GOD'S Design

# Praise for *By God's Design*

"STALWART" IS A WORD WE shouldn't use lightly, but what better term describes Alan Medinger? For decades he was a consistent voice of integrity, and for many of us, a reliable co-laborer and friend. Reading Judith Hartzell's book had me laughing and crying, remembering the man she's so well profiled. Anyone interested in ministry to the same-sex attracted, or in the rigors of ministry in general, will enjoy this much-needed account of a big hearted pioneer.

-Joe Dallas,
Founder of Genesis Biblical Solutions, Author of *When Homosexuality Hits Home* and *The Gay Gospel? How Pro-Gay Advocates Misread the Bible*

ALAN MEDINGER'S LIFE STORY NEEDS to be remembered simply because so many today are frantically trying to forget. His story remains a billboard of the power of Jesus to change a life. Many thanks to Judith Hartzell for writing a life history full of grace and truth.

- Peter Hubbard,
Teaching pastor at North Hills Community Church, Author of *Love Into Light: The Gospel, the Homosexual and the Church*

WHEN ASKED TO READ "BY God's Design" and offer my comments, I intended to read only a chapter daily as a part of my devotions. The book was so interesting that I often read two or three chapters, even when it put me behind on the rest of my day. Judith Hartzell recounts, with documentation, the planning by gay activists for "normalization" of homosexuality and how it shifted the culture of our country, juxtaposed with the early years and development of ministries to those same-sex attracted. Although both accounts are useful, the encouraging biography of Alan and Willa Medinger gives the book vitality: putting a human face on homosexual attraction and God's power to cleanse and heal. I know of no family that better typifies the growth process for manhood, how God can heal a wounded spouse and how God uses those healed to bring healing to so many others. Alan and Willa's conversion and multi-year struggles to live out God's design in their lives provides hope for all of us who struggle with life-dominating issues. These two finished well.

—Reid Lehman,
President/CEO of Miracle Hill Ministries,
Author of *God Wears His Own Watch*

FOR ANYONE WHO CARES FOR the LGBT community, this is a must read. Alan's story of transformation and his decades of ministry to the sexually broken gives him unique authority to share the power available in the gospel of Jesus. This book is an important addition to the current conversation about homosexuality: Jesus doesn't just accept and forgive people, he transforms them.

—Ron Citlau,
Senior Pastor of Calvary Church, IL, Author of *Compassion without Compromise: How to love our gay friends and keep the truth*

I AM SO THRILLED TO see the Medingers' story in print. Alan's testimony of transformation is amazing and genuine. I worked alongside him in ministry for years, and his Christian testimony was solid and enduring.

—Bob Davies,
Past president of Exodus International,
Co-author of *Coming Out of Homosexuality* with Lori Rentzel and of *Someone I Love Is Gay* with Anita Worthen

WILLA AND ALAN MEDINGER WERE an inspiration of hope and encouragement to me in the beginning formation of Whosoever Will Ministry. Their quiet, patient encouragement in allowing God to lead by His Spirit is something I'll always treasure. We were taught to listen to God for ourselves, and to follow His direction.

—Penny Dalton,
Co-founder Whosoever Will Ministry

I AM EXCITED THAT THE life and work of Alan and Willa Medinger have been saved for history. I can think of few better than Judy Hartzell to catalogue their lives. This man, this couple, meant so much to so many. He poured into my life and helped shape me as a man and as a leader. His book *Growth Into Manhood* helped start me on my journey of growing as a man. At his death, I drove eleven hours with my son to his funeral, telling my son it was important to respect this man of honor with our attendance.

—McKrae Game,
President, Hope for Wholeness

ALAN AND WILLA MEDINGER PROVIDED inspiration and stability, as well as love and laughter, to generations of men and women seeking hope and healing. Judith Hartzell has captured the essence and beauty of their presence in all of our lives. Thank you, Judith, for such a vulnerable telling of the life story of our beloved friends and valued mentors. This book is a must have for all who knew the Medingers, as well as for those who desire to know what God can do in the area of same-sex attraction with lives that are fully surrendered to Him (and to the vital experience of the authority of scripture). Judith's account is not all "rosy" but it is true in its recounting of the pain, the beauty, and the ultimate powerful transformation of Alan and Willa as individuals and of their marriage!

—Jeanie Smith,
Director of Set Free Ministry

IT'S WONDERFUL THAT MANY WILL have the opportunity to read about Alan and Willa and the work they have done as pioneers of the ex-gay movement. Alan was true to who he was when speaking to a group, writing a book or just sharing with friends. He was all about shining a light on the path for other men to follow, men who were trapped in the bondage of the homosexual life. Willa was his colorful life companion who had the same burden for wives of those men. We miss you dear friends and thank Judith for her tireless journey in making this book available to all.

—Anita Worthen,
Co-author of *Someone I Love Is Gay*

I AM SO GRATEFUL THAT the lives of these two remarkable people will be remembered through the pages of this book. They were pioneers in a difficult and often unrewarding work that brought new life to so many people. Both were always honest and open about their journey through life, and this openness brought the right balance between hope and the reality that nothing seems to be easy in this life. Alan was a bright light lighting the path to other men trapped in the bondage of homosexuality. The love Alan and Willa shared for each other was a true love story. Willa was always there for Alan, his encourager and his defense, and his burden was her burden.

—Frank Worthen,
Founder and Director of Love in Action in California and of New Hope Ministries; Author of *This Way Out* and *Destiny Bridge,* Co-founder of Exodus International and past president of Exodus International

# By God's Design

## Overcoming Same-Sex Attractions -A True Story-

Judith Hartzell

Ambassador International
Greenville, South Carolina & Belfast, Northern Ireland
www.ambassador-international.com

# By God's Design

Overcoming Same Sex Attractions -A True Story-



ISBN: 978-1-62020-519-8
eISBN:978-1-62020-426-9



eBook Conversion by Anna Riebe Raats
Author Photo by Tony Moore

AMBASSADOR INTERNATIONAL
Emerald House
427 Wade Hampton Blvd.
Greenville, SC 29609, USA
www.ambassador-international.com

AMBASSADOR BOOKS
The Mount
2 Woodstock Link
Belfast, BT6 8DD, Northern Ireland, UK
www.ambassadormedia.co.uk

*The colophon is a trademark of Ambassador*

*Like the woman who washed Jesus' feet with her tears,*
*he loved much because he was forgiven much.*

# Contents

# Introduction

DO YOU WANT TO LOVE gay people but also live and speak according to Bible truth? Did the closing of Exodus International in the summer of 2013 confuse you about how to minister to people struggling with unwanted attractions?

Bottom line: if teens find out they are same-sex attracted (SSA), should they accept what the world says—that this is who they are and happiness depends on same-sex partners? Or is the best hope for SSA Christians that they resist temptation and suffer with lifelong illicit attractions?

Here is the story of one man who discovered a better way. For him, following Jesus brought change to his beliefs, behavior, and attractions. He was convinced that "if it could happen to me, it could happen to anyone."

Not everyone experiences what Alan Medinger did, but you should know why he thought they could. Then you can more intelligently form wise opinions. This side of the discussion has been suppressed or ridiculed by gay activists, but it is true and relevant.

CHAPTER 1:

# The Story of a Man

*Every age has its own outlook. It is specially good at seeing certain truths and specially liable to make certain mistakes. We all, therefore, need the books that will correct the characteristic mistakes of our own period. And that means the old books.*

~ C.S. Lewis[1]

IF A CHILD ENTERING PUBERTY experiences unwanted same-sex attractions, is this a life sentence? Must he or she endure that same temptation and emotional torture forever or else give in to it?

Many—perhaps most—people today think it impossible to change sexual attractions, and therefore they say to same-sex-attracted persons, "accept who you are." From Alan Medinger's perspective, these people are wrong. Our true identity is in Christ, he believed, and Christ created our sexuality for use as He intends. He is able to change His children. As they are discipled in His Word, He will help them live abundant lives as the men and women He designed them to be.

Who is Alan Medinger, and why should his opinions matter to Bible-believing Christians? He is a man born in 1936, before the Christian worldview became obsolete in American culture and even before the word *gay* came into use. Because he was born with a male body, he believed, as a child, that God intended him to grow up to be a heterosexual man, and when in puberty he experienced unwanted same-sex attractions, he didn't change his mind. They were aberrations, he thought, so he stepped into the world he wished to inhabit.

He graduated from Johns Hopkins University, married his best friend (Willa), and became a successful accountant with a large corporation. But after five years of marriage, impelled by various stresses, he sought release through homosexual fantasy and, eventually, acts.

Alan's opinions would be inconsequential had his life ended then, which it nearly did. Instead, he encountered Christ at a prayer meeting, surrendered his life to Him, was born again, and experienced miracles. Christ took away his same-sex attractions[2] and set him free to love. In profound gratitude, Alan stepped into another life. He dedicated himself to Jesus. Empowered by prayer, he restored his marriage and with his wife reared three godly children. In 1979 Alan established a ministry, Regeneration, and he led it more than thirty years. It remains one of the oldest and most successful redemptive ministries to SSA people in the world. Through Alan's life and writings, thousands have learned to follow Christ. In so doing, they have gone on to either happy marriages with persons of the opposite gender or fulfilled single lives.

For thirty-five years, Alan studied same-sex attraction. For twenty-five years, he wrote about it. When he said choosing a homosexual identity is choosing a lesser life than the one Jesus designs for a person, he knew what he was talking about.

Do Alan's ideas have anything to say to us in this moral climate? Should we read them? Yes, if we follow C. S. Lewis's advice about how to find truth. Lewis considered it essential for people to balance their reading of new ideas with reading old ones. He warns against "the dangers of an exclusive contemporary diet," which, he wrote, "has to be tested against the great body of Christian thought down the ages."

Today our culture shares certain assumptions about sexuality. One "truth" many of us accept is the idea that persons experiencing same-sex attraction deserve special civil rights protection because of their orientation. Another is the belief that sexual activity is necessary for a full and happy life, and that the concept of family does not require both a mother and a father. Many of us believe that marriage can take

Most of our assumptions are WRONG & lead us to DEATH.

place between persons of the same gender. These ideas are relatively new. Will they endure the scrutiny of future generations?

Lewis advises wisdom-seekers to consider different perspectives. "None of us can fully escape this blindness [of contemporary thought]," he says, "but we shall certainly increase it, and weaken our guard against it, if we read only modern books. Where they are true, they will give us truths that we half knew already. Where they are false, they will aggravate the error with which we are already dangerously ill. The only palliative is to keep the clean sea breeze of the centuries blowing through our minds, and this can be done only by reading old books."

Can someone born in 1936 be considered the author of an old book? Yes, if the subject is human homosexuality. We live today in a different age from the 1950s, when Alan reached adulthood. Since the 1960s, when a sexual revolution began, and especially since the 1970s, when gay rights for the first time were vigorously advanced in this country, the pace of cultural change has been rapid and relentless. Are we drawing closer to a true perspective on sexuality than ever before? Before concluding, let us look at the life and teachings of a wise man from an earlier age.

This book presents Alan's discoveries about sexuality, showing how life events affected his philosophy and writings. We follow him from his lowest point—sunk in a whirlpool of SSA activity that soon would have destroyed his marriage, his prestigious and profitable career, and even his life—to a supremely content old age. What he learned along the way about homosexuality, how it occurs and how it changes in a person's life, can teach us a truer view of this phenomenon. He observed late in life that everything he learned as a novice Regeneration leader proved to be true. His beliefs were based on the Bible, unlike shifting worldly beliefs, and so they were "the same yesterday, today, and forever."

CHAPTER 2:

# The Story of a Marriage: Can It Be Saved?

*I felt powerless to stop [what I was doing]. Gradually sinking into a fatalistic attitude, I saw my life as being on a downward spiral that eventually would cost me my family, my job, maybe even my life, and there was nothing I could do about it.*

~ Alan Medinger[1]

WILLA ASKED HERSELF—IS THERE ANY way out of this marriage trap? Alan seemed worse each night—more drunken and ashamed. And when he came home, too late to put the girls to bed and hear their prayers, he reeked of secret sin. She was doing all she could to be a good wife. Even in his most wretched moments, she tried to encourage him. "You're a good man," she said firmly. "A good husband and a good father."

It wasn't true anymore, but in 1974 after fourteen years of marriage, she said it anyway. What else could she do? Willa had done all she knew to make Alan happy. And how did he repay her? By constantly criticizing her in front of their daughters, Laura and Beth. They were impressionable girls growing into young women, eleven and ten years old. Surely he was wounding them too. And what had happened to romance? She couldn't recall the last time they had made love.

Willa knew if she asked some of her friends what to do—which she would never do, because she could take care of this herself—they would say, "Divorce him." But she would never divorce Alan. Standing

at the altar, they had promised each other before God "to have and to hold from this day forward, for better or for worse, for richer or for poorer, in sickness and in health, to love and to cherish until death do us part."

And they had meant it. Everybody they respected considered wedding vows sacred. Willa's father, F. Murray Benson, an admired attorney in Baltimore, Maryland, and the law partner of a United States senator, represented a wide variety of clients. As a matter of principle, he never accepted divorce cases. Nor did Willa's older brother Frank, also a lawyer, ever help anyone divorce. No. Breaking a vow one had made before God was unthinkable.

So what *was* Willa to do? She saw no way out—except one. Possibly God could help her, though that seemed unlikely. He wasn't exactly accessible, not somebody she knew well. She and Alan were members of St. Margaret's Episcopal Church. But though she attended every Sunday service and directed the church choir, she hesitated to ask their pastor for help. How could she explain what was happening to Alan when she didn't understand it herself? Besides, everyone in church considered him a model Christian. He was a member of the vestry [the ruling body of a local Episcopal church] and a Sunday school teacher, after all. No, she couldn't embarrass herself and him by talking to their pastor. And she really didn't know how to discuss the situation with God Himself.

---

Alan was even more desperate and confused. By not telling Willa about his attractions to men before their marriage, he had betrayed her—that was plain to him now. But at the time, it had seemed the right thing to do. He married Willa not because he loved her as a husband normally loves a wife, but because he wanted to grow into that kind of love. He had been same-sex attracted since he was twelve.

Back in 1960 when they married, Alan was a good looking, intelligent accountant with excellent prospects. He didn't consider himself a homosexual. He thought of himself as a man, but one whose sexual attractions were toward other men. No concept of a gay lifestyle existed then as an acceptable alternative to his life. He wanted to live what he believed to be a healthy life, including marriage and children, and Willa was the right woman for him. That he knew for sure.

When he married her, Willa was a petite, shapely, funny extrovert who loved music. Ever since fourth grade they had been friends. Alan had watched her develop—through great will power—from an overweight, gap-toothed girl with thick glasses into a beautiful bride, and he remained her friend through all the changes. Even as a homely teen, Willa had always managed to be the center of a crowd of people enjoying themselves. This was one reason Alan chose her. He believed her social skills would be a happy complement to his quiet, somewhat nerdy personality. And he always enjoyed Willa's wit and sparkle.

What made Alan think he could have a normal family life with Willa, knowing his past sexual desires had been for men? The reasons are complex, but many resulted from the culture of the times, very different from our own.

Alan and Willa married in 1960, the year John F. Kennedy was elected president by a nation still buoyant and optimistic about its future, a nation that had pulled together to defeat evil regimes in Germany, Italy, and Japan—a nation sure of itself. The word gay was not yet in use, nor, of course, the word ex-gay. Psychiatrists treated people with unwanted same-sex attractions, and sometimes after years of expensive therapy, those attractions abated. Everyone knew some people were drawn to others of their own gender, but homosexuality was considered unnatural. Alan himself disliked having same-sex desires. He truly desired and believed he could live a full life that included marriage and children.

In his book, *Growth into Manhood: Resuming the Journey,* Alan wrote, "I was blessed to grow up in a time and culture in which there was no gay alternative lifestyle out there, calling me into it. . . . It never really occurred to me to bail out of the only world I knew and let homosexuality determine the course of my life. Like so many homosexually oriented men of that time, I would get a job, marry, have children, and cope the best I could."

Since he had avoided sex with men for six years before marriage, Alan hoped he could continue. He was not bisexual, that is, sexually attracted to both men and women. He was never "turned on" by seeing or fantasizing about women. Like many SSA men, he could enjoy the purely physical dimension of having sexual intercourse with a woman. And although he knew he would prefer being with a man, his youthful energy enabled him to make love to Willa in the early years without difficulty. He never fantasized about men when he was with Willa. Somehow, he knew this would be wrong.

Willa hoped for happiness marrying a man she trusted and respected. Alan knew this, and that knowledge tormented him now. He had long ago become so adept at leading a double life—showing one face to the world while covering up secret desires and behaviors—that it didn't even occur to him that he was deceiving his wife when he married her. He had told her nothing of his youthful experiences with boys because he believed those experiences were over, never to return, he hoped. During his undergraduate years at Johns Hopkins University, he enjoyed friendships with the heterosexual men in his fraternity and also in the Naval Reserves, and his same-sex urges decreased. Alan had not acted on these urges for six years before his marriage. He believed Willa need not know about the experiences that shamed him, since he planned to be faithful to her and keep his wedding vows. He hoped to succeed in living the life he desired, that of a married man with a family.

In the first few years, he succeeded. They had not made love before their wedding, but it was not a problem for them in the beginning. Alan explained later, "A young man can have sex easily if he wants to."

The early years, before their babies were born, were happy ones. Of course, living together posed a few difficulties. Willa "couldn't boil water" when they married. Her first meal for him, breakfast, was a disaster—coffee, eggs, toast, bacon, and Pillsbury cinnamon rolls, all burned and ruined, except the coffee. She could plan a menu. After that, she had no idea what she was doing, having grown up in a wealthy home where a hired cook handled all the meals. Because Willa loved to eat, she slowly taught herself to cook by reading recipes on her bus ride home from work each day and then practicing what she read.

In college Alan enjoyed social drinking, but Willa's family avoided intoxicating drinks. "Because my parents were Methodists," Willa said, "drinking was a no-no. My grandparents didn't even use vanilla extract because of its alcohol content."

Two and a half years after they married, Willa discovered—to her own and Alan's delight—that she was expecting a baby. Then in June 1963, when Willa was seven months pregnant, her father died suddenly of a heart attack, just after his sixty-sixth birthday. As Alan thought back to those times, he decided their unhappiness began with Benson's death, a grievous loss to Willa. She hadn't been aware before what a difference her father made in her life.

On August 15, 1963, two months after her father's death, Willa gave birth to a daughter, Laura. Alan, even more than Willa, loved this little one from the beginning.

He was succeeding in business because he was smart and hard working. After coasting through Johns Hopkins University with B's, he had earned the highest score in his home state, Maryland, the year he took his certified public accountant exam. Though not particularly ambitious, Alan was terrified of not living up to others' expectations. His low self-esteem made him dread failure, so he became a hard worker and began getting promotions and added responsibility at work. The stress that came with this success added to his growing unhappiness. At a downward spiral just keeps spirally down like a falling airplane.



Sucked into a sinkhole

church, he became a Sunday school teacher and was elected a member of the vestry, even though he disliked leadership roles. His life slowly grew complicated beyond his comfort level.

Another cause of ongoing stress was Alan's father's chronic depression that had robbed him of his father's care and attention throughout his childhood. Irwin Medinger remained for many years under a psychiatrist's care, taking prescription drugs that seemed only to make him worse. The drugs left his mind clouded. Enid Medinger depended on her younger son for counsel and support, which Alan conscientiously gave. But he felt the emotional drain of this ongoing situation.

Then, exactly twelve months and twelve days after Laura was born, Willa gave birth to another daughter, Elizabeth ("Beth"). She became Willa's especially loved baby, and her birth led to another problem. Willa developed postpartum depression. From that day forward, for more than ten years, Alan's home was a difficult place for him.[2]

Because of escalating tensions at home and at work, Alan began to turn back to homosexual fantasies as de-stressors. As a little boy, he had sought comfort in a make-believe world of heroic men who noticed him and liked him. In adolescence, erotic elements crept into these daydreams. The fantasies from his early years never stopped altogether when he married, but they had subsided. Now, however, they surged back, and Alan entertained them as an escape. He believed at first that he could control them. But the stresses intensified.

NO ONE CAN control sin.

Because of an undiagnosed thyroid problem, Willa was for some years emotionally unstable, fluctuating from depressed to happy and back again. She also fought a losing battle against weight gain. At one time she carried as much as 180 pounds on her five-foot-two frame, in contrast to the 120 pounds she weighed when they married. With all those extra pounds, she had little energy and often felt "down." To lose weight, she followed her doctor's advice and took Dexedrine, an amphetamine. After some months, Willa became addicted. She sneaked extra pills until one day when food and drug regulators banned them

Sin is always there waiting + watching like a mouse trap to crush you-

and she couldn't get more. Though she managed to go on without them, she started overeating again.

Because of Alan's SSA, he had never been sexually aroused by looking at attractive women, so Willa's weight was not an issue for him, except that he cared about her health.

To help counteract his own daily stress, Alan started drinking too much in addition to indulging in his fantasy life. Soon Willa also sought relief from stress, which she too was experiencing, by beginning to drink as well as overeat. She did so reluctantly at first, because it meant breaking a strong Benson family taboo.

Willa's emotional imbalance upset their daughters, adding to Alan's stress as well as her own. Because Laura was Alan's special little girl, when Willa was angry at Alan and couldn't express it to him, she vented on Laura. (Alan couldn't protect Laura, because he didn't discover Willa's mistreatment of her until much later.)

Even in this troubled atmosphere, because she deeply desired to be a good person, Willa introduced an ongoing project that escalated the emotional and physical demands on both her and Alan—taking troubled foster children into their home. The first was Jane*, a twelve-year-old girl who sang in Willa's church choir. Jane's mother was an alcoholic. One evening she drank herself into such a stupor that her frightened daughter called the police for help. That night Jane asked to move into Willa's and Alan's house. She remained with them until she was grown. The blind leading the blind.

Bobby** was the second child Willa and Alan helped. When he was fourteen, he came to St. Margaret's as their church organist. He moved into the Medinger home several years later. Bobby was "pretty obviously homosexual," Willa observed, so she set out to heal him. She had no clue that her husband shared this problem with the boy. Nor did Alan enlighten her.[3] More than a hopeless mess – more like a tunnel with no light at its end + it really never ends.

* Not her real name.
** Not his real name.

To educate herself, Willa read *Homosexuality: A Psychoanalytic Study of Male Homosexuals*, published in 1962 as a rebuttal of the 1948 study by Alfred Kinsey, *Sexual Behavior in the Human Male*. Dr. Irving Bieber, a psychoanalyst, led the research team of nine that wrote the 1962 book. For many years he had successfully treated men who wished to diminish their same-sex attractions. Based on a nine-year study of 106 men, Dr. Bieber and the other researchers concluded that they all suffered from the same family deficit—a relationship with parents that involved a dominant mother and disaffected father. Dr. Bieber believed homosexuality was a curable condition.

From her reading, Willa decided Bobby needed heterosexual male friends. She designed an area for young people in her basement, installing black lights, glowing posters, and a piano painted in fluorescent colors. Then she invited motorcycle gang members to her house, thinking their masculinity might rub off on Bobby. It didn't work. Bobby got along fine with the young men, but their heterosexuality had no effect on his sexual preferences.

Having two troubled teens living in his home in addition to his own daughters added to Alan's stress level, but he didn't stop Willa in her efforts, because he wanted the approval of his church friends. He basked in the admiration he and Willa received, especially in church.

Two other foster children came and went: a teen girl emotionally devastated after submitting to an illegal abortion (whom Willa helped restore to emotional health), and a boy just out of reform school. Authorities at Catholic Charities called him "incorrigible." He stayed a year, until Willa developed sciatica caused by stress and he had to leave.

Alan's prestigious Baltimore corporation had now promoted him to vice president and treasurer of their large real estate subsidiary. He was well paid and given perks that Willa enjoyed. But Alan wasn't comfortable with executive decision-making and hated being thrust into leadership roles. As his stresses grew, Alan turned more and more to the source of comfort he had enjoyed in his teens—erotic daydreams involving other men. Eventually, these dreams became deeds. At first he was careful. He drove to gay bars forty-five miles away in Washington, D.C., where he met men who became willing sex partners. He never loved them. He didn't crave romance with them. Sometimes, he barely knew them.

In the meantime, he maintained his carefully crafted public identity as a solid citizen: straight arrow at work, Sunday school teacher, church vestry member, husband, father to his two girls, and foster father to as many as three children living in his home at once. Alan had a strong desire to feel good about himself. "I actually had a huge amount of spiritual pride," he said, "and I thought I was a good person overall, except for this sexual problem. Especially, I was proud of my honesty."

In 1974, fourteen years into his marriage, Alan's SSA feelings had become stronger than ever—he was addicted to them, controlled by illicit desires demanding to be obeyed. He grew reckless and frequented gay bars in Baltimore, where someone he knew could easily have discovered him. Worse, he visited a park close to his house where men hid in the woods, waiting for sex partners. In *Growth into Manhood*, Alan wrote, "A major part of my homosexuality was masochistic, and I started answering ads for sadomasochistic sex."[4]

His theory (developed later) was that for any child to truly feel love, he or she must experience boundaries and discipline from the father. Because he never experienced this, Alan developed an infantile need for that discipline from men in an inappropriate way as an adult. And he continued to drink heavily.

Inexorably, Alan felt himself sucked down into a dark whirlpool.

He would tell Willa he had to work late. After working late, he would stop in a gay bar on the way home and spend several more hours. On Saturdays, he went to the woods. When he returned home, his face was etched with shame and guilt. Usually, he was drunk. During this terrible time, Alan had a keen sense that his life was falling apart. He was meeting men he didn't know who took pleasure in hurting him. He knew he could be killed by one of them.

But he couldn't stop. He explained later, "I never justified what I was doing, but I felt powerless to stop it. Gradually sinking into a fatalistic attitude, I saw my life as being on a downward spiral that eventually would cost me my family, my job, maybe even my life, and there was nothing I could do about it."

Like Willa, Alan had meant it when he promised before God "to have and to hold from this day forward, for better or for worse, until death do us part." He still remembered their wedding vows and wanted to honor them. But he felt powerless to confront the evil he was now courting. He hated his homosexuality, but he also loved it and didn't believe he could manage his life without it.

One evening during this time when Alan perceived himself pulled down into a deadly vortex, he attended a party of coworkers and their spouses that ended in a bar. His friends gave him nearly straight liquor, drink after drink, for the fun of getting him drunk. When the wife of one coworker, Sue, sat on his lap, he divulged to her that he was SSA. She was a friend of Willa's.

The next day she tried to tell Willa, but Willa wouldn't listen.

"I never fully felt the weight of what Alan was doing," Willa said of the time when Alan's life was spinning out of control. "I used denial as my defense mechanism. What was I feeling? A great deal of anger and stress." She also sensed spiritual darkness in their home, which she didn't understand. It manifested in her deep desire to escape somehow from the mess of her marriage. She felt trapped with no hope of escape.

Then one day, a woman from the Anglican Fellowship of Prayer came to an adult class on prayer at the Medingers' church. As she began talking of the Holy Spirit, her face was suffused with peace. Willa felt drawn to her. Ordinarily proudly independent, Willa, desperate, released her problems to the Lord. She asked the woman for help. "I don't know what you've got," she said, "but I want it."

The woman told Willa of her prayer group, and, like Ruth in the Bible, Willa said, "Wherever you go, I want to go with you."

Later, they went together to the home of a wealthy Episcopalian woman, where a group of older women, "mighty prayer warriors" in Willa's words, met to pray. Helen Shoemaker, author of six books on prayer and co-founder of the Anglican Fellowship of Prayer, led the meeting. Her late husband, the Reverend Sam Shoemaker, was a well-known, evangelical Episcopal priest.

The ladies took turns sharing their prayer requests. When Willa's turn came, she told the women she was unhappy with Alan. Not understanding the cause herself, she couldn't specify the exact reason for her troubled marriage. All twenty-five women in the group, in turn, prayed out loud for Willa and Alan and their daughters. Although Willa had never prayed out loud before, now she did not hesitate.

In September 1974, after some weeks of praying regularly with the women, Willa noticed a change in herself. She found herself wanting to be in church all the time. "I couldn't put the Bible down," she said. "It wasn't goodness that drove me to church—it was need." As she read the Bible, Willa found that "God started showing me things. He showed me things in my life that displeased Him. He tore down the deception and control and disobedience my life had been built upon." This process was gentle, as if God were making allowances for Willa's sensitive nature.

One day, she received a thought that she understood to be God saying, "Willa, I want you to stop living for Alan and start living for Me. Stop being something you're not. Be yourself. Be authentic." A month later, in October, as she sat at home on her piano bench, she encountered the Lord again. Looking back on this experience, Willa believed it was this meeting with God that constituted the new birth for her, because, all at once, she knew for certain that He was real, that she was a sinner, and that God wanted her to submit her life to Him. She did, although reluctantly at first. At this time she understood God to say, "I want you to give me Alan. I want you to stop playing God."[5]

At first this suggestion made her angry. In her mind, she had been behaving like a wonderful person—loving and enduring. Whenever

Alan came home at night drunk and miserable, she consoled and reassured him.

Despite her initial resistance, the Lord continued to instruct her. "You know Alan is stubborn, and the only way I can reach him is through pain. You're taking his pain away and negating what I'm trying to do."

Finally, Willa relented. "Okay, God," she said. "I give him to You, but I sure hope You know what You're doing. Who's going to love him if I don't?"

When she heard her own words, she realized they were wrong, and she felt convicted. She promised again to let go of Alan.

CHAPTER 3:

# "Lord, I Surrender!"

*As a disciple of Jesus I am . . . learning from Jesus how to live my life as he would live it if he were [me].*

~ Dallas Willard in *The Divine Conspiracy*

ONE MONTH AFTER WILLA PROMISED God to let go of her husband and stop interfering, her prayers for Alan were answered. On Tuesday, November 26, 1974, he accepted an invitation from Jim, a friend at work, to attend a prayer and worship meeting of the Lamb of God Community. This interdenominational charismatic group met in the basement of a Catholic school. Jim had invited Alan earlier, but he had resisted going, sensing that if he responded at the meeting as Jim had already done—by giving his life to Christ—it would mean he would have to deal with his homosexuality. He both hated it and loved it. He didn't know if he could live without it.

As Alan left for the evening meeting, he said to Willa, "Say 'good-bye.' The man who comes back will be a different man." He had no idea why he said that.

He joined over 200 other men and women in the basement of St. Joseph school in Texas, Maryland. The people sat on folding chairs in a big circle, singing praise songs and listening to testimonies and some prophesies. Despite Jim's warning that Alan might see expressions of worship he wasn't used to, Alan felt comfortable in the big crowd. He was happy to be anonymous. Nobody approached him personally. Nobody there knew his problems.

At this time, Alan didn't understand what it was to be "born again." Though he was a churchgoer, he hadn't been taught about giving one's life to Jesus. He did realize that God was his last hope for escaping the downward momentum of his life. "He will either kill me or cure me," he thought.

After listening to testimonies awhile, as others around him worshipped the Lord, Alan prayed a desperate, silent, sincere cry from his heart. "Lord, I surrender! My life is a total mess. I've tried and tried, but I can't do anything about it. I'm willing to let You take over now, God. Do whatever You want—no limitations, no restrictions—just set me free, Lord. I'm willing to do it Your way now. Forgive me, Lord, and let me start over!"[1]

In this prayer, Alan relinquished his entire life, including his sexuality, to the Lord. Jim, sitting next to him, knew nothing of what was happening in his friend's heart. They left the meeting as casually as they arrived, and parted saying, "See you at work!"

Alan returned home that evening unaware of any spiritual change. He sat down in his usual chair, picked up the newspaper, and took out a cigarette to smoke, a habit he began when he was twelve, the same age he started engaging in homosexual activities. As he lifted the cigarette to his lips, the thought came to him—he didn't know why—"This is the last cigarette I'll ever smoke." It proved to be true. He never smoked again, nor did he ever crave another cigarette.

The next morning Alan awoke to an awareness that his life had miraculously changed, that is, that God had changed him in a way beyond what happens in nature. He experienced not just one miracle, but three, and it took him years to understand what had happened so he could describe it. Later he said, "Most of our spiritual growth in life takes place with surrender. Our lives are marked by a series of surrenders. Before my surrender to the Lord in 1974, I was so consumed with meeting my own needs that I was unable to love others."

The first and most important change when Alan woke up "in Christ" was his awareness of Jesus' presence and His love. At once, Alan responded by loving Jesus in return. He felt himself "a new creature." He began to pray and especially to praise.

Then Alan became aware that the Lord had broken an emotional wall of protection—a wall he had built within himself long ago. That wall had prevented Alan from loving anyone except his daughters, his young niece Stephanie, and his childhood friend Bill. Now with the wall tumbled down, God enabled Alan to experience agape love, a self-sacrificing delight in the well being of another. Before, Alan's affection for others had been self-serving.

God Himself was the first one Alan responded to in this new way, and then people, especially Willa. These changes in his ability to love he called "Miracle Number One."

"Miracle Number Two" followed. In addition to the deep love he now felt for Willa, and born of this love, he experienced sexual desire for her. He was healed of the old mental habit of fantasizing about sex with men. He didn't want sex with men at all—his sexual addiction was gone.

"Miracle Number Three" was slower in coming; the need for it was not apparent at first.

Because Alan's conversion was so dramatic, he later related, "I was high on the Lord for a long time afterwards." He began spending an hour in the early morning and time after dinner every day with the Lord, reading the Bible and praying. He now looked at the Bible differently. Though he had often before tried to read it, it had seemed just another book. Now he experienced it as God's Word freshly spoken to him. He discovered that his usual drink before dinner interfered with the spiritual quality of his after-dinner devotions, and he stopped drinking it.

For several weeks, Alan and Willa had wonderful times together—like a second honeymoon. He enjoyed making love with her. In every way he tried to please her. He listened to her, laughed with her, enjoyed her stories, praised her cooking, and joined her in caring tenderly for their daughters. He even helped with the foster children.

Some of this was not new. He had always liked and enjoyed Willa. But now that Alan was at home and sober, he wanted a whole new life for Willa, himself, and his daughters. Each new day he would say to himself, "Everything's all right now!" At this point, he didn't anticipate how difficult it would be for Willa to adjust to the knowledge of his secret life. He was unaware of how severely he had wounded Willa.

Things were nearly perfect for a month. Then, as Christmas approached, Alan felt the Lord urging him to confess to Willa all that he had been doing for the previous ten years. At first he demurred, asking the Lord, "Do I have to tell her? Everything is so great now." But he was aware of a firm leading to be honest with his wife. Transparent. Finally, he initiated that talk with her.

Willa knew Alan had changed, so she was prepared for some explanation, but not the one she got. "I feared you would get into deep trouble," she said.

"I *was* in trouble," Alan replied tentatively.

Willa fixed her hazel eyes on him. "You're a homosexual, aren't you?" The words just popped out of her lips.

"I was one," he admitted.

Willa felt deeply betrayed. "How could you have done this to me?" she asked. "How could you lie to me?" That was the worst sin to her—lying from a husband who prided himself on honesty.

A deep rage fell over her. How could she ever trust him again? All her life, Willa had worked hard at being "a good girl." And she had worked equally hard at being "the perfect wife." Now this.

To Willa, the way to be loved was to become necessary to a person by working to please him or her. And she had worked hard, so because of her efforts, she thought she deserved to be loved in a solid marriage. But how could she succeed when Alan was hiding this terrible problem?

For months Willa remained bitterly angry with Alan. Even years later, her anger smoldered. In the early days, she would beat on his chest with her fists, yelling, "I hate you! I hate you! I hate you!" But the Lord gave Alan such supernatural love for her that he endured her attacks with a mild and forbearing temper.

Shortly after Christmas, Willa's friend Sue, the same Sue who had sat on Alan's lap several months before, dropped by for a visit. Willa said, "Sue, there's something I just found out about Alan, and I can't tell anyone."

Sue answered, "I already know. He's homosexual."

To Willa, these were words of comfort. She saw that God had gone before her, and, understanding her need, provided a friend who could be a confidante. Before Alan's confession, Willa was so set on always being strong that she would never have sought such a friend on her own.

In addition to Sue, Willa could talk with her pastor and with Alan. She also confided in Gwen, a trusted member of the Anglican Fellowship of Prayer. Later, when she would counsel distressed wives of men acting out homosexually, she told them to find at least one wise and trusted woman to help through difficult times.

Even with someone to talk to, Willa felt threatened by Alan's revelation. She feared becoming vulnerable to him and trusting him to love her. Willa had never experienced emotional intimacy with anyone, not with either of her parents growing up. She had a deep fear of losing control in a transparent relationship. She even prayed for the Lord to let Alan become homosexual again. Though it was neither rational nor biblical, she prayed "let him be gay again" for years. She would, of course, have been devastated had he gone back to the old ways, but she prayed that prayer as a person who was comfortable with codependency. She found it hard when Alan looked to the Lord and not to her.

As for Alan, he began to pray constantly, "Lord, please change Willa," but he sensed the Lord saying, "Let's work on you." Because of the radical way God had intervened, Alan didn't harbor fears or anger. But he still had to learn much before he could conform his thinking to the Lord's thinking.

He attended a seven-week "Life in the Spirit" seminar at the Lamb of God Community, where he learned how to let the Holy Spirit guide

Victims who find life's meaning in being a victim

and empower his life. When the class ended, another class began for all who wanted to continue to learn, as Alan did, but he was not invited to join it. He was disappointed until he discovered the reason—this seminar was for couples only (if you were married), and since Willa didn't want to go, he didn't qualify.

For years Alan's main source of spiritual edification continued to be daily quiet times with the Lord—on average, ninety minutes a day, five or six days a week. He used this time to pray and meditate on the Bible. He later called his time with God "one of the main fruits of my conversion, [my] primary source of power and direction."[2]

Though Alan wanted a new pattern of relationships in his home, initiating this was not easy. Willa would explain, "This is how a father should behave—he should lead his family." The Christian books he read agreed with her. But much as he wanted to, he couldn't govern anyone. For instance, Alan tried leading family prayers. He would start off with all four of them praying a set prayer together, and then, without warning, "It was me alone. The girls wouldn't cooperate. They just sat there."

He discovered that being a completely different, totally new, Christian husband and father didn't come naturally. In fact, his children, especially Beth, rebelled and wanted the old daddy back, the one who was tipsy sometimes and lots of fun. Alan said that the *before* and *after* contrast in him was hard for the family: "All of a sudden, I was this super Christian, in terms of I couldn't get enough of Jesus, and Willa and the girls were left where they were."

Later he learned that he wasn't totally healed of the homosexual neurosis in the beginning of this new life, and that was why he had trouble with leadership, both in the family and elsewhere. "Homosexuality is more than just sexual attractions and behavior," Alan says in *Growth into Manhood*. "I was thirty-eight years old at the time of my conversion and healing, but in the development of my masculinity and sense of manhood, I believe I was about eight years old. I had to start growing up. This process took years, but again it was a mighty work of God."[3] This was Alan's "Miracle Number Three."

For a while, Alan was "a little of the obnoxious new Christian," telling others that he had met Jesus. But he didn't mention giving up his homosexual life. None of his friends or extended family had known about it, so why should he mention it to them now?

At length he did tell his family though, his mother first and then Willa's mother. Enid Medinger had a hard time accepting the news, but Willa's mother took it well. She had always liked Alan, and this new information about his past didn't bother her, especially since it was already irrelevant to the man he had become.

Three or four years later, Alan told Willa's two brothers, Frank and Arthur, and they were fine with it. "It didn't bother them a lick," Willa said. Her sister, Janice, didn't change toward Alan either. "There's so much else good about Alan, and she didn't forget that," Willa said. "Janice liked Alan always and respected him."

After his conversion, Alan was hungry for Christian male friends. Four other men at work had come to Christ about the time he did, but they didn't meet together. He didn't see Jim much outside of work either. Alan continued seeing his Johns Hopkins friends socially, but they were not on the same spiritual path. He perceived, much later, that the Lord had protected him from slipping into dependence upon another man or even creating a false idol of a male friend. Beginning in early childhood, Alan had developed a mental habit of "just accepting what is." At this time, he accepted not having close male friends.

The first five years after his conversion, Alan depended on Jesus alone for male companionship. Because the Lord was so real to him in those first years, Alan's natural need for a man's love and affirmation was satisfied by Jesus. "Developing a relationship with the Lord," he discovered, "is the key to healing for any person from any sin."

One day during his private devotions, he had a vision of the Lord coming to him. Alan was a boy in the vision. Jesus picked him up and carried him on His shoulder as He walked around the Medingers' old

Liberty Heights Avenue neighborhood in Baltimore. Alan's playmates in the vision saw how strong he was as Jesus' friend. This spiritual experience helped Alan change his attitude toward his childish self.

He especially liked the words of a hymn based on Psalm 23 that he said "express perfectly what happened to me . . . when I encountered the Lord and He brought me out of homosexuality."

"Perverse and foolish oft I strayed, but yet in love He sought me;
And on His shoulder gently laid, and home rejoicing brought me."

---

In late August 1975, nine months after Alan's conversion, Willa conceived their third child. She kept her pregnancy secret from him at first. She'd had two miscarriages during the early years of their marriage and was convinced she would never complete another pregnancy. If Alan had known they were expecting, and the baby miscarried, Willa believed it would have broken not only her own heart, but his as well.

At the end of her fourth month, near Christmas 1975—just one year after Alan's confession to her of his SSA past—Willa finally told him the news. He was overjoyed. With affection and humor, Alan began referring to the unborn baby as a boy, "Baby Leroy."

Willa was thirty-nine and Alan just forty on May 27, 1976, when their third baby was born. Willa, who was often late those days, arrived at the hospital after her 8 a.m. appointment for an induction. The doctor was busy with other appointments until noon. Then he did induce the baby, which caused immediate, hard contractions. The unborn baby was in a transverse lie, and for two extremely painful hours Willa suffered as the doctor and his assistants repositioned him. Only then did the anesthetist give her sodium thiopental to help her endure the birth. She didn't remember much of anything after that. Some muscles were torn during the birth process.

When the baby emerged about six p.m., he didn't breathe for a short time, and at first he scored only three of the ten required for a perfect Apgar rating. He did revive quickly after the first test though. (The Apgar test is commonly given to newborns, once when they are one minute old and again when they are five minutes old. It tests appearance, pulse, responsiveness, muscle activity, and breathing.)

Willa needed surgery to repair her body. Afterwards, still groggy, she heard the beautiful words, "Willa, you have a healthy boy." Late in the evening when the drugs wore off, she was able to sit and rock her treasured son.

Alan and his mother-in-law, Meriam Benson, waited anxiously more than six hours in the waiting room. They heard next to nothing of what was happening until the doctor at last came with the news, "You have a boy, and everything is okay."

The news thrilled them. Alan was so elated he began to cry. Besides being relieved, he was also at first "scared to death to have a son." He loved the baby, whom they named Stephen Alan, from the first moment, and he prayed to be capable of rearing the boy to complete manhood.

The next day Laura, twelve, and Beth, eleven, came to see their mother and brother in the hospital, a difficult errand because of restrictive hospital rules. They managed to peer through the window of a door near Willa's room. It was Alan and Willa's sixteenth wedding anniversary, and they quietly celebrated having a healthy son, two delighted daughters, and a restored marriage.

On May 30, Willa went home, but Stephen stayed one more day so the doctors could monitor his jaundice, a condition not uncommon in newborns. Willa said that when the family reunited at home, "It was just perfect—Alan and me, the healthy baby, and the joyful girls. It was just the way it should be in a really happy marriage."

Cooperating with the incomparably great power of the Lord, Alan had climbed out of a pit of compulsive sin. He dared to hope that a happy future awaited him and his family.

often so STUPID & ANTI-HEALING

## CHAPTER 4:

# BACK STORY—A "STUNNING VICTORY"

*Psychiatry is the enemy incarnate. Psychiatry has waged a relentless war of extermination against us. You may take this as a declaration of war against you.*

~ Gay activist Frank Kameny in 1971 to a convention of the American Psychiatric Association

AS ALAN'S LIFE SPIRALED DOWNWARD into sexual addiction in the late 1960s and early 1970s, he followed news of the gay community with mild interest. About the Stonewall Bar confrontations between gays and New York City police in June 1969, which some say began the gay rights battle, he said, "I remember reading about it with amusement, but because I really didn't identify with a gay community, I had no strong feelings about it one way or the other."[1] Nevertheless, the struggle of gay activists to change America's perception of homosexuality would, in time, affect him in ways he could not have predicted.

---

In the first year of John F. Kennedy's presidency, Dr. Frank Kameny, a father of the gay rights movement and a brilliant astronomer with a Ph.D. from Harvard, started a chapter of the Mattachine Society in Washington, D.C., with his friend Jack Nichols. This gay group, begun in the early 1950s in California and New York, was named for a medieval French secret society of unmarried men. The original Mattachines were "mysterious masked medieval figures" who performed plays critical of the social order, according to historian John D'Emilio. (The word *mattachine* is from an Arabic word meaning mask-wearer.)

At first, the American society was composed of same-sex attracted (SSA) men meeting in their own living rooms to discuss gay issues. In its early days the groups were, in Kameny's words, "very unassertive, apologetic, and defensive." He wanted his Mattachine chapter to be different. The U.S. government had fired him years earlier from his job at the U.S. Army Map Service because, they said, "We have information that leads us to believe you are a homosexual." He protested in court all the way to the Supreme Court and lost his case. By this time, he said, "I had become radicalized."[2]

Kameny decided to confront the mental health profession, and especially the American Psychiatric Association (APA). Psychiatrists considered homosexuality a mental disorder, and society believed those doctors to be experts. Consequently, many gays also considered themselves mentally ill. Kameny said, "My answer to that was, 'Drivel! We are the experts on ourselves, and we will tell the experts they have nothing to tell us!' Giving all views a fair hearing didn't suit my personality. And the Mattachine Society of Washington was formed around my personality." So the society in Washington became "an activist militant organization," in his words.[3]

Kameny understood, as few others did in the 1960s, the importance of the American Psychiatric Association's little book that officially listed mental illnesses—the *Diagnostic and Statistical Manual of Mental Disorders (DSM)*. In its second edition (*DSM-II*), published in 1968, homosexuality was listed as a mental disorder. Most Americans knew nothing of this spiral-bound paperback that described about 100 disorders in 134 pages, cost $3.50, and sold to large state mental institutions. Kameny believed the *DSM* had potential to be important—to change the status of gays in America. He proved to be right.

Today the *DSM-5* is very influential. A hardback/paperback/e-book published in May 2013, it revised the *DSM-IV-TR* from 2000. In 947 pages, this *DSM* describes over 300 mental disorders. Hundreds of thousands of copies, each costing $149 hardback or $106 paperback, sell each year. Insurance companies require a *DSM* diagnosis before they will reimburse mental health workers. Courts, social service agencies, schools, prisons, governments, and mental health therapists all use the manual. Since 1973, the *DSM* no longer lists homosexuality as a disorder. Therefore, the condition is commonly considered normal and healthy.

How did this change happen? Was it a scientific breakthrough?

Led by Frank Kameny, gay activists decided to force the American Psychiatric Association to delist homosexuality. They began their fight at the association's May 1970 annual convention in San Francisco. It took them only three years to succeed. Their method? A "systematic effort to disrupt the annual meetings of the American Psychiatric Association," according to Ronald Bayer, who wrote a book on the 1973 decision. Bayer's book carefully gives views of both gay activists and APA members and is praised by both sides. It is *Homosexuality and American Psychiatry, the Politics of Diagnosis.*[4]

At the 1970 convention, feminists and gay activists, intending to "direct their wrath against a common organizational foe," (Bayer's words) infiltrated meetings of psychiatrists. As the doctors spoke, activists surprised them with harassing interruptions. Dr. Irving Bieber was a prime target because of his successful work in changing sexual orientations of SSA clients, which was well known and disliked by gays. Loud, derisive laughter greeted Dr. Bieber when he tried to read a paper on his findings. One activist denounced his book with a hint at violence, saying if its subject had been black people, "you'd be drawn and quartered, and you'd deserve it."

It wasn't Bieber who attracted the greatest protest, however. At this time, behavioral psychiatrists were using electric shock treatment on SSA patients. When Dr. Nathaniel McConaghy, a young behavioral psychiatrist from Australia who practiced "aversive conditioning techniques," spoke on how to treat sexual deviation, he met loud anger. Shouts of "torture," and "Where did you take your residency,

Auschwitz?" interrupted his talk, culminating when demonstrators broke up the meeting, exploding with demands to be heard. "We've listened to you, now you listen to us. . . . We've waited 5,000 years!"[5]

One angry psychiatrist denounced a shouting gay activist as a "maniac," while another called a feminist "a paranoid fool." Some enraged psychiatrists demanded refunds of their air fares to the conference, and one said the police should be called "to shoot the activists."

The following year in Kameny's hometown of Washington, D.C., psychiatrists worked with him to prevent problems. He helped plan their convention, arranging for a panel of gays to give a positive account of their mental health, "Lifestyles of Non-Patient Homosexuals." However, Kameny also secretly arranged disruptive protests in several rooms from a violence-friendly group, the Gay Liberation Front Collective. Activists were unwilling to give up a threat of "disorder or even of violence" at this time, feeling "yet another jolt" to the APA was necessary to move them quickly to delist homosexuality in the *DSM*.

The APA by now provided security at conventions, but gay activists forged credentials and easily gained access. At one meeting, Kameny himself took the microphone and announced to psychiatrists that they had no right even discussing homosexuality. "Psychiatry is the enemy incarnate," he shouted. "Psychiatry has waged a relentless war of extermination against us. You may take this as a declaration of war against you."

A mood of intimidation prevailed. Activists forced the removal of one exhibit on aversive conditioning, saying if the psychiatrist didn't dismantle his own booth, they would tear it down themselves.[6]

The 1972 convention in Dallas was calmer. Kameny and a lesbian activist friend, Barbara Gittings, ran an exhibit, "Gay, Proud and Healthy: The Homosexual Community Speaks." Kameny wrote a flyer asking psychiatrists to consider the harm they were doing to gay people by stigmatizing them as mentally ill. His tone was conciliatory: "Psychiatry in the past . . . has been the major single obstacle in our society to . . . our full happiness and our basic human dignity. Psychiatry *can* become our major ally." He asked the doctors to reject their "sickness theory."

Later in 1972, activists broadened their attacks on mental health professionals beyond just the APA. In October the New York Gay Activist Alliance produced a "zap" at a meeting of the Association for the Advancement of Behavior Therapy. Over 100 demonstrators picketed outside the New York Hilton Hotel, and another group infiltrated the psychiatrists' meeting and distributed a flyer, "Torture Anyone?"

Dr. Robert Spitzer, who attended the meeting and observed the demonstrators' ardor, promised to sponsor a panel to consider delisting homosexuality at the 1973 APA convention. This was an important breakthrough for gays because Spitzer was a member of the APA Committee on Nomenclature that was revising the *DSM*.

Consequently, in February 1973, Charles Silverstein of the Institute for Human Identity (a homosexual and bisexual counseling center) spoke to the nomenclature committee. In a long statement he surveyed some current psychologists and psychiatrists who argued that homosexuality is not a mental disease. He also listed instances of SSA people who were refused jobs because they were deemed mentally ill. For instance, the New York Taxi Commission required SSA drivers to undergo psychiatric evaluations twice a year to prove their fitness to drive. Silverstein argued against psychoanalysts who believed that homosexuality was a disorder. He called their theories "subjective," "unsubstantiated," and a series of "adult fairy tales." His passion, plus his statements presenting current pro-homosexual doctors' opinions, impressed the nomenclature committee.

Psychoanalysts on the Council of the Association for Psychoanalytic Medicine passed a resolution in 1973 saying that exclusive homosexuality was a kind of "disordered psychosexual development" caused by early childhood experiences. They said it could be cured by means of psychotherapy. But psychoanalysts were not asked to speak to the nomenclature committee.

By May 1973 when the APA convened, Dr. Spitzer had come to believe that homosexuality should no longer be considered a disorder. He was persuaded by gay activists who said they "were fully satisfied with their sexual orientations."

The matter was dealt with in October 1973, when five psychiatrists, members of the APA Council on Research and Development, voted unanimously to take homosexuality off the list of mental disorders. None of them was an expert on the subject. They had done no research but were responding to Dr. Spitzer's proposal to delist, though they modified it. Spitzer was uncomfortable with the possibility that deleting homosexuality as a disorder might be interpreted as a declaration by the APA that the condition was "normal." He recommended that the research council say, "Homosexuality *per se* is a form of irregular sexual development and like other forms of irregular sexual development, which are not by themselves psychiatric disorders, is not listed."[7] The council rejected this advice.

Two months later, thirteen members of the APA Board of Trustees added their votes for delisting homosexuality to those of the council, officially delisting homosexuality from the *DSM*.

To announce this decision, gay activists pressured the APA to organize a media event. At the press conference, Frank Kameny, Barbara Gittings, and other activists celebrated their victory.

The research council's votes were ratified a few months later after the APA sent a referendum letter to more than 30,000 members. The letter was signed by APA members, including Dr. Spitzer, but it was secretly co-written by a gay activist, Ronald Gold, and paid for by the National Gay Task Force. It urged psychiatrists to agree to delist homosexuality, not because science had demonstrated that the condition is normal, but because "it would be a serious and potentially embarrassing step for our profession to vote down" the well publicized board of trustees' decision. In fact, the reasons for delisting homosexuality were not even mentioned in the letter.

Only 5,854 psychiatrists marked their ballots "yes," less than twenty percent of the APA membership, but this was a majority of those who mailed in their votes.

Gays believed it was politics, not science, which yielded this favorable outcome, the beginning of a total change in the secular culture. "It never was a medical decision," Barbara Gittings said in an interview. "And that's why I think the action came so fast. After all, it was only three years from the time that feminists and gays first zapped the APA to the time that the board of trustees voted in 1973 to approve removing homosexuality from the list of mental disorders. It was a political move. When the vote came in, we had a wonderful headline in one of the Philadelphia papers, 'Twenty Million Homosexuals Gain Instant Cure.'"[8]

This "stunning victory," in Ronald Bayer's words, resulted from two causes: first, psychiatrists wanted to make the harassing at their conventions go away. But second, and more important, the APA decision came at a turning point in psychiatry. Power was shifting from pro-psychoanalysis doctors to a new type of psychiatrist. Dr. Spitzer typified the new type, which called itself DOPs, "Data-Oriented People."

Leaving the decision about whether a patient is mentally ill up to the patient can obviously be problematic. By this thinking, a happy, satisfied, friendly pedophile could be considered mentally healthy. But how can the doctor be sure the pedophile is honest in his self-description? And what about the victim?

The DOP doctors' method of looking at the patient's symptoms and prescribing medicines contrasted to the method old-fashioned psychoanalysts and other psychotherapists preferred—discussing with patients what caused their suffering and helping them understand and ameliorate it. These changes had far-reaching consequences and potential weaknesses. One of these is exposed in the current DSM-5. According to it, a person can be diagnosed with depression, a problem characterized by loss of interest in everyday activities, sad feelings, difficulty concentrating, decreased energy, etc., if he shows these symptoms after a bereavement, even one as grievous as losing a spouse or a child. If the sufferer's symptoms are those of depression, he is eligible for drugs.

Changing a criterion for mental disorder to "subjective distress" worked for delisting homosexuality, and it worked for classifying many new mental problems. Attention-deficit disorder, autism, and post-traumatic stress disorder are among the mental ills that officially came into being when they were given names and agreed-upon lists of symptoms by those writing the DSM-III—Spitzer and his Nomenclature Committee.

Rewriting the *DSM* was the central activity by which these doctors gained control of psychiatry and minimized the power of psychoanalysts. DOPs wanted a standardized list of mental illnesses with standardized symptoms so that psychiatry would become more "scientific" and reliable in its diagnoses, treatments, and research. Simply calling a behavior a "neurosis," as psychoanalysts did, and saying that internal conflicts—all unique—caused mental disorders wasn't good enough for the DOPs. They needed a list of symptoms and insisted that all disorders be identified "by subjective distress and/or some generalized impairment in social . . . functioning."[10] This is why testimony from gays that they were happy and didn't consider themselves mentally ill had weight with Spitzer and the other DOPs. If gays said they were not experiencing "subjective distress," who should know better than they? And if they maintained satisfactory friendships, then how could a doctor call them disordered?

As for the old school of psychoanalysis, the research and experience of Dr. Irving Bieber and others who treated SSA people was not rebutted; it was ignored. Alan Medinger and his friend Sy Rogers described what happened: "Over 75 years of psychoanalytic knowledge underscoring homosexuality as a disorder was disregarded."[11]

Psychiatrists today rely less on talk therapy to solve problems than they did before 1973. They prescribe drugs to control symptoms.

Christian ex-gay ministries invite clients to discuss their pasts and problems, but they do not consider this talk therapy. They rely on the power of Christ as expressed in Scripture, healing prayer, and participation in a healing spiritual community to bring about change. These ministries still offer hope for people who wish to resolve same-sex attractions.

Gay people might have celebrated the 1973 APA decision, but for the rest of the world, it was, at the time, a non-event. It escaped Alan Medinger's attention completely. He wrote, "I didn't know about the APA decision until later. When I got into ministry, I saw this as one of the gays' greatest victories and a real obstacle to us."[12]

CHAPTER 5:

# BUILDING AN ARK BEFORE THE RAINS CAME

*God's standard of righteousness and holiness . . . declares that homosexuality is sin and affirms His love and redemptive power to recreate the individual.*

~ Statement of intent for Exodus International

STEPHEN'S BIRTH WAS A BLESSING to the family as a whole and to every member of it, a daily reminder of God's goodness. Laura and Beth, just beginning adolescence, were at the right age to nurture a baby and learn to care for him. Stephen gave them training for the future, when Laura would mother three children and Beth five. Willa, who was by nature an expert nurturer, was deeply content to feed and cuddle this new soul. And as for Alan, he knew the Lord had planned the timing of Stephen's birth, since he was healed enough to rear a same-gender child effectively, a task that can be daunting to an unhealed parent. Now he had extra incentive to grow into his own manhood and abandon the insecurities of his SSA past.

In his book *Growth into Manhood,* Alan calls Stephen's birth, "the new start in life that we were . . . given."[1]

Life in the Medinger house soon settled into patterns of contentment. Since little Stephen was, in effect, a boy with three mothers, Alan was careful to give him plenty of masculine attention. Early on, Alan encouraged Willa and the girls to sleep late, and he fixed breakfast for himself and Stephen to enjoy together. This began when Stephen was still only taking a bottle. Willa's deep underground anger at Alan resurfaced from time to time, but as the couple interacted with Stephen, they knew deeper happiness than ever before. Things were harmonious too between Laura, Beth, and Stephen—the girls delighted in their baby brother. However, though Alan had been set free to love, the girls and Willa still suffered from unresolved issues. Their slow healing and forgiveness of Alan belonged in the future.

Willa continued to enjoy St. Margaret's as her church home. Here, she said, she learned about loving people "where they are," though she did have one disagreement with her pastor. After Alan shared with him his story of miraculous healing, the pastor told Willa, "Well, if you are a homosexual, you can't change. Alan just thinks he's healed."

Willa disagreed. "You and I apparently believe in two different gods," she said. "I believe in a God who heals." But even after the confrontation, Willa wanted to continue in this church where she loved the people and also her work directing the choir.

Alan, however, grew dissatisfied with St. Margaret's Church after his conversion. He found it a spiritually dry place, and so he looked elsewhere for spiritual encouragement. In the early years he supplemented worship at St. Margaret's with activities at the Lamb of God Community and at St. Timothy's Episcopal Church in Catonsville, where Father Philip Zampino held healing services. Father Z "would pack them in," three or four hundred at a service, and whenever he could, Alan drove the eighteen miles to Catonsville to participate, in prayer, with what Father Z and the Holy Spirit were doing. In addition, Alan faithfully listened to Father Z's radio broadcasts. Fifteen years later, Alan credited "much of my early Christian nurture" to Father Zampino's teachings.[2]

With his eyes now open to the efficacy of prayer, Alan thought of his father's need one day and wanted to pray for him. Bill Karcher, a close friend from Alan's childhood, was living with Alan and Willa at the time. When Alan's mother was away for a few days once, Irwin spent some nights with them too. For more than thirty-five years, most of Alan's life, his father had suffered from severe depression, and now Irwin's life was so restricted by his mental illness that he had no social life and could only deal with the simplest tasks. A year before, Irwin had gone forward at a Billy Graham crusade in Baltimore and given his life to Jesus, but he remained depressed.[3]

Alan reflected later on the events of that evening. "We believed that God could heal him," he said, "not that He necessarily would." After dinner, Alan, Willa, and Bill decided to pray for Irwin. Alan's thought was, "It can't do any harm!"

The three of them laid hands on Irwin, who sat in a wingback chair in the living room, and prayed in turn for half an hour. They anointed him with oil and prayed some deliverance prayers.[4] They were all four surprised when Irwin, as soon as they stopped praying, came out of the depression. From then on, Irwin was able to lead a normal life. He began playing bridge again, and he traveled with Enid—to her native England and to many places in America. Enid at last enjoyed the companionship of a loving husband. As long as Irwin lived—another ten years—the depression never returned.

---

From the day of Alan's conversion, he had wanted to help other men who were conflicted by a homosexual drive. He said, "I believed if being healed could happen to me, it could happen to anyone. I still think this."

At first, he knew of no one else who had experienced change from same-sex attraction to freedom to love, value, and be one flesh in marriage with one woman for life. Then in 1977, twice in one week he saw articles (in *Christian Life* and *The National Courier*) about an ex-gay ministry. He wrote to Love in Action, the San Rafael, California, group mentioned, saying "Almost three years ago I received the greatest blessing any of us can experience—I came to know the Lord. At the same time, in His indescribable love and mercy, He healed me of homosexuality." Alan said he prayed "for those in homosexual bondage" because "my heart aches to participate in such a ministry, and I do believe the Lord is calling me to serve in this area."[5]

The ministry director, Frank Worthen, answered with a letter encouraging Alan to write his testimony for a book or an audiotape: "We need taped testimonies to send out to pastors who do not believe that Christ has life-changing power. Sad to say, many still believe 'once gay, always gay.'" He signed his letter "Brother Frank."[6] So began the friendship between Alan and Frank Worthen, which eventually included their wives.

---

Frank Worthen is a man with a story of God's grace as impressive as Alan's story. He began homosexual activity at age eighteen, when his SSA pastor convinced him he was fit for no other life. At forty-two, Frank came to believe that homosexual acts were against God's will. He contemplated suicide, working out the details of how to do it—he would jump from the Golden Gate Bridge. But one day, driving across the bridge, he thought he heard God say to him, "If you're willing to take your life, are you willing to give it to Me?"

This so startled Frank that he consulted the only Christian he knew, a young employee of his, and told him, "God spoke to me!" Mike responded by taking Frank to his church, asking him to kneel by the altar, and leading him through a lengthy sinner's prayer. The Lord, by means of that prayer and the continued support and teaching of Mike's church, changed Frank from a person who believed that homosexuality was his only option to a

In 1976, homosexuality was not considered a disorder by the American Psychiatric Association. They had voted to remove it from the DSM in 1973. Officially, then, the condition was not a mental disorder. But what was it? Neither psychiatrists nor psychologists (who followed along with the APA delisting) made a statement to define it medically. The man who led the APA to delist homosexuality, Dr. Robert Spitzer, had called it "a form of irregular sexual development," and also, a "suboptimal condition." Some people continued to call it a "neurosis," following the old psychoanalytic thinking. Exodus International called it by another name—"sin." Exodus members believed that same-sex acts were contrary to God's intent for sexuality, outlined in the Bible.

Christian who walked out the process of freedom leading to a vital ministry and marriage to a delightful woman.[7]

Frank's ministry, Love in Action, was one of twelve that met together in September 1976, to establish Exodus International. This group organized itself with the intention of becoming "an international Christian effort" to reach SSA people with the news that "God's standard of righteousness and holiness . . . declares that homosexuality is sin and affirms His love and redemptive power to recreate the individual."[8]

---

Alan corresponded with Frank Worthen and Bob Davies, who joined the staff of Love in Action in July 1979. He sent them a tape giving his testimony and another letter saying he was thinking of starting a ministry in Baltimore.

Bob listened "with real interest" to Alan's story of healing. As he thought about the testimony, Bob "felt a strong confirmation" in his heart that Alan's desire to minister to SSA people was from God. He had read a verse in Ezra (10:4 NASB) that he believed was for Alan, so he enclosed it in a letter written October 17, 1979: "Arise! For this matter is your responsibility, but we will be with you; be courageous and act." Bob wanted to assure Alan that Exodus ministries would support him.[9]

This message, plus a recent event, convinced Alan that the Lord was calling him to establish a new ministry in Baltimore. The current event involved five men who had just been arrested in a park and charged by the police with same-sex activity, which was illegal. One man was a married Baptist minister with two sons. When a local newspaper published the names of the accused, the minister shot and killed himself rather than experience disgrace. This was in 1979, only five years after Alan himself might have been apprehended in a park. It might have been his name in the paper and his disgrace.

Alan tracked down the surviving men from the article and told them about his experience of miraculous change. He invited them to his house to talk. One of them came, along with Bobby, the Medingers' former foster child, who said he believed it was time to be healed.

The three men met on October 29, 1979, in Alan's home, and a new ministry, Regeneration, was born. A fourth man, Ned, joined them soon afterwards.

Alan was surprised when the fifth Regeneration member showed up at his door—an SSA woman, Ashby. He had thought the ministry would be only for men, but he couldn't turn this individual away, so the ministry broadened its reach. Within a year, other women joined; early on, SSA women outnumbered men, though this was for a short time only.

Since Ned played the guitar, Regeneration people began each week's meeting singing praises to the Lord. Then they shared their stories and prayed for one another. Soon, Alan added a teaching that he put together from ministry newsletters (especially the one from Love in Action), the few books available, the Bible, and insight the Lord gave him during his personal devotions. His desire for Regeneration was to "give a very unique witness as to how God can and will change the lives of homosexual persons."[10]

Later, Alan discovered that Christians created redemptive ministries for SSA people all over the world in the 1970s—in Minneapolis, San Francisco, Los Angeles, Baltimore, London, Cape Town, and Amsterdam, each independent of the others and even ignorant of the others. It was some years before those creating the ministries found out about each other.

Why was this? "Surely, this was God's hand," Alan said.[11] "He cares about homosexually-inclined people. He wanted His truth heard at the time of great need."[12]

Willa added, "I used to think God healed Alan for me. Then He filled Alan's heart with desire to start a ministry. God was preparing Frank Worthen, Alan, and others because only He knew what was coming—the decade of the eighties and AIDS, as well as acceptance of homosexuality in the church."

God was sending an ark before the rains came.

Soon a group of nine or ten people who heard of Regeneration from interested persons came to the Medingers' living room each week. Alan wanted his ministry to grow by "attraction, not promotion," so he didn't advertise it except through local denominational newspapers but depended mostly on word of mouth to bring the people who wanted to come. A Southern Baptist minister with a church on Alan's street referred five people who wanted to come out of homosexuality. The pastor became the ministry's board of trustees president, despite his church's refusal to allow an Exodus ministry to meet in its building.

In the 1970s and 1980s, most churches did not reach out with a redemptive approach to SSA people because they didn't know same-sex attractions could be healed. Instead, they stood against the gay agenda, usually "with honorable intentions but most often . . . wrong methods," according to Alan Chambers, who later became president of Exodus International.[13] The official church messages and actions "only led to further estrangement from anyone personally affected by homosexuality and a resolve within the activist gay community to get organized and get even," said Chambers.

Originally, Regeneration members were SSA men and women, parents, friends, and women who liked gay men. (Willa said many girls like gay men, perhaps because they find them nonthreatening.) In a few years, members were exclusively SSA men and women; the others dropped out.

At first, Alan said, "I was a weak leader who didn't know what I was doing." His leadership was challenged once, when several angry lesbians tried to take over the meeting. Alan left the house in frustration, but Willa ran after him and brought him back.

Wanting to learn how to minister more effectively, Alan eagerly attended the Exodus V conference in June 1980 and met the people whose newsletters he was reading. He and Bobby flew together to Seattle, Washington, and gathered with fifty others at a conference site on Puget Sound. Exodus leaders Frank Worthen, Bob Davies, and Roberta Kenney were there. Roberta is the woman who had given Exodus its name at the organizational meeting four years before. She thought a reference to the people of God leaving Egypt, land of bondage, was apt.[14]

"Meeting these people was such a thrill," Alan said. "They were heroes to me."

His initial reaction to Frank Worthen was respect with no presumption of friendship. Frank was older (51 to Alan's 44 in 1980) and had already spent seven years in ministry. He was considered a "father" of this kind of ministry, having been a charter member of Exodus. A year earlier, the group had elected him its president.

Lifelines Ministry (now "Metanoia"), directed by Sharon Harrington, hosted the conference. People came more out of faith than hope, remembering the dissension at the 1979 Exodus conference in Johnstown, Pennsylvania, which some had dubbed "the Johnstown Disaster." There they had argued about the goal of their ministries. What did "healed" look like? Was it lifelong homosexual celibacy because sexual orientation can't be changed, or was it the potential for attraction to another-sex person, resulting in marriage and a family?

At Exodus V, this question was, for most conferees, put to rest. The keynote speaker, Art Katz, a messianic Jew, gave a powerful talk with a call to personal holiness. He vividly described the slaughter of a pig and concluded, "That's what the sin nature is like. It kicks and squirms and squeals until it's totally dead." Katz said we need to put the sin nature to death daily by God's power working in us.

Responding, the board of directors agreed that not only homosexual acts, but also the homosexual identity is neither acceptable nor neutral. They said that to be tempted toward acts (that is, to experience same-sex attraction) is not sin. They based this on Hebrews 4:15. Describing Jesus, this verse says he "was in all points tempted as we are, yet without sin" (NKJV). But even while tempted, they said, persons must stop identifying themselves with homosexual desires, thoughts, and acts. The board declared, "The homosexual orientation is an expression of humanity's sinfulness and cannot co-exist within the context of a total commitment to Jesus Christ."[15]

Years later, Alan quoted the Catholic Church on this subject. In *The Pastoral Care of the Homosexual Person,* that church had called the homosexual condition "a strong tendency ordered toward an intrinsic moral evil and thus the inclination itself must be seen as an objective moral disorder."

Alan said, "To define oneself as a homosexual, and to not go on further from that place, is to define ourselves in a way that is contrary to the identity that God wants us to have . . . a willing manifestation of disposition toward sin." A person almost never chooses to have same-sex desires when they first develop, Alan said. But clinging to a gay identity is choosing to "be my own person, not God's."[16] He added that since homosexuality "is an expression of rebellion against God's order, we can legitimately call it a stronghold of evil, a stronghold of the enemy. As Christians we are called to tear down such strongholds."

The idea of sinfulness involves the perception of choice. Later Medinger and others emphasized that we are sinners by birth (our fallen state) *and* by choice. The feelings of same-sex attraction are part of fallenness, sometimes called "brokenness." Acting on them belongs to choice.

---

When Alan told the Exodus V conferees his amazing story of miraculous, overnight healing, they listened with great interest, but also incredulity. Nobody else present had been instantly changed. None of the delegates accepted Alan's experience as the norm others could expect to duplicate, since the process of healing they knew was slower. As he patiently observed the experiences of others, Alan was led into understanding and writing about them.

About Alan's potential as a future leader of Exodus, the conferees had no doubts. He came wearing a business suit and tie, looking like an executive. The others were more casually dressed. Some of them were former California "flower children" wearing jeans and t-shirts. Frank Worthen said later, "Alan was the most sophisticated, intelligent, together guy. We saw him as a great resource to Exodus—a star. He was answered prayer before we ever prayed."[17]

The Exodus board heard that Alan was an accountant with a prestigious firm in Baltimore, and they were ready for him to step in and rescue their organization. "Probably there wouldn't have been another Exodus conference without him," Frank said. "He was our first strong pillar after years of turmoil."[18]

The organization had two serious problems in the summer of 1980: a tax problem and an incorporation problem. Frank had succeeded in getting Exodus incorporated in California, but whenever he applied for tax-exempt status in San Francisco, the papers were "lost." On top of this, the corporation papers had been kept in a locked box in the Exodus office, and now this box was missing.

Alan did step in and rescue Exodus. Shortly after he returned home, he successfully applied for reincorporation of Exodus as well as tax exemption in his home state, Maryland. Then he secured start-up money for a renewed Exodus by contacting the Christian Broadcasting Network in Virginia Beach, Virginia, which gave ten thousand dollars for necessities like stationery, postage, and phone expenses.

---

After the conference, Alan was buoyed by faith in the validity of ministry to SSA strugglers and also by hope that he could develop friendships with other leaders. He flew to Kansas City to meet Willa and the children, who had traveled there for the wedding of her niece, Lisa Paulsen. Little Stephen Medinger, four years old, was ringbearer.

Back home, Alan plunged back into his busy life. At work, he continued to be fully engaged in his corporation's leadership. Regeneration was growing, attracting people from Virginia and Pennsylvania now as well as Maryland. Alan's library of books and tapes on redeeming homosexuality was also growing. After 1980, it included twenty audiotapes from the Exodus conference.

In the meantime, Willa's anger at Alan still smoldered deep in her soul, though she lived in contentment sometimes too. She decided to consult a counselor, Mr. P, a psychologist whose father was the psychiatrist who had worked with Irwin Medinger for years and failed to cure him of depression. After some sessions learning about Willa's problem, Mr. P aggressively confronted her and asked, "What is this thing you have with control? I think it's masochistic." She always left his office with a severe headache and continued to be on an emotional yoyo.

Because of their failure with his father, Alan didn't believe psychiatrists and psychologists would be of any help, so he convinced Willa to find a different counselor. She eventually found Larry Dietrich, who had been a Catholic priest. He believed in the therapeutic value of the confessional and of prayer. Now an ex-priest, he was married to Nan, a woman whom Alan and Willa both liked, and he was a Christian counselor.

Larry had experienced profound spiritual renewal, and he desired to follow the Holy Spirit. To Willa, Larry "personified the love of Christ." During counseling sessions, he didn't criticize Willa or Alan. He would pray privately before each session. Then, with Willa reclining on a lounger, he would listen as she spewed out her anger as well as her deep feelings of worthlessness. From time to time Dietrich walked behind Willa, put his hand on the lounger, and prayed silently. He also asked Willa to pray. He "never shamed me or came down on me," Willa said. Each time when she left the session, she felt relieved and freer. But this was a slow process; her total freedom from anger was several years away.

In early 1981, more than six years after Alan's conversion, a gay man spoke at St. Margaret's Church. He told the congregation how comfortable he felt in his life, in his homosexuality, and in his religious faith. The church people listened with interest.

Soon after, Alan gave his testimony for the first time at St. Margaret's, telling how God had miraculously taken away all his SSA desires and replaced them with normal sexual desires for his wife as well as a fervent desire to love and serve God Himself. The people listened quietly, and afterwards began to avoid him, using the time-honored method of shunning to express their dislike for his message. Even though Willa was attached to many people at St. Margaret's, Alan knew then that he and Willa had to leave that church.

CHAPTER 6:

# Anger Management

*Anger is a secondary emotion; the primary one is fear.*

~ Willa Medinger

LAKE MEAD NEAR LAS VEGAS, Nevada, was probably not the best place for Willa to experience her first Exodus. For a woman who struggled with anger, the extraordinary heat in June 1981 was not helpful. She found outside daytime temperatures of 120 degrees Fahrenheit unbearable. (It was so hot in one class on how to counteract pro-gay theology that the teacher, Bob Davies, encouraged his audience to climb in the pool to keep cool as they listened.)

But Willa didn't need the trigger of torrid days to ignite her anger; Alan did it by himself. He pressured her to act like a model wife, submissive and supportive. Still in the "spill it all out" stage of her recovery, she resented Alan for pushing her to conform to others' expectations. She wanted him to care more about what she thought and felt than about the conferees' opinions of him or her.

On the other hand, Alan was insecure in leadership, and here, at his second Exodus, he was already expected to lead. The board of directors asked him to teach a workshop. Doing so was stressful, because he believed the other conferees were more skilled and knowledgeable than he, especially in quoting the Bible. They came from evangelical church backgrounds, where Bible memorization was common. He came from a liturgical church, where it was uncommon. Alan wanted to make a good impression on the other conferees—to display what it was to be a man healed miraculously by the Lord and in a good marriage, so he wanted Willa to behave. He had strong feelings about what was appropriate behavior in a public setting. Indeed, he felt any husband would have been distressed and embarrassed by the way she acted. Willa wasn't concerned about public decorum at all.

She gave an hour-long workshop on "What Wives Go Through,"[1] speaking in an angry tone. Frank Worthen said later, "We were a little scared of Willa, but she was able to articulate the problem." She couldn't help wives find the solution though, because she had not yet worked through her own suffering.

Privately, Willa complained to people, saying she believed Alan "loved the ministry more than me." She told them that Alan was giving all his time and heart to the ministry. He was always on the phone. He invited SSA friends over to their house frequently. She said, "Homosexuality ruined my life before, and it's ruining it now."

Seeing how hurt and angry Willa was, Frank Worthen hugged her and said, "Willa, I love you." This meant a great deal to her. She never forgot his kindness, which she interpreted as God loving her through Frank. He was the first person who seemed to understand what she was going through, unlike Alan, who obviously didn't understand. Instead, "Alan was furious with me," she said. Willa cried all through the night after the last conference session and all the way home on the plane.

This Exodus attracted leaders in ministry from the Netherlands and South Africa. A Dutch film crew conducted interviews with leaders for a televised report in Holland later in the summer. Word of healing from same-sex attractions was spreading around the world.

One of the leaders interviewed on film was Sy Rogers, whom Alan and Willa brought to the conference from his home in Hagerstown, Maryland. For a year and a half, Sy formerly lived as a woman. He had even scheduled sex-change surgery at Johns Hopkins University Hospital. But three days after he asked the Lord, "Please show me if You *don't* want me to pursue this sex change," he received an unmistakable answer. Johns Hopkins cancelled all such procedures, saying this was not the best treatment for transsexuals.

Barbara Johnson, an author and friend of Frank Worthen, spoke at the conference. She had founded SPATULA, a ministry for parents of SSA people, after she said to some friends, "I need about a dozen big spatulas to pull these frantic mothers down off the ceiling when they first learn their kid is homosexual." Barbara had survived triple tragedy: two of her sons died, one in Vietnam and one in an automobile accident, and the third son announced he was gay, changed his name, and left home saying he never wanted to see his parents again. (A fourth son did remain at home, loyal to God and his parents.) Barbara had developed her faith in God to the point where she was so full of joy that a publisher approached her, asking her to write her story. She wrote it in eight weeks—a miracle in her opinion—and it was published in 1979 under the title, *Where Does a Mother Go to Resign?*[2]

Barbara gave her testimony at the conference about fighting severe anxiety attacks and depression after her third son disappeared into the gay culture. During a year of therapy, Barbara had promised herself, in writing, that if she survived, she would use what she learned to help other hurting parents. "After knowing the heartache of this child going into homosexuality," she said, "I have gradually been accepting the blanket of God's comfort. Maybe from this stinging experience I can help lighten the pain for others, if I don't die before I get through."[3]

The main thing she learned was "I can only love him [my son]; I can't fix or change him. . . . Only God can take a heart of stone and make it a heart of flesh. Love them right where they are, because parents aren't to blame, and they can't fix them."

"She was hysterically funny," Willa said. A counselor had told Barbara that her sense of humor would help her survive and become emotionally whole again. He was right.

Like Barbara, the main speaker, Perry Desmond, spoke from a grief-filled life transformed by faith in God. He was born in the same year as Alan, 1936, and born again the same year as Alan, 1974. However, Perry's life was very different: he had been a transsexual, beginning as a little boy. For six years, he wore women's clothes exclusively. He also submitted to the first surgical step of a sex-change operation. Then he became a Christian and decided that since God had created him a man, he was a man. He bought men's clothing and "the great adventure of ministering for Jesus began."

---

Alan's problems with Willa destroyed his sense of well being at this conference, but the delegates were so sure of his abilities that neither his anger nor hers harmed his position as a leader. He was elected to the Exodus board of directors at Lake Mead.[4]

After she returned home, Willa went back to Larry Dietrich for more counsel to control and understand her anger. He asked Alan to come along with her. For several sessions Alan listened to Willa expressing her anger. Then one day Larry said, "Willa, I think it's time for you to forgive."

She agreed. There followed "quite a session," Willa said. Larry and Alan listened while Willa tried to say, "Alan, I forgive you." The words stuck in her throat. Willa worked for half an hour to say them. As she finally began to enunciate the four words, she felt a sensation of something moving in her which seemed to have roots. Then it came out, roots and all, and the words "I forgive you" came in a roar. Willa didn't feel she controlled the event.

Even though Larry pronounced her healed after this and said she needed no more counseling, her struggle was not quite over. Forgiving Alan was a wholesome, necessary experience, but even so, Willa felt the need for self therapy and prayer to understand her more manageable but continuing anger. She read a book by Nancy Groom on codependency, *From Bondage to Bonding,* and found the definition of codependency fit her situation. This condition is, in Willa's words, "a huge need to be needed. You place your own life on hold, and you become addicted to being loved by that person." Why was she codependent? Willa learned that "the way my life formed was not God's way."

Beneath her long-time anger, she discovered, had been fear of becoming vulnerable to anyone. Deep down, she felt unworthy of being loved.

"What was so upsetting," she said, "was that I couldn't keep the perfect world I thought I had, and without that world, Alan wouldn't love me." This was why she held onto her anger for so long. The anger helped her avoid looking deeper and seeing her own worthlessness, or rather, her perception of worthlessness.

Willa said, "Anger is a secondary emotion; the primary one is fear."

Even after understanding her anger, Willa struggled sometimes with her automatic assumption of the role of "good girl." Like many women, she was the peace-maker in her family, and often this came at the expense of her ability to express herself, to be "honest and open." She wrote in a letter to a dear friend, "I'm angry that I always have to be perfect, and I'm angry that God doesn't seem to change Alan. . . . I'm tired of being the one who always has to make things work. And I'm angry with a God who would expect this of me. Where do my needs come in? . . . The intensity of the anger goes way back to my childhood. I'm soooooooooooo mad at my mother who didn't fill my deepest needs and always wanted me to not cry, not ask, not bother her—just be a good girl. My little girl is so angry with her, with God, and now with the adult Willa who went along with this. And under the anger is this pitiful little child whose heart has been mortally wounded because no one cared what she needed, or loved who she was."[5]

---

Anyone observing Willa Benson during her childhood would have assumed she was content in a loving family. Her father's big, beautiful white frame house, one block from Alan's parents' home, was impressive. Willa called it "a gorgeous place." Benson loved to garden. Everyone knew him by his pansies, grown from seed, which bloomed profusely in the front yard in a big plot next to the sunroom. He cultivated delicate tea roses, which needed constant care, and a large garden of flowers in clumps: columbines, marguerites, Shasta daisies, delphiniums, foxgloves, marigolds, and others.

But with his successful, demanding law practice, Benson had no extra time for cultivating his children. He left that to his wife.

Unfortunately, her energy was required for the care of four dependent adult family members who also lived in the big house. These adults were Benson's mother, "Grandmom Benson;" Meriam's parents, Grandmother and Grandfather Seipel; and their son, Meriam's brother, Bill Seipel.

Grandmom Benson suffered from sundowners syndrome, a mood disorder that afflicted her when evening came. After dinner, she would become irritated and irrational toward her son and daughter-in-law until bedtime, and sometimes again during the night. Often, the only person who could comfort her was little Willa, who curled up in her lap and spoke soothingly to the old woman.

A stroke had paralyzed Grandfather Seipel from the neck down. His wife and especially his son did the necessary work of lifting to wash and tend him, but his care took Meriam's time too. And Bill himself needed Meriam's attention. He had returned from World War I severely shell shocked. The electric shock treatments doctors ordered for him left him unable to work. After he told his wife she could divorce him because he "wasn't going to be much good," she did. By the time Willa was born (January 30, 1937), Bill depended on his sister and her husband for support and care.[6]

These four adult family members brought heavy responsibilities to Meriam Benson, and on top of these, she was diligently trying to do what she considered her most important job—managing the demanding social life her attorney husband wanted and needed for his career. Willa, the third child born into this household, was mostly handed off to the maid. Willa's sister, Janice, eight years older, busied herself with her own friends and activities. Willa's older brother Frank didn't include her either in his masculine world. And Frank was a terrible tease. He annoyed Willa constantly, perhaps contributing to the development of her strong will.

Willa's early memories were not happy ones. Craving the attention of her mother and father, she found them always either busy or away. She remembered walking around the house alone, with a cookie in her hand. Her beloved baby dolls were her closest companions. Every night she put them to bed and prayed over them. She only stopped playing with dolls when she was so old she worried that others might laugh at her continued attachment. One day when she was twelve, she moved the dolls and their crib from her room to the attic. Doing this broke her heart. For the time being, Willa's dolls satisfied her need to be needed. Later she would be surprised by the anger she felt at a real baby who behaved differently from a lifeless doll.

During her childhood, Willa kept a calendar with big squares for each day. She blacked out every day she considered a bad day. Her sister, Janice, remembered seeing it one month with every square black but one.

As a neglected child in her parents' busy household, Willa (wrongly) concluded that because her parents didn't pay attention to her, she was unimportant and unlovable. At one point, all alone, she vowed to cut herself off emotionally from others, especially her father, who commanded great respect in the family and in the world but never had time for her. She was obeying a persistent, misleading thought that kept occurring to her. It told her if she cut others out of her life, "No one will ever hurt you. You won't be in pain again."

Willa said later, "The evil one is very present where children are hurt. I became like a robot when I was very young. I vowed to cut my father out of my life. To me, he was dead."

---

After studying Nancy Groom's book *From Bondage to Bonding*, and led by the Lord, Willa finally renounced the old vow to cut herself off emotionally from her father. She experienced "the end of me—of the old me." Psychologically, it was an important event. She had come slowly to soften her heart so it could receive love from God, Alan, and others.

"God showed me things piece by piece. He looked beyond my faults and saw my need," Willa said. This is why, when she later spoke to wives of SSA men, Willa didn't give them a list of "things to do to be holy." She wanted them, after they gave their lives to God, to put Him in control, uncovering their buried hurts and allowing Him to heal them. "God's timing is so perfect," Willa said. "The Lord was gentle with me. He knew just how much I could stand at a time."

After she renounced her childhood vow, Willa was ready to take her place beside her husband in ministry and in marriage. What resulted, except for one relapse, "wasn't a partnership with God and with Alan," Willa said. "It was a union."

---

One weekend in 1981, Bobby, the Medingers' former foster child, went to a spiritual retreat sponsored by an Episcopalian church group. At this time, Bobby's parents were leaders of the Baltimore Regeneration parents' group. Bobby had faithfully attended Regeneration meetings for almost two years and was making progress overcoming his same-sex desires. However, some priests at the retreat, who were themselves homosexual, told him he didn't need to give up his homosexuality to be a Christian. "You can be actively gay, and God will still love you," they told him. Their teaching contained an important truth, "God loves you no matter what." However, they said nothing about Bobby responding to God's love by loving and obeying Him in return.

Bobby decided to go back to homosexual relationships. Alan deeply regretted seeing him drop out of Regeneration. Though Bobby never came back to the ministry, his parents continued their work with Regeneration, and succeeded, over time, in reestablishing a close relationship with him. Alan said he "grew quite close to them in the years before they died."

Fourteen years after Bobby left Regeneration in 1981, he was dead at age 43 of AIDS, a disease unknown when he returned to his homosexual life. During Bobby's last days, Alan and Willa visited him often in a hospice. "I made some wrong decisions, didn't I?" he asked them.

Alan commented in *Regeneration News* about Bobby's death, "We mourn that he chose to lead the life that he did, but we trust in the goodness and mercy of our God."[7]

Years later, Frank Worthen remembered Bobby as an outgoing, loveable man. They had met at the Exodus V conference. Frank said, "The pro-gay movement took his life."

CHAPTER 7

# Healing Prayer

*As a sexual neurosis, homosexuality is regarded as one of the most complex. As a condition for God to heal, it is . . . remarkably simple.*

~ Leanne Payne

A CHURCH THAT WOULD OFFER a meeting place for Regeneration was on Alan's prayer list in the spring of 1982. Ministry groups were growing too large for his living room, and his two-year quest for another place to meet had not met with success. Alan did not usually "put down a fleece" as Gideon did in the Bible—that is, ask God for a sign that a certain action is pleasing to Him. But one day, thinking about a church some friends recommended, Alan prayed, "God, if You want us in this church, let the first person who talks to us after the service today be wearing green."

He, Willa, and Stephen were about to attend St. Mary's, a charismatic church belonging to the Episcopal Church United States of America (ECUSA), as St. Margaret's did. As Alan and Willa prepared to leave after the service, the first person to speak to them was a lady in a bright green dress. She said, "Welcome to St. Mary's!"

The real clincher to their decision to make this their new church home came from Father Richard Lipka, the rector. Alan and Willa told him about Regeneration. He had never heard of it, but after the Medingers described the ministry, he asked, "And where do you meet?"

Alan said, "In our home."

"That's terrible!" Father Lipka responded. "If you ever need a place to meet, consider yourselves welcome here."[1]

Alan and Willa started attending St. Mary's regularly, and "it felt like home" to them. Willa said the walls of her heart opened there because of the love she encountered. She became fully able to receive love from God, Alan, and other people in this place and to give her love in return. Alan also grew spiritually here. For Stephen, almost six, St. Mary's was the right place for the Christian training that he, like any child, needed. After a while, Willa became co-director of St. Mary's choir, and she enjoyed it immensely, just as she had enjoyed directing the choir at St. Margaret's.

In July 1982, when Alan and Willa attended Exodus VII, they were a couple in one accord spiritually, emotionally, mentally, and physically. Both had a wonderful time on this trip. To reach the conference site in Vancouver, British Columbia, they first drove to Toronto with two other conferees, Sy Rogers and Roger Rue. Then all four took the train to Vancouver to enjoy the spectacular scenery. They stayed overnight in Banff for the refreshment of seeing Lake Louise and the Canadian Rockies up close.

At Trinity Western College in Vancouver, they met seventy other Exodus conferees. Leanne Payne, four years older than Alan, was the principal speaker. She had recently incorporated her Pastoral Care Ministries in Milwaukee, Wisconsin. There, Payne and her helpers taught and practiced "healing prayer" during five-day retreats for doctors and medical professionals, pastors, church lay leaders, counselors, and persons needing healing. In Payne's long-time study of C.S. Lewis, she had found inspiration to teach people how to seek God's presence and find their ultimate healing, using Scripture as their guide to what is real.

In healing prayer, counselors and counselees begin by praying, invoking, and visualizing Jesus present with them. Led by counselors, the counselees ask Jesus to bring up from the subconscious any memory of a submerged hurt that needs healing. Then, in the prayed-for presence of Jesus, the counselees are led to forgive those in the remembered scene.

They also are led to forgive themselves for any wrong done because of the old hurt, and, if necessary, they forgive God too. (Payne discovered, during years of counseling, that when children are grievously hurt, they sometimes blame God Himself for the event, since they cannot bring themselves to blame the perpetrators.)

Payne did not come from an SSA background herself, but she had seen in her ministry dramatic recoveries from homosexuality. These she described in her just-published book, *The Broken Image: Restoring Personal Wholeness Through Healing Prayer.* She states in its preface, "As a sexual neurosis, homosexuality is regarded as one of the most complex. As a condition for God to heal, it is (in spite of the widespread belief to the contrary) remarkably simple."[2]

"Matthew" is one SSA man Payne prayed with and then taught how to continue his healing by means of "listening prayer," another of Payne's techniques, which means keeping a prayer journal and "receiv[ing] the healing word God is always speaking in the place of . . . misleading or lying words." He returned several years later, joyful at his changed life. Payne said, "He knows beyond all shadow of a doubt that if God could and would heal him, He can and will heal anyone. He knows also that there is really no such thing as a 'homosexual' person. There are only those who need healing . . . and the knowledge of their own higher selves in Christ."[3]

Alan read Payne's book just before the conference, so he was well prepared to learn from her. He said the book "opened me to healing prayer."

At this time, Payne was meditating on "one of the most satisfying and richly rewarding studies"—what she called "the true masculine" and "the true feminine." She had learned from C.S. Lewis's writings that God "is so masculine that we are all feminine in relation to Him." God the Father initiates, creates, plans, and leads, which are all masculine acts. Yet He also loves us, nurtures us, and draws us to Himself—feminine acts. Payne stated that "The essence of masculinity is initiation. The essence of femininity is response." As a person matures in Christ, she said, and learns to practice listening prayer, he or she will discover the gift of gender and celebrate it.

From Payne, Alan began to understand his problems with leadership. He had grown up unaffirmed in his masculinity by his father, who experienced chronic depression almost all of Alan's life. In Payne's terms, Alan "suffered severely from the lack of a warm and loving father to pattern after, the necessary masculine role model."[4]

As Alan described himself later, "I could not do the things that men do because I had never grown up to become a man. In many ways my growth into manhood had ground to a halt in my early adolescence."[5] Without an affirming male in a boy's life, Payne said, his body grows to manhood, but he remains immature in his gender identity development.

However, she believed masculinity can be learned later, even in adulthood, when a man is affirmed by Jesus Himself and by psychologically healthy men, whom she calls "whole men." Payne said "a study of homosexuality turns out to be a study of arrested growth in at least a part of the personality: it is a study in immaturity."[6]

Understanding this growing-into-masculinity process, Alan stopped blaming himself for failures to lead. He became patient with himself. This was freeing to him, but even more freeing was the realization that God was not condemning him for his failure to lead. The Lord "knew I had to grow up, and He would be very patient as the process took place," Alan wrote.[7]

At the same time, though no longer condemning Alan for his weaknesses, God expected him to overcome them. "Well, that's just the way I am" would never be an excuse in God's eyes to stay at an "acceptable" level of sin, Alan said, for His standard is always "absolute purity." God is "the perfect father, totally loving and accepting us while always urging us to change and grow." Just as physical growth into manhood is slow, so is psychological growth. As Alan continued to develop and identify as a man, no longer as a homosexual (who feels himself a non-man—neither a man nor a woman), he would develop as a leader. This insight gave him needed confidence to attempt leadership roles.

---

An explanation for Alan's problems can be found in his childhood. His father, Irwin Medinger, graduated from law school but never practiced law. Instead, he found a job with the Maryland Department of Social Services, counseling physically and mentally handicapped children and adults to help them find job training and employment. This was his life's work. He was never promoted.

When Alan was born (May 18, 1936), an unplanned child, his parents, Enid and Irwin, were a little disappointed. They would have preferred a daughter, for they already had a four-year-old son, Peter. Since Pete was more athletic, more "all boy" than Alan as they grew up, "he became Dad's, and I became Mom's," Alan said.[8]

Shortly before Alan's birth, his paternal grandmother died, and the family moved into his grandfather's house. Clarence Edward ("Ed") Medinger lived in a corner row house on a busy street in northwest Baltimore. A dominant person, Ed always sat at the head of his table and led family discussions during meals. Irwin slowly became passive and depressed as his father usurped the position of family leader.

Irwin's depression, in time, dominated the family's life. During his worst episodes, he drank excessively and fought verbally with his wife. Sometimes he was hospitalized in the psychiatric wing of the local hospital. Because of his illness, Irwin was never able to mentor Alan as a father mentors a male child to be comfortable with masculinity. To Alan, his father became a nonentity, always sitting in his chair reading the newspaper, never interested enough in his younger son to play with him, supervise homework, or discipline him in any way. Though Alan never hated his father or even felt conscious anger at him, he shut him out of his emotional life.

Alan especially regretted that his father never disciplined him—never set limits on his activities. "Children thrive with limits," he said, "especially limits set by fathers."[9] His father's inability to discipline him he considered a lack of protection as well as a lack of affirmation and direction. During his childhood Alan suffered a recurrent bad dream that he interpreted as a view of his life with no limits. In it, he flew through the air and then crashed into a wall.

Often in an unhappy marriage, the son becomes a confidant of one parent. Alan was his mother's confidant to some extent, but not excessively. He had fond memories of his mother, who loved to read the Bible and Shakespeare and to quote from those sources. Born in England, she moved to America in her teens, along with her parents, Dorothy and Thomas Paxton, and her sister, Jessie. "Whatever character I have, my mother gave me," Alan said. From her he learned to be honest, honorable, and loyal, and also to attend the Episcopal church. "Good people go to church," was Alan's perception of this, "and we are good people."

As time passed, the cloud over Irwin Medinger grew blacker as his doctors prescribed pills and treatments that confused his mind, though they failed to relieve his depression. Once, when Alan was eleven, he stood by and watched his mother alternately throw cold and hot water on his naked father, who stood in the bathtub. She was following a psychiatrist's orders. At times Irwin received electric shock treatments, from which he recovered slowly. These impaired his memory, and he was "out of it" for weeks afterwards. Nothing relieved his suffering.

Like Willa, Alan as a child vowed to make himself invulnerable. In his own words, "I have a vivid memory of lying in bed one night as a young boy, listening to my parents fight, and saying to myself quite smugly, 'They can never hurt me. No one will ever hurt me.' I believe that . . . as a consequence of that decision, until my conversion years later, I would never be free to truly love anyone."[10]

This vow established the defensive wall in Alan's soul that came down only when Jesus broke through it in 1974 and poured His love upon him.

---

With the help of Leanne Payne's teaching and prayer at the Vancouver Exodus conference, Alan could accept the little boy in himself, and he could strongly affirm that boy's desire to be a man. His realization that he was growing into manhood, and thereby becoming more capable of leadership, came in good time, for Alan's challenges to lead were continuing. He taught a workshop on self-esteem at this Exodus conference, while continuing on the board of directors. At home, he was now chief financial officer of his firm's large real estate branch. He learned to handle this leadership position despite the stress because it operated through a formal structure, and he had a clear role. But assuming leadership positions in Exodus, Alan said, "was an unbelievable challenge to me; I was scared to death." He feared looking foolish in front of the other conferees. Also, he felt challenged by the lack of structure in the growing and evolving organization.

According to Willa, Alan at this time expressed his lack of confidence during public speaking by holding his head down and clearing his throat before uttering a word. Still, she thought he spoke well.

Willa loved Leanne Payne and her teaching. "I could absorb Leanne and understand her message," she said. "She was so pretty and energetic and graceful. Her personality was so real."

For a woman to experience "the true feminine,"[11] Payne teaches, she must learn to welcome her intuitive, contemplative, symbolic, and feeling mind. Because our culture values rational thought inordinately, it fails to value the special gender gifts of women, Payne says, especially the "intuitive capacity" that helps us "see, worship, adore, and respond to God." In healing prayer, Payne tries to help women understand how important their special gifts are and how impoverished men are when intuition and contemplation of God are ignored. A "whole woman," Payne teaches, values herself as a responsive and nurturing person, receiving love from God and giving it abundantly to those about her. She delights in being "creaturely."

This teaching helped Willa advance in the process she had already begun, learning to love others and express more richly her nurturing capabilities, and it came at the right time. At home Willa faced the challenge of helping her daughters resolve the hurts they had endured from her during many angry years. Laura, especially, had suffered from

Willa's out-of-control anger, some of it aimed at Laura when Alan, the cause of it, was unavailable. All throughout high school, Laura was terrified of her mother. For years she desired counseling. In the spring before the Leanne Payne conference, when Laura was a senior in high school, she had reluctantly shown a mediocre report card to her mother. Willa raged at Laura, and for the first time in her life, Laura spoke back. Having done this, Laura left the room and collapsed, shaking.

At last, Willa was confronted with the evidence that her anger was corrosive. She told Laura to sit down, and then she spoon fed her daughter a cup of tea. Willa asked, "Do you want counseling?" and Laura answered, eagerly, "Yes."

Willa took her to a skilled Christian counselor who prayed with Laura and sought to find the cause of her problems. But Laura couldn't get beyond a certain blocked memory, so the counselor asked Laura to bring Willa to the next session. Then Willa shared a memory of Laura at age one. She had wanted attention from her mother, and to get it, she knocked an ashtray on the floor. Willa beat the baby so badly that Willa's mother came running from a nearby room to rescue Laura. Remembering this, Willa said to Laura at the session, in a matter-of-fact tone, "I didn't love you."

To Laura, that was okay, because after Willa described the incident, she could now remember it and her mother's lack of affection at the time. The recalled memory, and the prayer that followed, set Laura free to begin forgiving and loving her mother. From this time, mother and daughter slowly healed.[12]

Beth's issues with both her parents took longer to resolve because no event precipitated them into the light for many years.

---

Frank Worthen, another attendee at the Leanne Payne conference, said, "Vancouver was a healing time." He appreciated Payne's hopeful message, for she was totally convinced God could heal SSA people. "This certainty resonated with everyone," he said. "We all grew up with Leanne. It was a time of putting the past behind us."[13]

Results from healing prayer, of course, continued long after the conference ended. Payne had prayed with Sy Rogers to help him forgive his mother. Sy accepted her prayer, though at the time, he said defensively to himself, "I've already done that—forgiven her."

His mother, an alcoholic, had died in a car accident when Sy was five. Her abrupt and unexpected death caused the little boy not only immense hurt, but anger at her for leaving him. He also suffered from what he perceived as his father's failure to love him. Sy's father, while he confronted his own grief, had sent the boy away to live with relatives for over a year.

On the way back to Toronto on the train, sitting behind Alan and Willa, Sy began to weep and couldn't stop. (Alan and Willa were unaware of this.) Sy saw an image of his mother's body lying in her coffin, and the intense pain of that long-submerged memory came back to him. He cried for hours.

At one point, the conductor came through the car and said, "Is there something I can do for you?"

Sy answered, "No, I'm fine really; I'm processing, and this is good."[14]

Nearly twenty years later, as the chief speaker at Exodus XXVI, Sy taught that one way to keep from falling back into homosexuality is to "Be instantly ready to forgive." He might have said, "Forgive, and if necessary, forgive again."[15]

---

Moving to St. Mary's church for its weekly meetings proved a blessing to Regeneration. Alan began to understand the importance of partnering with a church. Eventually, the ministry asked the church to "take it under its wing" and provide oversight and accountability—to approve all Regeneration Board of Trustee appointments and to provide a pastor or vestry member as board president.[16] Alan and Father Lipka met each week to discuss ministry needs.

Both Alan and his administrative assistant, Luanna Hutchison, were commissioned by St. Mary's as healing ministers so that Father Lipka could mark them as belonging to one of the church's three ministries—preaching, teaching, and healing. St. Mary's also helped Regeneration financially and granted it use of the pastoral counseling staff (for individuals needing special help) and intercessory prayer ministry.

Alan came to believe, "In the perfect world and in the perfect church, all of the ministry that a homosexual [person] needs would be found in the local church." After writing this in *Regeneration News*, he corrected himself by saying, "Wait a minute, in the perfect world there wouldn't be any homosexuality. Well, you know what I'm getting at."[17]

He continued to believe the local church should be the primary place for SSA people to heal and grow. But at that time (the end of 1986), he said, "In actual practice not many churches have done well in ministry to homosexual [people]." He mentioned four that successfully modeled care to them—his own St. Mary's Episcopal Church, College Hill Presbyterian Church in Cincinnati, The Church of the Open Door in San Rafael, California, and the Vineyard in Santa Monica, California. Each of these had three characteristics:

> They considered themselves fellowships of sinners and not congregations of righteous people,
>
> They believed in God's power to change lives, and
>
> They responded to the gospel with total commitment.[18]

Regeneration was never the sole property of one church. It retained its interdenominational outreach, considering itself "a ministry to the body of Christ." The board of trustees was always interdenominational.[19] Alan and other leaders spoke at any church open to the Regeneration message and accepted as clients anyone struggling with homosexuality, no matter the denomination. Unchurched people were also accepted if they wanted help.

Nearly five years after the Medingers began attending St. Mary's, Alan formally thanked them for helping Regeneration. The church had lost some members, who preferred not associating with former SSA persons. And the singles group had grown smaller because so many

Regeneration participants attended St. Mary's that people in the community thought if you were young and single and went to this church, you must be gay. For some young people, this stigma caused them to seek another church home.

Still, Alan believed the church was helped by associating with Regeneration: "I think it is basically good that St. Mary's reaches out to a people who have been rejected, those neglected by the church. God is blessing St. Mary's for its boldness and willingness to reach out to the lost and truly hurting."[20]

Father Lipka agreed. When asked, "On balance, has your association with this ministry been good or bad for the church?" he answered, "I think it's been very, very good for the church in the sense of helping us to have some real healing ministry in an area which is . . . not being dealt with in a manner that's very positive and helpful."[21]

He said he considered Regeneration an important reminder that "there is still a basic, fundamental statement made by God about this. . . . It's creational, not a particular denominational or faith thing. It goes back to creation. 'God made them male and female, male and female He created them.' And God's creational intention is that male and female come together in marriage."

When in 1989 Father Lipka and his family left St. Mary's to serve in another St. Mary's Episcopal Church in Hawaii, Alan felt great loss. Receiving the Eucharist from Father Rich on his last Sunday at St. Mary's was an emotional experience. "I was hit," Alan said, "with the sudden realization that no man in my life has believed in me like Rich has." Seven years before, when Alan and Willa first came to the church, Alan said, "I was quite a different person . . . filled with insecurities with respect to the ministry that I was starting." The growth Alan experienced, he said, is "in no small part due to the way that Rich has believed in me and in Regeneration."[22]

CHAPTER 8:

# Surviving on Radical Faith

*I have to do what God wants me to do. I can't do what pleases you.*

~ Alan Medinger

WILLA WAS AMBIVALENT ABOUT ALAN'S involvement in Exodus International after he was elected to its board of directors. Although she believed God had called him to his own local ministry—Regeneration—she was concerned about the extra burdens he assumed in the much larger organization.

At a January 1983 Exodus board meeting in Denver, Alan challenged the other board members, saying, "Exodus has tended to be an inward-looking group. Our vision has been too narrow. We have not been on the offensive in proclaiming Christ's power to deliver people from homosexuality."[1]

The Exodus board elected Alan its president[2] at the June annual conference that year and responded to his earlier challenge to expand their vision. Under his leadership, they voted to assist new ministries and encourage publication of books, tapes, and other materials useful to SSA people who wanted to change, as well as to their families, pastors, and churches. They also decided to increase advertising for the annual conferences and to establish a new "board of reference" to watch over and advise the Exodus board. On this board were ten Christian leaders from various denominations who, unlike the Exodus leaders, had never experienced same-sex attractions. Because these leaders were known and respected in the wider Christian community, Exodus hoped they would help it gain credibility. (After ten years, Exodus was much better established, and the board of reference was discontinued.)[3]

Clearly, Alan intended to do his best as board president, even enlarging the scope of the organization, no matter the cost to himself. This worried Willa.

At this conference, however, Willa enjoyed herself. In fact, Frank Worthen said later that Alan and Willa were "like lovebirds. They danced together. They got everyone else dancing too." It appeared to Frank that Willa was now totally healed of her anger.

Whether recovered SSA people should seek to marry was still a thorny question for some ministry leaders, but not for Alan and Frank, who believed in healing with the potential of marriage as a goal for single people. They also believed God wanted to restore marriages threatened by discoveries of homosexuality in one of the spouses. Obviously, the Medingers themselves were demonstrating a restored marriage now, Frank said.[4]

In November 1983, Alan's family grew when Willa's widowed mother, unable to care for herself, came to live with them. At age 83, Meriam Benson was diagnosed with breast cancer that had metastasized into the bone. More than twenty years earlier, in another bout with cancer, she had had a radical mastectomy. This time, the doctors gave her six months to live.[5]

Alan loved Meriam and had always treated her affectionately. Now he was especially tender with her. He suggested she come to the Episcopal church where Father Philip Zampino conducted healing services, but Meriam, a Methodist, was afraid to go. She thought a charismatic service would be too odd and scary. Gently, Alan and Willa persuaded her. They took her in her wheelchair to a healing service and afterwards to the sacristy, a private place in the church. There, Father Zampino greeted Meriam, laid his hands on her head and, after praying aloud quietly, said, "Be healed, Meriam, in the name of Jesus."

Meriam was docile and received the prayer without a murmur. She said later the church service reminded her of Methodist camp meetings she went to as a child.

The three went home that evening with Meriam seemingly unchanged. Soon afterwards, she got out of her wheelchair. Her mind, which had sometimes been confused, cleared. She continued living with Alan and Willa as her strength slowly returned. And the cancer disappeared.

After some time, when Meriam was strong enough, she moved to a Christian retirement home, Asbury Village Apartments in Gaithersburg, Maryland. She lived there awhile and then moved into the home of her son and daughter-in-law, Arthur and Gloria Benson, for another six years, except for occasional visits to the homes of her daughters, Janice Benson Paulsen and Willa. Alan wrote in 1989 that she was "in wonderful physical condition for an 89-year-old lady." Meriam died on February 22, 1990.[6]

---

Meanwhile, day-to-day life continued. Alan was handling the load of stresses in his life, but he felt "stretched too thin." He was an executive at work, and on top of that, he was president of Exodus, director of Regeneration, and the head of his family, six in all including Meriam. Most of the time, he was "just overwhelmed with things and totally exhausted."[7]

The following year, in the summer of 1984, Alan was in charge of Exodus IX in Baltimore, which attracted about 120 people. He planned to teach on spiritual warfare, and, strangely, felt oppressed and harassed as he worked on organizing the event. When the Exodus board arrived a few days before the conference and met together in the Medinger home, Alan asked for prayer to help him deal with the stress. Board member Bob Davies recalled that as the members gathered around Alan to pray, he sobbed under the weight of all the pressure he felt. Bob believes their prayer was answered, because "the conference went wonderfully, and it seemed very well run to me as a participant."[8]

Even with this prayer support, Alan said that speaking on spiritual warfare "tore me apart." He described the extra dimension he saw in battling sexual perversions—the work of evil spirits drawing people away from God and His desires for His people. After his message, Alan remembered nothing of what he had said. He believed the Holy Spirit helped him deliver it, because his message had the desired impact. Andrew Comiskey told him, "That's when I realized this was spiritual warfare."[9] (Comiskey, a former student of Leanne Payne, was at this time director of Desert Stream Ministries in Anaheim, California, and author of the Living Waters program.)

Alan had arranged for Robert Frost, author of the book *Our Heavenly Father,* to speak at the conference. Using Scripture, Frost taught that we should all see ourselves as children of God and experience the Father's love, because He has given this love to be the energy empowering a growing spiritual life. Then, especially for those in the audience who had not experienced the love of a natural father, he described from the Bible what it is to be loved by a heavenly father who is so intimate that we call him "Abba!" or, in our terms, "Daddy!"

Following his talk, Dr. Frost asked anyone who needed the Heavenly Father's touch to come forward. Nearly the entire audience responded. Christian leaders asked the people to behave like children with fathers—to lay their heads on the leaders' shoulders and accept hugs. Then the leaders prayed one by one for them. The room filled with grateful sobs from men and women receiving divine love they had needed all their lives. Mario Bergner was one of these. He said, "For the first time in my life I believed that God is a real Father who genuinely delights in me and loves me."[10]

A professor of math from Messiah College in Mechanicsburg, Pennsylvania, Gene Chase, came to Baltimore for his first conference and heard Frost speak, a moving experience for him. He chose a front row seat and "spent most of my time crying," because the talk touched an emotional nerve. Gene had been same-sex attracted in his youth but had been healed for twelve years, since 1972, "following the same principles that Exodus teaches, except that I learned them on my own." From the Bible and prayer he had discovered that "putting Christ first" was the essential step to becoming holy and becoming whole.

A blessing came to Gene at the conference, though he didn't see it as a blessing until several years later. Alan and Willa, as well as other Exodus leaders, served communion the last day. Gene went forward, picking the shortest line, which was the Medingers'. When Alan and Willa prayed over him, they believed their message was inspired by the Holy Spirit: "God, in His good time, will raise up an Exodus group in Mechanicsburg with Gene as the leader."[11]

This was not Gene's desire at all. "When you're being freed from homosexuality," he said later, "this is the last thing you want to proclaim." He believes this is one reason why the statistics that tell how many people have been helped by ministries to SSA strugglers are unreliably low. Those who are healed want to fit into society, and they think, "What would my kids and my kids' friends think?" So they hide their former experiences.

One conferee, Katherine Allen from upstate New York, felt herself "an odd fish" at this Exodus, because she was not same-sex attracted and did not come seeking healing for herself or a loved one. She was an administrator in a small liberal arts college in Pennsylvania. Finding herself an unofficial counselor there to female students caught in the intersection of the sexual revolution and feminism, she looked for answers to puzzling questions in various books and from various people. So much of what she found was "without hope" and, in fact, "stupid," she said, that she was relieved to find wise teaching in Baltimore. Many of the conferees were pursuing a radical relationship with Christ, something she had not experienced. "They were salty," she said, and "they made me thirsty for a closer walk."

Katherine noticed the prayer/intercession room that Alan had set apart for the week so that people could retire there, one hour at a time, and cover the conference with prayer. The task of these prayer warriors was to support those who were engaging in spiritual battle. As one who prayed there, Katherine said, "It was a very special time for me."[12]

This ninth Exodus attracted more press than any previous conference. A reporter, Beth Spring from *Christianity Today* magazine, visited for a day and wrote a major report with photos, which gave the organization international publicity. "Until more churches learn to address the acute spiritual and emotional needs of homosexuals," she said, "groups that are part of the Exodus coalition intend to fill the gap." She praised these ministries because they "offer authentic models of change for men and women still struggling with a misplaced sexual identity."[13]

Conferees were encouraged when Frank Worthen announced he was engaged to marry Anita Thomas, and they planned a November wedding. To everyone's delight, a picture of Anita, a tall, good-looking redhead, was projected on a screen. This news backed up Alan's position that ministries should support more than just "white-knuckling it" for their clients, that is, living celibate lives but tortured by ongoing same-sex attractions.

In the fall of 1984, having led Regeneration for five years, Alan felt the Lord telling him, "Go public." So when he was invited to give his testimony on the 700 Club television program, he accepted. The interviewer, Ben Kinchlow, told him before the show, "You're here because God wants you here. If we don't ask the right questions, you lead the discussion where you want it to go." Consequently, the interview went well. Alan spoke about what God had done and was doing in his life.

At this time, both Medinger daughters were in college, incurring expenses that Alan covered. Regeneration didn't bring in any income; rather, Alan spent from his earnings to support the ministry. He could do this because he was well paid as vice president of his firm's real estate development wing.

Following up on the 700 Club interview, a reporter from a local newspaper, the *Baltimore News American*, interviewed Alan for a feature article to be published later. Soon after that, what Willa called "the huge event" took place in Alan and Willa's private lives. It began with a prayer. Not believing he could tolerate any longer the burden of the combined stresses from his job, his duties in a rapidly growing Regeneration, his leadership of Exodus, and everything else in his life, and feeling "totally overwhelmed," Alan prayed, "God, You've got to do something! I can't go on any longer this way."

Later that same day, his boss at the company called him into the office. He said he knew about the 700 Club interview—his wife had seen it and told him "an ex-gay is working for you." This was "embarrassing to the company," he said, cautioning Alan not to publicize his past, because that made the firm look bad.

He warned, "You have to remember where your priorities are."

Alan answered firmly, "I know where my priorities are. I have to do what the Lord called me to do."

Very soon after, the *Baltimore News American* interview appeared in print, and it was not buried on a back page. It appeared on page one of the Sunday paper, right beside a picture of Alan. The next day, "feeling totally naked," Alan went to his job. "That Monday was one of the most difficult of my life,"[14] he said later. His boss called him to his private office and asked for Alan's immediate resignation. Alan complied and drove home early.

He was already there by the time Willa returned from some errands, and he was worried about breaking the news to her.

"Why are you home?" she asked in surprise.

"I lost my job," he told her simply.

Willa's immediate reaction was to console him. She was sympathetic, and then—he grinned. It was a smile of relief.

Alan believed God had called him to ministry, and God was now answering his prayer for relief from manifold stresses. Whether it was the wish of his boss or his wife, he said, "I have to do what God wants me to do. I can't do what pleases you."

Seeing him smile, Willa instantly grew angry. She realized their financial security was gone. Not only was his paycheck not going to be arriving anymore, but they had almost no savings. And Alan didn't seem to care. Controlling her emotions, she climbed the stairs to Stephen's bedroom. Then she lay down on the floor and screamed. Kicking felt good, releasing her tensions, so she kicked the floor.

The phone rang, and Alan answered it. It was their pastor, Father Lipka. Alan told him what had happened.

"How is Willa?" he asked.

"Well, she's on the floor, kicking and screaming," Alan answered.

Willa had lost not only her financial security but also her pleasure in being the wife of a man who for twenty-two years had been with the same important company, the last years as an executive. While Alan was vice president of the company, "we were looked up to," Willa said. Now that was gone. She imagined them forced to sell their home and move to a run-down olive gray slum house in downtown Baltimore. They would live in poverty, and "everything would be drab, our whole existence." Not only were Laura and Beth still in college, but eight-year-old Stephen needed to be fed, clothed, and educated.

Later that day, Willa went to St. Mary's Church, arriving early to assist with choir practice. She broke down sobbing. Four men who were good friends prayed with her, which put her back together emotionally, and she went on to lead the choir. She said, "Those men showed me God's heart of love that evening."

That same night, a phone call came for Alan from his daughter Beth's boyfriend. He invited Alan for lunch the next day because he wanted to ask for Beth's hand in marriage, which he then did, and it was granted. When Willa heard about this, her concerns about money intensified—they now had a wedding to plan and pay for.

For a long time after Alan lost his job, Willa worried about money.[15] Her friend Sue O'Neill said Willa collected "about a thousand" coupons for food, and when they shopped for groceries together, it took Willa three hours to make her choices. She also became an expert at shopping in discount stores, where she examined each item carefully before selecting something to buy. Often she left empty-handed.

Soon after, Alan consulted his attorney brother-in-law, Frank Benson, for advice on a settlement with the company. Then Alan asked for and received a year's severance pay, a year of health insurance for the family, and continuation of Beth's college scholarship, which the company had promised her. That these requests were granted, Alan considered "a miraculous answer to prayer," because he saw no other way that he could have survived financially without the job. With these provisions from his company, Alan had one year's cushion before he needed to begin receiving a salary.

Asked five years later if leaving his job and going full-time with the ministry was a difficult transition, Alan answered, "I've never looked back and never regretted a minute of it." It did stretch him though. He said, "I've probably grown more through having to be in a faith ministry than in anything else that's happened to me in the last five years."[16]

---

After losing his job, Alan spent several days praying and fasting over finances. Then he started raising money for Regeneration, for which he now worked full-time. He needed rent money when he leased a small office from a Christian counseling group.[17] In January 1985, Alan drew up a budget of $21,390 for the upcoming year with no salary for himself. Six months later, the ministry had received only $8,810.25 in "contributions received . . . and in view," that is, pledged.[18]

Participants in Regeneration increased after Alan went full-time. So many came that Regeneration, in time, started a second group in northern Virginia for people from northern Virginia and Washington, D.C. The two groups kept in close contact.

Ministry speaking engagements also increased, and Alan now had time to accept them. In May he conducted a leadership development class for sixteen people who wished to minister to people struggling with unwanted same-sex attractions. Topics included "The Basics of Homosexuality," "Healing Expectations," and "Inner Healing." Dr. Larry Dietrich, Willa's former counselor, conducted a session on "The Wounded Healer."[19]

In April 1985, Alan hired his first paid employee, Luanna Hutchison, as his administrative assistant. She became the first editor of an ambitious six-page monthly newsletter, *Regeneration News*, which began in July. It inaugurated a new logo, a flourishing tree that clarified the ministry's name: "We hope that the tree clearly symbolizes change and growth—regeneration—through our Lord Jesus Christ."

Alan now worked as an unpaid volunteer. He knew he needed to become a fund-raiser but said, "With my personality, asking people one on one for money was very difficult."

Nevertheless, one day Alan sensed the Lord leading him to ask a fellow member of St. Mary's Church for a donation to Regeneration. This man was non-committal during their talk, but later he pledged and gave $12,000.

With this encouragement, Alan went to other Episcopal churches. He had reason to be nervous when he asked for an interview with Father John W. Howe, rector of Truro Episcopal Church in Fairfax, Virginia. Several years earlier, this church had sponsored a ministry to SSA strugglers that failed because its leader became sexually involved with a client. Would Father Howe and the vestry want to commit prayer and money to another leader, one whom they didn't know?

Alan imagined Father Howe entertaining suspicions, but he prayed earnestly, asking the Lord for help, and phoned for an interview. Father Howe was cautious. He agreed to speak with Alan, but he also phoned Alan's rector at St. Mary's, Father Lipka, and asked, "What about this man, Medinger? Is he all right?"[20] The answer was a hearty "yes," and the Truro church became a faithful Regeneration supporter.

Two other big Episcopal churches in northern Virginia also gave—the Church of the Apostles in Fairfax, and Falls Church in Falls Church, near metropolitan Washington, D.C. Other churches, especially Presbyterian ones, and many individuals supported the ministry. Alan said that Regeneration "was a fairly radical faith ministry." He believed God always provides for ministries He calls into being. Except for once or twice in thirty-two years, Regeneration has met its entire yearly budget.

When the ministry had unusual financial needs, Alan would call the board and staff to observe three days of fasting and prayer. Once they needed five thousand dollars by a certain day, so they all fasted and prayed. When that day arrived, Luanna opened the mail.

"Is there a check for five thousand there?" Alan asked.

"Yes!"

Another time, they fasted and prayed again for a specific amount by a certain day. Nothing came in the mail the morning of the due date. In the afternoon, a woman who had worked with Alan in his corporate job stopped by the office to see him. She hand-delivered the donation check that covered their need.

At Christmastime each year, Willa wrote personal thank-you notes to supporters. As time passed and the ministry grew, she would write several hundred personal notes. Their peak year, she wrote one thousand notes. Alan and Willa were especially touched by the faithfulness of those with few resources who supported them. One Catholic brother who had no provision would send them two dollars a year.

Alan did eventually receive a salary from Regeneration, only forty percent of the salary from his former corporation job. Sometimes, if too little money came in, his salary would be paid late, though it was almost always paid by the end of the year. He said, "God led me to a series of surrenders. One was the willingness to accept a substantially lower standard of living."

Having accepted this eventuality, though, Alan and Willa found their lives didn't change drastically. They invited three boarders to share their big home, and these people helped support them. Willa's great economy in shopping was an important contribution to their well being. Five years after leaving his company job, Alan could say, "God has tested me over and over . . . and now I'm pretty peaceful about [my income]. . . .The one area where I still have some way to go is with insecurities about retirement.[21] God is still working with me on that."

In October 1989, after ten years of ministry, Regeneration could thank ten churches for ongoing financial support. Six were Presbyterian—Atonement, Columbia, Grace, Central, Timonium, and Fourth. Four were Episcopalian, the same ones Alan had approached and asked for help—The Falls Church, Church of the Apostles, Truro, and his own St. Mary's. These ten were steadfast in their giving.

At this time the ministry employed five people: Alan, Willa (part-time), Marty Hylbom (who edited the newsletter after Luanna resigned because of marriage and motherhood), Bruce McKutcheon (who became manager of Regeneration Books), and Earl Miller, the office manager. Regeneration was serving about seventy individual clients each week.[22]

As the months and years passed, Willa and Alan discovered day by day that doing the Lord's will did not mean they had to sell their home and live in gray poverty, for by God's provision, enough money arrived—sometimes just in time. Over the years, Willa said, "I came to love Alan's faith for finances."

CHAPTER 9:

# What Does It Mean to Be a Man?

*We are faced with grown men . . . in whom the masculine has not developed.*

~ Alan Medinger

ON SATURDAY NOVEMBER 24, 1984, Frank Worthen, 55, married Anita Thomas at the Church of the Open Door in San Rafael, California. Alan flew out for the event, happy to be participating as a witness in the wedding of a man he deeply admired. Frank's faith that God would heal him from homosexuality, not just part-way but all the way to the potential for healthy heterosexual marriage, was being abundantly fulfilled. (Frank and Alan always said that marriage doesn't confirm that an SSA man or woman is healed; the transition toward holiness confirms it. Not every healed person will find a mate, because some can serve the Lord better as single people.)

The ceremony was a "bare bones wedding," in Anita's words. They chose Carpenter Hall for the event, the building where their church held services, large enough for two hundred guests. Union slogans covered the walls. Leftover Thanksgiving flowers doubled as wedding flowers. Frank, who had a bad cold and had recently lost weight, wore a brown suit that no longer fit. Anita wore a lovely knee-length peach-colored dress with a lacy skirt, and she carried peach carnations. On her head, perched to one side, she wore a white hat trimmed with lace.

The church worship team sang several songs, one especially memorable: "Wait on the Lord. Be of good courage. Wait, I say, on the Lord." Many of the guests were in tears during the ceremony because of the intense emotions they experienced. Bob Davies said on a video interview of wedding guests, "Your getting married told me I can do it." (He married, one year later, a woman Frank had introduced to him.)

When Frank married Anita, they had not had sex and didn't know if it would be possible for them. Frank had been celibate for eleven years, and he half believed what the world says, "If you don't use it, you lose it." But they both agreed that they wanted to spend the rest of their lives together. Anita decided she would accept a marriage of hugging and no sex, if necessary. It would be better than living apart from Frank.

Before the wedding, they agreed not to try having sex on their wedding night, because they knew in advance they would both be exhausted, and indeed, they were. "Wait on the Lord," they thought, was good advice.

However, Frank wrote in his autobiography, *Destiny Bridge,* "Sometime after midnight, we broke our agreement."[1]

They understood God saying to them, "A marriage of convenience would not honor me. I want to give you a testimony of my power to restore life."

According to Anita, "God brought passion into our marriage, and we're still sexually active today. It makes everything different." She added, "Since we've been married, being loved by Frank has made me more secure in the Lord—knowing how deeply He loves me."[2]

---

At the end of 1984, Alan was teaching his Regeneration group new lessons that he'd written himself, based partly on his meditations during quiet times with the Lord and partly on his readings. These teachings were well received. He was eager to learn whatever he could about healing from same-sex attraction.

One topic on his mind was the perennial question: Can a person be both homosexual and Christian? He defined Christian as "a person who has had a conversion experience wherein they have accepted

Christ's atonement on their own behalf and are seeking to lead a life in which Jesus is their Lord."[3]

He defined homosexual as "a man or woman whose primary sexual attraction is toward people of the same gender and who struggle with homosexual lust, whether they act it out or not." (Alan disliked the word "gay" and used it only to refer to SSA persons actively working for a gay rights agenda.)

His answer was—of course God can save people with any involvement in homosexuality, whether action or just attraction. But conversion does not usually mean instant loss of same-sex attractions. The person will be led by Christ to come into a new life and to avoid homosexual acts and thoughts as sin, Alan believed, but not all at once. Similarly, the glutton doesn't convert to a person with healthy eating habits without a struggle. The SSA person will change as the Holy Spirit reveals truth, and in the meantime, Alan's main concern was that church people should love the new Christian. "Jesus takes us as sinful, blind people, often blind to the worst of our sins," he said, "and makes us new creatures. . . . In ministering to the [SSA person], Jesus is the first issue, not homosexuality."

---

One snowy night, after Alan drove twenty-five minutes to St. Mary's Church for a Regeneration meeting, he discovered that nobody else showed up. Was he discouraged? No. He said he never doubted that God wanted him to do this ministry and that He Himself would help it succeed.

Eight people from Regeneration attended the tenth Exodus International conference in San Francisco the first week of July 1985, including Willa and Alan.[4] This was the first time Willa met Anita Thomas, now Anita Worthen. Frank and Anita were back from a three-month honeymoon in Europe, where they had met with Exodus Europe leaders in Switzerland, England, North Wales, France, Germany, Denmark, Norway, Sweden, and Finland. Frank assisted leaders of fledgling ministries in these places, and Anita spoke at meetings, especially to parents of SSA people. (Her only child, a son born before she met Frank, is SSA.)

After Frank married Anita, and Alan and Willa discovered they liked them both, their four-way friendship flourished. As time went by, younger Exodus people called the couples "the four fossils," a term Willa both laughed at and liked, repeating it so often that it stuck.[5]

Many gays came to the conference that year, some of them to picket outside the building. People from pro-gay Metropolitan Community Church spent all week attempting to talk to attendees and explain their theology. Evangelicals Concerned, a pro-gay group from the Episcopal church, mounted what Alan called "a small protest."[6] He and others took this opportunity to tell SSA people, as permitted, about God's power to heal their attractions. A San Francisco gay newspaper also interviewed Alan, and he spoke on a call-in show on San Francisco's largest radio station.

Conference guest speakers were the Reverend Dennis Bennett and his wife, Rita, who spoke on "Release of the Holy Spirit" and "Inner Healing."[7] Reverend Bennett, an Episcopal priest, had written *Nine O'Clock in the Morning* about his experiences with the Lord. He understood healing prayer and wanted to encourage people to practice it. Alan and Willa were happy to meet and befriend Bennett and his wife.

Alan taught a workshop on masculinity in which he asked, "Once we start becoming free of homosexual behavior and identity, what is it we are becoming?" He said Leanne Payne offers one answer in her book, *The Crisis in Masculinity* when she says that "the essence of masculinity is initiation. The essence of femininity is response."

Alan explained that though God the Father is the ultimate masculine model as he initiates and leads creation, He is also feminine as He loves and nurtures. These, he said, are transcendent gender characteristics—that is, they are not limited to physical bodies. All people, created in the image of God, at times display masculine and/or feminine traits—all in accord with God's plan. The important thing for an individual is for masculine traits to predominate in men, and feminine traits in women.

Another explanation of the differences between masculine and feminine, Alan said, is based on brain anatomy. Brain structures suggest that God made men to be "better equipped to handle the visual and spatial and less well equipped to handle the verbal." That is, God made males with a "bias toward action" and females with a bias toward "understanding [people] and communication." One might say a man is made to build and protect, a woman to nurture and create community.

Alan discovered that being able to define masculinity makes a difference to males who want to recover from SSA. Often they have failed to develop a basic masculine character. They feel emotionally cut off from their fathers and from manly men. So when they come for help, "we are faced with grown men . . . in whom the masculine has not developed. . . . How do we lead an adult through adolescence and into manhood?" He was working on that question in 1985; in 2000 he published *Growth into Manhood* with his mature answers.[8]

Alan wrote practical suggestions at this time to help men develop manliness. "Seek to understand masculinity (in terms of the Bible)," Alan advised, and also "come to terms with what society says a man is." (These definitions are not always the same.) Alan discovered that many Regeneration participants, in rejecting their father's influence, also rejected our culture's definition of maleness.

Sometimes a sensitive boy with artistic interests was shunned by male athletes in his high school years, and in anger and hurt he cut himself off from them emotionally. He defined himself as "other" than them and began seeking the company of girls and other artistic boys. This detachment sometimes led to same-sex attractions. Alan did not say that artistic talents *per se* are feminine. Boys who are designed by God to become artists are not less masculine than other boys. But the shunning these sensitive boys endured sometimes made them rebel against the prevailing male prototype of a macho-man-worshipping culture, and in so doing, they cut themselves off from masculine self images. However, even if a society has a warped idea of what it is to be masculine, Alan said, a recovering SSA person must come to terms with what his own society accepts. "Our masculinity will grow in response to other men responding to us as fellow men."

"Accept masculinity as desirable," he advised, and "Repent . . . of arrogant and defensive" attitudes toward manly men. "Practice masculine attributes such as deliberately choosing leadership positions (even when they are difficult)."

Another bit of advice was "Learn to relate to other men . . . on their own terms." Alan pointed out that men who are comfortable with their manhood usually establish friendships and satisfy their need for male bonding not through talking, as women do, but through sports and working with other men—active and physical inter-relating. He suggested socializing with non-SSA men by an activity such as watching a football game together or working with them to build a fence or to landscape property.

Finally, Alan made another suggestion, "Thank God for your masculinity." Over more than ten years, Alan said, God had formed his masculine character so that now "I rejoice in my manhood. My masculinity is truly a blessing." He believed that an accurate definition of masculinity and the desire to live up to it were essential in his own growth as a successful leader of Regeneration and also as a husband. For many years his marriage with Willa, though improving, was marred by anger and faulty communication. Their relationship, both sexual and in daily life, got better as Alan grew into manhood.

Years later, Andrew Comiskey commented that Alan was one of the first leaders to "speak definitively of masculinity." Comiskey said this was important because "the women [we minister to] feared enslavement from traditional men, the men feared a replay of the unrelenting shame they had experienced from them [traditional men]."[9] Both these women and men needed to overcome their old fears and learn to relate to men as fellow Christians.

As Alan and Willa grew in understanding masculinity and femininity, they learned to enjoy their gender differences. Josh Glaser, who much later directed Regeneration, said, "In an area of ministry so focused on the value of gender and complementarity, Alan and Willa exemplified the masculine and the feminine to all of us." Alan was manly in his "linear thinking and relatively stoic demeanor," while Willa was womanly with her "ability to intuit and her well known 'Awwww' that has brought many an aching soul to at last let out needful tears."[10] Over the years, Josh said, hundreds of persons came to Regeneration needing "accepting, loving, prayerful parents. God used Alan and

Willa to re-parent us—with both words of loving and firm truth, and more patience and grace than most of us could ever dream possible."

---

Back home after the conference, Alan was beginning to see fruit in his ministry. He liked being able to work at it full-time. Though he continued to feel insecure as a teacher, Frank Worthen observed that, "Alan was good at teaching. He knows how to make his points clearly, and he doesn't digress. He has always been a pillar."[11]

What helped Alan as a teacher was his belief that about one-third of the healing for an SSA person has already taken place when he or she comes to the ministry. Just by showing up, that person is making the statement, "I'm going to seek help, God. I'm going to do something to please You that is scary to me."

Then by meeting with others in a group, SSA persons gain self-acceptance, Alan believed, for they see that "others have been through what I've been through." They gain support for persevering in trying to live holy lives as they see others trying to do this. In the group too, people learn to forgive, which is basic to healing.

Alan also encouraged participants to depend on quiet times with the Lord, knowing these times were very important to his own healing process. "Let God be your Father," Alan counseled. "Let Him minister to you. Open up to the Healer."

---

In late 1985, Alan was handling the load of stresses in his life well, but he felt unable to take on more. He was executive director of Exodus, director of Regeneration, its chief fund-raiser (an uncertain and worrying job), and head of his family, six in all including, once again, Meriam Benson. She had moved back in with them temporarily. (In late 1984 she moved to the home of her son Arthur and his wife, Gloria, as she recovered from double pneumonia. But after Arthur suffered his second heart attack a year later, Alan and Willa offered to care for Meriam.)

One day Bill Karcher, Alan's childhood friend, phoned the Medingers. Bill had been an alcoholic for many years—since he was a young man.

He had often begged to "come home" to the only place that would take him in after his mother and grandmother died—Alan and Willa's.

"When can I come home, Pax?" he would ask. (He called Alan "Pax" from Alan's middle name, "Paxton," his mother's maiden name.)

"When you've stopped drinking!"

Now Bill phoned with a different message. "Hey, Pax, I stopped drinking, and I'm coming home!" Alan felt he had to keep his word to Bill, even though the timing was inconvenient.

"Okay," he said. "Come ahead."

But Alan didn't see how he could care for Bill on top of everything else. To this problem he reacted strongly in private. "I was so mad at God for bringing Bill home now," he said, "that I shook my fist at Him."[12] Never again did he do this!

On the morning Willa knew Bill was about to arrive, she cowered in bed, dreading how her gentle, cultured mother would react to this man who had no teeth and was greasy and yellow-skinned. She heard Bill ring the doorbell, and as Alan answered the door, she pulled the covers over her head. After awhile, she heard her mom and Bill laughing. When she went to check, they were having fun together. Mom wasn't put off by appearances. She enjoyed Bill.

He cleaned up and soon got some new teeth. Willa provided a bed for him in the basement by the furnace, a place he liked because the sound of the furnace reminded him of a tugboat he had once worked on as a cook. Bill became a valued member of the family, always kind and loving to Meriam and the others. He liked to make breakfast, especially for Meriam. Alan said, "After she got to know him, my mother-in-law wanted me to be more like Bill!"

The children loved Bill too. Steve was nine at this time, and Bill became his favorite baby-sitter. The girls were older too. They had always loved Bill, who called them "Lovely Laura" and "Beautiful Beth."

After two weeks living with Alan and Willa, Bill was ready to accept the Lord. Alan prayed with him to do this. Afterwards, Bill was spiritually "on fire," a changed man.

CHAPTER 10:

# Back Story: GRID, the Mystery Disease

*When [AIDS] first surfaced, I figured we are going to be swamped with people seeking change.*

~ Alan Medinger

ONE DAY IN A NEW York medical center, Dr. Jeffrey Satinover examined an unnamed young man sick from "Gay-Related Immune Disorder" or "GRID," which was what the condition was called at that time—1981.[1] The patient was gaunt, dead white in the face, his arms covered with large purple bruises that also wrapped around his abdomen to his back. He could neither speak nor focus his eyes. Though the purple bruises were symptoms of Kaposi's sarcoma, this cancer was only the opportunistic infection that took advantage of the patient's immune weakness. GRID caused that weakness.

The doctor's medical assessment was "will not survive the week." Soon a famous medical journal carried the story of this death and seven others just like it. A mystery disease had appeared in America. It struck people—men—mostly in San Francisco, Los Angeles, and New York City.

Along with the sexual permissiveness of the 1960s, lifting taboos on all types of sexual activity, came a new influx of sicknesses spread by sexual activity. Gay-related conditions increased in startling numbers: hepatitis B, bowel parasites, and so on. Two decades later, Dr. Satinover said, "One thing seemed obvious: Medical sanity would soon have to prevail over our clearly catastrophic . . . experiment in sexual liberation." Not for religious, moral, or political reasons, but for medical ones—in order to survive—gays would swiftly seek ways to abandon homosexual acts.[2]

The gay community did react swiftly, but not as doctors expected. They attacked the name "GRID" and forced a change in July 1982 to a new name, "Acquired Immune Deficiency Syndrome"—AIDS—, obscuring the link between the disease and the behavior that caused it in a majority of cases. The first priority of gay activists, Satinover said, became "to *protect homosexuality itself as a perfectly acceptable, normal, and safe way of life.*" [Italics are his.] Protecting themselves from illness was a lower priority. Massive funding to handle the disease followed, but none of it addressed the risk factor that was, and continues to be, number one—men having sex with men.

In 1981, only 234 people in the United States died of GRID. By the end of 1983, the number grew to 2,304. Not until 1985 did the Food and Drug Administration approve the first HIV antibody test after scientists discovered that the human immunodeficiency virus (HIV) causes AIDS. Until then, no means of diagnosing AIDS existed, and no cure was in sight. In 1985, 5,636 people died of AIDS, one of them the movie star Rock Hudson. Escalating at a rate of about 2,300 percent in five years, the disease by then claimed public attention.

Alan Medinger heard of AIDS early in the 1980s. His first encounter with it in ministry came when Timothy, 26, came to him. Tim was very tall (six feet six) and handsome. He had had only one lover, and after they both gave their lives to Jesus, they stopped having sex. Nevertheless, he feared he had AIDS. Since he tested negative for the HIV virus, Alan counseled him through this scare with little difficulty. Then, knowing that discipleship is important for a man to grow out of homosexuality, Alan encouraged him to continue in a Regeneration support group. For some years Timothy played an important part in the ministry, encouraging others and leading groups.

After Alan learned the nature of AIDS, he, like Dr. Satinover, expected gay men to want to stay healthy by changing their behavior. "When it first surfaced," Alan wrote, "I figured we [ex-gay ministries] are going to be swamped with people seeking change, because we are the only groups offering a way out."[3] Some married men who knew they had to stop living double lives did come to Regeneration and received help.

However, when asked in September 1985, "What impact is the AIDS epidemic having on your ministry?" Alan responded, "Not much." He explained the reason: "Most homosexual [persons] genuinely believe that they cannot change. They believe they are trapped."[4] This belief, he said, comes from accepting what the world and many liberal churches are telling them: they are created same-sex attracted and, since they cannot change, must accept who they are and celebrate it, if possible. Alan called it "tragic" that pastors and church leaders are buying this argument without looking for evidence of it, since there is none. Even worse, they are not examining the lives and arguments of those who have experienced change.

Years later, Alan gave another reason why the AIDS scare did not cause gays to flock to Regeneration in vast numbers. "Homosexuality grips people too tightly," he said. "The desire to change is almost always motivated by spiritual [not practical] concerns."[5]

Nevertheless, from his own experience in Regeneration, Alan said when the SSA person hears about change in a clear, bold, and loving manner, "many respond." Lesbian women in the 1980s came to Regeneration, bringing their friends. These women, one by one, entered life-changing relationships with Jesus Christ. "What a blessing this has been," Alan wrote. He was looking forward to a time when this "quiet, slow process" accelerated, caused by Christians lovingly "proclaim[ing] the message of freedom." He said then "those who have been trapped for years by the lie that change is not possible" will be freed. And when that happens, he said, "What a joy it will be to get caught in the stampede that will follow."[6]

Alan, Willa, and Luanna, Alan's administrative assistant, took an active interest in combating the new disease. They all believed in healing prayer and had seen it effectively administered for those with other illnesses. So they attended a series of AIDS healing services sponsored by a coalition of downtown Baltimore churches. Luanna wrote in the newsletter that she was disappointed at the second such service.[7] Though it was well advertised in the local gay press, and fifty had come to the first service, only ten showed up this time, including two pastors, two ushers, Alan, and herself—six people to pray for four sick men. Gay men were not responding in large numbers to the ministry's message that Jesus could and would heal their same-sex attractions; they didn't respond to Him as Healer of AIDS either.

About the traditional church's reaction to ex-gay ministry at this time, Alan wrote, "Conservative Christians, who will listen to us, don't like to talk about homosexuality. Liberal Christians, who like to talk about homosexuality, won't listen to us."[8]

However, in the mid-eighties, pastors in many churches became more supportive of Exodus-type ministries. They were shocked to find some of their own church members infected with the new disease. These pastors called into being ministries that sought to affiliate with Exodus, which prompted the Exodus board to draw up qualifications for new ministries. They had to be supervised by local churches, and their directors had to actively participate in the local church and be free of all same-sex activity for at least one year before applying to join the network.

Alan was encouraged by these changes. In June 1987, at the Exodus XII convention in St. Paul, Minnesota, he addressed two hundred men and women from forty-five ministries. "We are in a spiritual battle of staggering proportions," he said. "Until now, widespread church support for redemptive ministry to homosexual [people] has been lacking, but AIDS is changing that. Voices in the church previously speaking out in defense of the homosexual lifestyle are now strangely silent."[9]

Alan dedicated the August 1987 issue of *Regeneration News* to AIDS. He said, "A number of Christian men involved with Regeneration . . .

know they are carrying a virus that, any day, could produce symptoms that would signal their imminent death. . . . To help us all understand what they are going through, and hopefully to help us better minister to them, we offer the following testimonies."

Roger, 24, had graduated from college in 1985. There he had accepted the Lord because of the witness of friends, and then he ceased all same-sex activity. However, after returning from an overseas short-term mission the summer after graduation, he tried to donate blood through the Red Cross but was refused when his blood tested positive for HIV. He was trying to find a clinical trial that might offer a cure. Most people, even Christians, Roger said, "want you to act as if nothing is wrong. . . . People don't deal very well with death. . . . It's not something we talk about in our society." He was confused and unhappy.

Craig, 28, became a Christian ten years ago and "had some periods of stability" during that time but also lapsed into homosexual acts. He tested positive for HIV one year ago, and he said that since "I had nowhere else to turn . . . I turned [back] to God." He came to Regeneration and joined a support group, which helped, but he was looking for Christian support groups specifically for people who test positive. He said he didn't consider HIV "a punishment for homosexuality" but rather "a consequence of promiscuity" that the Lord was using "to draw attention to my sin and draw me back to Himself." Craig was beginning to worry about his spiritual walk because "I sure don't feel worthy of the kingdom." He was hoping, with counsel and inner-healing prayer, "things will start to come around."

Finally, Alan told the story of Ken and Anne and their two children. While they were dating, Ken told Anne that in his past he had been sexually active with men. He had hoped to scare her away. That was in 1980. But Anne loved him, and they married. She gave birth to a little girl and later became pregnant again. When she was eight months pregnant, Ken tested HIV positive, and the doctor said, "I'm sorry, but the risk of infection is too great. This pregnancy must be terminated."

As Christians, both Ken and Anne believed "it's wrong to kill this child because of fear of what might be. . . . Even if it's sick, God loves it, and we love it too." So Anne gave birth to Matthew. In August 1987, he was a healthy, active eighteen-month-old toddler. Neither he, his sister, nor his mother tested positive for HIV. Ken was praying for a miraculous healing, but he also continued to have sex with his wife. Both he and Anne wished for a support group for AIDS-affected families.

---

Because the people Alan interviewed said they wanted a group specifically for AIDS victims and their families, he prayed about establishing one. But he seemed to hear from the Lord, "Wait." Instead, he supported the work of Jeff Collins, a Regeneration alum who established Love & Action, headquartered in Annapolis, to work with AIDS victims. Jeff's ministry served people in Maryland, Washington, DC, and northern Virginia. In one year, he recruited 140 volunteers from 40 different churches, who visited AIDS patients in hospitals after they requested Christian visitors. Alan wrote that often "they are already reading the Bible" when volunteers first visit. In one year, Love & Action ministered to over one hundred patients. About ninety-five percent of them "either made professions of faith or . . . rededicated their lives to Christ."[10]

Through *Regeneration News,* Alan appealed for volunteers to work with the Annapolis ministry in three ways: to pray and fast for God's intervention against AIDS, to visit patients in hospitals, and (or) to become "care partners" for AIDs patients, inviting them to stay in their homes.

---

In the mid-1980s, while Alan was dealing with this new disease, Willa was mostly at home caring for Stephen, who was in elementary school, although she also volunteered at Regeneration. She started part-time work with pay in November 1987, when Steve was in middle school. This was the first time Willa worked outside her home since

1962. She gained a new sense of purpose, Alan said, and "she really blossomed with her work in the ministry."[11]

Willa became "an integral part of the ministry," he said. She "is my balancing factor and . . . the best counselor I have. She gets after me if I'm going to some extreme, so she's a tremendous asset for me." Willa soon discovered that God gave her the gift of an empathetic heart for suffering people.

In 1987, Alan published a pamphlet, "The Safe Sex Illusion," because many gay men told him "safe sex isn't working"—condoms didn't entirely prevent viruses and other pathogens from entering the systems of sex partners. Gay activists, Alan said, cling to the argument that SSA men can safely have sex with men not because it's true, but because they want to promote the image of homosexuality as being equally as normal and healthy as heterosexuality. "They do not want to admit that for a great many, homosexual behavior is compulsive."

Regeneration staff and volunteers took Alan's new pamphlets with them when they went street witnessing in gay neighborhoods. After the first night of passing them out, Regeneration got a call from a twenty-year-old man who said, "I think I need your help."[12] They happily provided it.

---

In October 1987, a number of Regeneration people drove to Washington, D.C., to watch the National March for Gay, Lesbian and Bi-Sexual Rights. They experienced an "overwhelming sense of sorrow" and "grim despair." Over 200,000 persons participated in the march, led by AIDS victims in wheelchairs. Two thousand handmade banners named those who had died with AIDS, and as people marched past the banners, some wept, recognizing names of dead friends.[13]

---

In October 1993, Alan wrote about Mike, "one of my favorite men in our ministry," who had a sordid past, one of the worst among Regeneration's participants. During two years he had lived in San Francisco—as Mike put it—"working and living so he could have sex."

He identified himself as belonging to the Kinsey Institute's category "twenty-eight percent of homosexual men who had sex with more than 1,000 sex partners." His desperate heart finally drove him home to the Washington, D.C. area for help. Mike turned to Jesus after he discovered he carried the HIV virus.

Alan said what was so appealing about Mike now was his innocence. "I look at Mike today and I see a righteous man; I see holiness."[14] Mike's most obvious characteristics now, Alan said, are his joy in the Lord, his eagerness to live as a Christian, and his desire to serve. This comes from Mike's new life in Christ that he learned at Regeneration. He can now satisfy his longings for love and affirmation by cultivating a close relationship with Jesus as well as close and wholesome relationships with other people. He is replacing his diseased thought life, following the advice of Philippians 4:8, by entertaining thoughts of what is true, noble, just, pure, lovely, of good report, virtuous, and praiseworthy. He meditates often on these things. Mike also had prayed, "God, I want to be innocent. I want to be as if I had never known those things which were a part of my former life. I want to be restored to the person I would have been if I had never seen a piece of pornography."

Alan said the innocence of spiritually reborn persons, who "are new creatures washed in the blood of the Lamb," can be as beautiful as the innocence of the physically newly born. "I have seen it happen," he said. "I have experienced it."[15]

---

After years of sponsoring a ministry to SSA people where they gathered in gay bars and pornographic bookstores, Alan decided this was an unfruitful use of ministry time, and he ended the street witnessing. He had perceived that the culture was now firmly divided between those who believe in God the Creator, who has a purpose for our lives and for our sexuality, and those who don't believe in Him. He wrote, "Little we say or do has much effect on the broader culture. We operate among believers. Others ignore us."

This realization disappointed him, for he had founded Regeneration believing he could succeed at street ministry, but he didn't blame himself. Alan said, "This is where we [as a culture] are today. But God is responsible for results. We just do our work one day at a time."[16]

"Our ministries prosper where the Christians are," he said, "not where the homosexual [people] are. Most people come to Christ first, and then they leave homosexuality." For this reason, Alan advised Christians in the beginning of a friendship with an SSA person to pray for him or her to come to Christ. Then after this person has accepted Him, pray for the new Christian to realize that homosexuality is not the Lord's will and that the Lord will forgive and heal a penitent. "The Holy Spirit is the one who convicts," Alan said, "and the One who gives power to change."[17]

CHAPTER 11:

# THE MINISTRY OF CHAIRS

*We bonded as a group, we cried together, we prayed over one another. . . . We always came away encouraged and uplifted with hope to continue on.*

~ Penny Dalton

ONE DAY WHEN ALAN WAS still new in ministry, he asked the Lord, "What is my ministry gift?"

He thought the Lord answered "administrator" (from 1 Corinthians 12:28)—that is, someone who organizes and builds up a ministry. At first Alan was disappointed to receive such a prosaic gift.[1] After all, he had been an administrator for a long time, usually a treasurer, since he was good with numbers. He wanted to do "real ministry"—to work directly with people, by counseling, teaching, and praying. He didn't want to do something in the background.

Eventually, Alan accepted what he called his "chairs ministry." He believed he was to do the same work as people preparing a building before a church meeting. He was "to set up chairs so others can minister."[2] God's plan turned out to be wiser than Alan's plan, and he said later, "I accept that role gladly, and as you might expect, God has blessed me [also] with many opportunities to teach, counsel and minister individually."[3]

Alan's work with Exodus was part of this chairs ministry. In the early years, as president of the board and then executive director, he helped give structure to the organization, whose purpose was to strengthen ex-gay ministries throughout the world. He also worked directly with people beginning fledgling ministries. Gene Chase, Carrie Wingfield, Penny Dalton, Elaine Sinnard, Katherine Allen, and others all benefited from this gift over the years.

After Alan and Willa prayed over Gene Chase at the 1984 Baltimore Exodus conference about a future Exodus group led by Gene, Alan followed up by phoning Gene to become better acquainted with him. Gene told Alan about his healing and marriage. He said he had written a professional, academic paper on "Homosexuality and Holiness," describing how to overcome SSA desires, and published an abstract of it in the 1974 *Bulletin of the Christian Association of Psychological Studies*. He had also read the paper to the faculty at Messiah College, where he taught math, and it was well received.

In January 1986, Bob Davies, executive secretary of Exodus, referred two SSA professional men from Pennsylvania to Gene for counsel, though Gene was neither a counselor nor a ministry leader. Gene called Bob and asked, "How do you know I can help these people?"

Bob replied, "I hear from Alan that you are a trustworthy person." In those days, the Exodus conferences were small enough so attendees could meet everyone attending and assess their characters. Having met Gene in Baltimore in 1984 and again in San Francisco in 1985, and having spoken with him on the phone, Alan respected both his testimony and his character.

Gene agreed to meet the two men Bob referred to him, and soon they invited some SSA professional friends to join them. In the first year and a half, the Thursday luncheon group of two men plus Gene grew to seven men plus Gene. Some younger men asked for help too, so Gene started a separate Saturday night group to give the young men an alternative to the gay bar scene. He called his ministry "Free!" for several reasons. It was supported by his church, the Evangelical Free Church. Their ministry Scripture was John 8:32. "If the Son will set you free, you will be free indeed." ("We offer the freedom Jesus offers," Gene said, "freedom to be strong and succeed, even with temptation.")

Finally, the name refers to the expense for participants. "When people ask what it costs," Gene said, "we say—it's free!"

During his early years of ministry, Gene regularly phoned Alan for advice. He also used Alan's articles in his newsletter, *Regeneration News*, for teaching materials. After Alan developed a series of teachings called "New Directions," Gene used this twice, once from notes as it was developed, once in its final form.

Gene said Alan was generous with his help. "If I were to pick a word for Alan," Gene said, "*gracious* is the word."[4]

Carrie Wingfield is another who was profoundly touched by the Lord at the 1984 Baltimore conference led by Alan. She went on to establish Transformation Ministries in 1985 with the support of her pastor at St. Luke's Episcopal Church in Seattle, Washington. When her ministry changed, several years later, to a non-profit with a board of directors, Alan helped her with the paperwork to establish the articles of incorporation and bylaws. Like other leaders, she used Alan's *Regeneration News* articles in her support groups, and she consulted him by phone for extra help.[5]

Another way Alan exercised his chairs ministry gift was through the Exodus East Coast leaders' conferences. These were informal events, designed to encourage new leaders from Maine to South Carolina with prayer, counsel, and friendship. The first small meeting was in October 1985, when representatives from seven ministries met in Oyster Bay, Long Island. Alan and Willa both attended. At this point, leaders were encouraged by just knowing that other similar ministries existed nearby. They spent the weekend getting acquainted and sharing stories.[6]

In April 1987, Day One Ministries hosted a meeting led by Earl Miller for almost forty people, representing thirteen ministries, at a Mennonite retreat center, Camp Men-O-Lan, near Allentown, Pennsylvania.[7] Participants worshipped and prayed together, talked informally, and walked in the springtime Pennsylvania woods. One of them, with a love for alliteration, described the event afterwards as "a refreshing, restful respite of reevaluation and relaxation."[8]

Penny Dalton of Whosoever Will Ministry in New Hampton, New York, said Alan and Willa quietly led this and subsequent conferences. They didn't stand and give speeches; they didn't even give advice, unless asked specifically one on one. Instead, they "watched." Penny and Elaine Sinnard had started their ministry the previous year with the support of their church, Trinity Assembly of God, and their pastor, the Reverend Jerry Bricker. For twenty years, until 2006 when Dalton and Sinnard retired, the ministry flourished, helping many people, some of whom came from far away—two hours away in Albany, New York, an hour and a half away in New York City, or from Connecticut or Pennsylvania.

In the beginning, Penny and Elaine needed encouragement. They had lived as a lesbian couple until, in 1978, God supernaturally saved them both and led them out of homosexuality without the help of any human counselor. They heard about Regeneration, phoned the office, and began receiving *Regeneration News*. For some years they used Alan's teachings in their personal lives. After Whosoever Will began, they planned their small group discussions around whatever topic Alan discussed in that month's newsletter.

When Penny and Elaine came to Camp Men-O-Lan, Penny said, "Alan and Willa just embraced Elaine and me. They observed us for a year, and in time, they saw this would work and they accepted us."

The conferences "were sweet times," Penny said. "They weren't structured at all. Just a bunch of people that God had called to do something." The people ate together and shared their stories. Penny said, "Alan and Willa would sit there, and finally Willa would say, 'Well, get up and pray for each other,' and we would. Willa would take part in the prayer. It was her heart."

Willa and Alan were practicing "healing prayer," the method they learned from Leanne Payne. Penny said, "The way God worked in my heart in those early days of ministry was so profound. God used Willa and Alan in a deep healing way."[9]

Alan and Willa's private prayer before these meetings was always that the Holy Spirit would lead the conversations and bless and build up the participants. That prayer was answered, according to Penny. "The early years of regional weekends are some of my greatest memories. [The meetings] were of tremendous help and influence. We bonded as a group, we cried together, we prayed over one another. We laughed, we loved, we were all touched by God deeply and always came away encouraged and uplifted with hope to continue on with the Lord in the area of ministry that He had called us all to do."[10]

After the Camp Men-O-Lan meeting, Alan encouraged Penny and Elaine to host another leaders' conference, and they did so eight months later, in December 1987, in their home in New Hampton. Fourteen ministry leaders came. A couple from their church, who supported their ministry, made all the meals. Alan came to watch, to pray, and to advise, if asked. (Willa stayed home this time.)

Katherine Allen, who had just founded Sought Out Ministries in 1987, came to this meeting. After attending the Baltimore Exodus conference in 1984, she decided to leave her work in college administration and earn a master's degree in counseling. This accomplished, she set up a counseling office in Virginia Beach, Virginia, and established Sought Out "to provide support, prayer, and information to those desiring freedom from sexual and relational brokenness through the redemptive power of Jesus Christ." Unlike many Exodus ministry leaders, Katherine had never been same-sex attracted. Hers was one of few ministries at this time addressing a wider spectrum of problems than homosexuality alone. She chose her ministry's title from Isaiah 62:12, "And you shall be called 'Sought Out, A City Not Forsaken.'"

Alan exercised his "ministry of chairs" even in his car on the way up to the Dalton-Sinnard conference in New York State. At his invitation, Katherine rode from Baltimore with Alan and returned with him. He spent the time teaching her about ministry.

Katherine saw Alan and Willa after this mostly at regional leaders' conferences. She attended all of them from 1987 to 2000. In October 1989, 70 leaders—nearly twice the previous year—met at Camp Men-O-Lan for the fourth annual conference. Eventually, because of many more ex-gay ministry start-ups along the east coast, the leaders divided into two regions, the Northeast and the mid-Atlantic. Both Alan and Katherine belonged to the mid-Atlantic region.

Katherine said she used Alan's newsletter articles in her ministry. She also used a small booklet Alan wrote on how to start an Exodus ministry. The biggest chapter in it was on "knowing that you are called," because Alan believed problems develop when leaders go into ministry for reasons other than a call from God—for instance, to satisfy their egos. He instructed leaders to operate "within the body of Christ" and find other people to "keep you accountable and confirm your call."[11] Even Alan operated with less than one hundred percent pure motives, he admitted, so he too needed people to keep him accountable.

Katherine found Alan "very helpful as a mentor."[12]

Another ministry, "Set Free" in Richmond, Virginia, grew stronger in its early years because of Alan's chairs ministry. In the late 1980s, a Richmond AIDS Ministry served men infected with the HIV virus. Ministry rules forbad any workers from mentioning the name of Jesus to clients. Some women from the group, dissatisfied with this rule, began praying on their own about it. In time a small group of those interested in beginning a new ministry went to Baltimore to find out how Regeneration worked. Alan was "a key factor" to the founding of a new ministry, according to the ministry's current director, Jeanie Smith. Set Free officially began in November 1990, and celebrated its twenty-fourth anniversary in November 2014.

Set Free leaders, in support groups, used Alan's program, "New Directions," which he had introduced to Regeneration in January 1989, as a means of providing more structure to his teachings. Participants were asked to commit both time and money (for materials) to a seven-week segment; after this, they could commit to another segment, and then to a third, making twenty-one weeks of teaching altogether. Then, if they desired, they could repeat the rotation. With "New Directions," Alan believed, participants would gain "a sense of completion"—of having mastered important material.

Like most similar ministries, when Set Free began, their mission statement said they would serve same-sex attracted people. After Jeanie Smith became director in 1998, the board initiated a two-year study of why people consulted the ministry. During this period they kept track of all incoming calls. "Why are you calling Set Free?" they asked callers. All answers were recorded. Some people called because of heterosexual addictions, pornography, or emotional dependencies unrelated to homosexuality.

The ministry changed and broadened its mission statement in 2000 because of this survey and "a watershed moment," Jeanie said. A woman came to one of their dinners who had been sexually abused from an early age. She was seeking help, but she was not same-sex attracted. Believing that Set Free could help her, this woman told Jeanie, "I'm so broken that if I have to go out one time and have sex with a woman to get help, I'll do it."

Jeanie was horrified.[13] "No!" she said. Set Free now offers "hope and healing through the Lord Jesus Christ to those who are sexually and relationally broken." Many other Exodus ministries, including Regeneration, have similarly broadened their missions.

---

In 1998, Alan and Willa spoke at a two-day conference in Richmond, Virginia, sponsored by Set Free. Paul and Jani D. heard about the conference and attended it, driving two hours from their home in Lynchburg, Virginia, and two hours back home. They were so encouraged by what Alan and Willa said about God's desire to heal same-sex-attracted people that they began attending Set Free. Paul was an SSA struggler, and Jani "stuck with me," he said, because she wanted to honor their marriage. "What an impact" Alan and Willa had at the conference, they said. For the next seven years, they attended Set Free each week, and "it was a difference-maker in our lives."

From this small beginning, Alan again had an opportunity to exercise his ministry of chairs. Paul and Jani attended mega church Thomas Road Baptist Church in Lynchburg. They told their pastor, Jerry Falwell, about the Medingers, and he invited them to spend a day with his staff in 2004. Paul said, "Their visit opened the eyes of our church staff."

The following year, the Thomas Road Church started a "Freedom Ministry" to offer help to people with relational problems, including same-sex attraction. It continues today, with about 200 people attending the various Monday night groups, including a same-sex-attraction group for men, led by Paul. Over the years, Alan and Willa talked on the phone to Paul and Jani many times to mentor and encourage them and the Freedom Ministry.

Alan had observed that ex-gay ministry flourishes where Bible-believing Christians gather, not where large groups of gays gather. This is true of Lynchburg. Not only is a church ministry flourishing there for SSA people, but Liberty University, affiliated with Thomas Road Baptist Church, was impacted too. Ever since Freedom Ministry began, an Exodus leader has been invited to speak about sexual issues to 12,000 resident students at a chapel service once a year. He or she stays on campus several days, conducting seminars for anyone interested. Mike Haley and Joe Dallas are leaders who have spoken there.

Paul said that Freedom Ministry at the church as well as chapel talks at Liberty University "would never have happened without Alan and Willa laying the groundwork."

In the spring of 2010, Alan agreed to a conference phone call with the men of Paul's Freedom Ministry group after these men had spent a year studying Alan's book, *Growth into Manhood*. "Quite a privilege for us," Paul said, adding, "Yes, [Alan and Willa] now, and will always, have a special place in our hearts."[14]

---

In late March 1999, Alan received a letter that caused him to rethink his ministry of chairs. A Jewish woman who took the Hebrew Bible seriously, Elaine Silodor Berk, wrote him from her home in Harrington Park, New Jersey, asking if he would encourage his Jewish colleagues to start ministries to SSA strugglers since she had been unable to find any. She mentioned "some influential Jews speaking out"—Dennis Prager and Norman Podhoretz—but said that, especially in the New

York City area, "the average Jewish temple . . . has completely bought the gay rights agenda."

Alan prayed about how to respond to this inquiry. He had just completed an article for the May *Regeneration News* saying that Jesus holds a "central place" in our ministries, and he hoped this focus would never change, because healing comes through the power of the Holy Spirit. But he said "Christian charity requires that we be willing to take what we have learned and offer it to others who . . . are not Christian."

Elaine's letter reminded Alan of an event years earlier. An SSA married rabbi had asked him to start a Jewish ex-gay ministry, and he had refused because he was over-burdened with other duties and also because he had thought that, without Jesus, he had nothing to offer.

Now he reconsidered. Alan knew that help for non-Christian people who struggle against unwanted same-sex attraction was available. He referred such people to a professional counselor friend who was a religious Jew and a member of the National Association for Research and Therapy of Homosexuality, a group with many Jewish members. So he wrote to Elaine with the message, "I would truly love to see a Jewish ministry established and would do what I could to help it." He promised to run a notice in *Regeneration News,* which had a circulation of about 3,500—including many Exodus ministry leaders—asking for the names of any Jewish people interested in starting a ministry to Jews.

Later Elaine said, "To my great shock on April 6 . . . I received my first reply in my pleas for help." Subsequently, she met Arthur Goldberg, who became co-director with her of the ministry, JONAH, an acronym for Jews Offering New Alternatives to Homosexuality (www.jonahweb.org). The new ministry benefited from Alan's advice and used some of his teaching articles, which he allowed to be "Judaicized" by JONAH editors before they were posted on the website or used in classes. JONAH uses Alan's book, *Growth into Manhood,* which Elaine called "a treasure."[15]

Alan also offered suggestions on Arthur's book, *Light in the Closet: Torah, Homosexuality, and the Power to Change,* in its manuscript stages, and he reviewed the published book.

After thirteen years, JONAH, still directed by Elaine Silodor Berk and Arthur Goldberg is "the only worldwide Jewish organization that deals with the volatile subject of homosexuality and other areas of sexual confusion from a Torah and healing perspective."[16] In 2007 the co-directors further extended their influence by creating the Jonah Institute for Gender Affirmation, a non-denominational clinical and research center. Arthur called Alan "a true friend who was able to reach across religious lines to help those in pain and distress over their unwanted same-sex attractions as well as provide organizational direction."[17]

---

Alan, and Willa too, operated in the chairs ministry another way, informally, by opening their vacation home, Pelican Palace, to ministry leaders and their families as a place of retreat and refreshment. This lovely home is located on the Atlantic Ocean beach in North Carolina. "Willa was such a sparkling personality," Jeanie Smith said. "She always played an important role at these gatherings."

At the first retreat, Willa organized a "play day" for the women. She announced to the men at breakfast that the women would be gone all day, but "we'll come home to cook dinner."

She told McKrae Game of Truth Ministry in Spartanburg, South Carolina (now Hope for Wholeness), that he must take care of his children, because his wife needed time off. Willa wanted to make sure the wives were not neglected, because she wanted them to fully support what their husbands were doing and not resent the ministries as she had once resented Regeneration for stealing her fun time. So she took the female ministry leaders and the wives of male leaders out to lunch in a Mexican restaurant and then to an arts and crafts consignment mall for shopping. She ended the afternoon by treating them all to ice cream.

---

Truth Ministry is another one aided by Alan's ministry of chairs. Alan mentored McKrae over the telephone. Alan called often—once a week for a while—with encouragement after Truth began in 1999.

When Alan retired as Exodus mid-Atlantic Conference director, he asked McKrae to take over that position. McKrae hesitated, wondering how he could assume another responsibility. He said to Alan, "I don't know how you did all you did. How did you find time to run your big ministry, direct the region, and also pour into ministry leaders?"

Alan laughed and said, "I only called you, McKrae. I didn't call the others as often."

"Why?"

"Because I see something of myself in you, and I see long-term leadership for Exodus in you."

"That was so encouraging!" McKrae said. "It made me realize he had been mentoring me and I hadn't even realized it. I thought he was phoning me as well as others as part of his job, not something he chose or wanted to do. It was extremely encouraging that someone like Alan saw promise in me. Alan fathered me, and I am forever grateful for those talks."[18]

---

Willa delighted in God's creation. Every afternoon about 5:30, she went out on the Pelican Palace ocean-side deck, carrying a basket of bread. She rang the big bell hanging there. Hordes of seagulls—trained to respond to Willa's bell—flew in. Then she invited the little children present to throw out handfuls of bread and watch while the birds scrabbled to grab the food.

"It was a Willa moment," Jeanie said.

One afternoon, Alan was looking for Willa about this time.

"Where is she?" he asked Jeanie.

"She's doing her bird ministry."

---

On many occasions Willa walked the beach with another Regeneration leader, Bob Ragan.[19] She and Bob had similar temperaments and interests. They had fun on long walks, talking and collecting sharks' teeth and seashells. Once with Bob and some others, who walked along the beach at night with flashlights, Willa picked up fifteen ghost crabs. She took them home and put them in the bathtub to watch before releasing them back again into the ocean.

---

Over the years the Medingers continued offering Pelican Palace as a retreat place for Exodus mid-Atlantic directors, and whenever they could, Alan and Willa came too. Monday through Saturday for a week in October, leaders assembled to discuss regional business, but mostly to relax and enjoy the place, pray, walk on the beach, and talk. One year so many directors came, Alan rented the next-door house for the overflow.

Jeanie Smith said, "Willa was one whose heart for women and wives impacted us all deeply." She said both Willa and Alan provided stability and wisdom. They had a "sense of ease and immediacy in prayer." And Alan had "such a heart to see other ministries succeed and prosper."

"One of the things I noticed about Alan's ministry," Gene Chase said, "was that he developed leaders, seeing the benefit of working himself out of a job, allowing the ministry to multiply."[20]

Through Regeneration ministry, over the years, Alan influenced hundreds of SSA people to change and seek holiness. Through his ministry of chairs, he influenced thousands more.

CHAPTER 12:

# Help for Lesbians

*So sweet on the inside and so tough on the outside—she was scared to death to be a woman.*

~ Willa Medinger

ALAN AND WILLA BOTH CLEARLY remembered the first time they met twenty-eight-year-old Harriet. She drove up to their front door in an Army pick-up truck wearing jeans, a flannel shirt, and combat boots.[1] Days earlier, her phone call had excited their interest, because few people phoned the ministry at that time—it was just over a year old and little known.

This caller identified herself as "a Christian woman in the Army" who wanted to know about Regeneration. Alan invited her to the next meeting, and she came January 19, 1981. She stayed through the evening, one of a large group of same-sex-attracted men and women, parents, and "interested people," but she said next to nothing before climbing back in her truck and driving away.

Willa loved Harriet from the start, perceiving that she was "so sweet on the inside and so tough on the outside." Willa saw the toughness as a thin veneer covering a person who was "scared to death to be a woman."[2]

Already, Harriet knew the Lord. After being encouraged by a former lover (a woman who had become a Christian) to read the Bible, she began studying the Bible and praying. Then the same Christian friend who had witnessed to her ex-lover witnessed to her, and, at age twenty-five, Harriet accepted the Lord and decided not to act out homosexually anymore. But she still fought sexual temptation and fantasy.[3] She prayed to find a fellowship of believers in the Army to help her endure loneliness and resist temptation, and she did find them. But she still needed someone to talk to who could understand her same-sex attractions and help her overcome them. Her friends directed her to Regeneration. After the first meeting, she kept coming.

When Alan and Willa joined St. Mary's Church, Harriet joined with them. Willa and the rector's wife, Susan Lipka, counseled her for nearly four years. Toward the end, they met with Harriet every day at 7 a.m., before her job began. Since Willa preferred to sleep late, her willingness to rise early showed her commitment to the counseling process, especially with this woman at this time. Experiencing affection for Harriet was important to Willa's own healing, as the Lord continued setting her free to love. Sometimes, Willa found it easier to understand Harriet than her own husband. "I loved that girl," Willa said. "She was so dedicated. She was a very intelligent person!"[4]

At St. Mary's, the Medingers encountered more women seeking healing. Two church ladies, who demonstrated the love of Jesus by cleaning homes of old people, found two women one day when they had cleaned the house of a man who had living with him his middle-aged daughter and her girlfriend, Vi. The women were in a lesbian relationship. Vi was "the toughest woman you ever saw," Willa said. "Tattoos covered both her arms." (At this time, women almost never got tattooed.)

Prone to start fights, Vi once beat up two policemen in a gay bar. They sent in two more officers, and she beat them up too. The fifth policeman to take her on—at this point she was tiring—managed to push her onto the floor and tie her up.

One time she threatened to take Alan to the parking lot and beat him up. "I would have been mincemeat," he said. Instead, he convinced her to change her mind and talk to him.[5]

After the cleaning women from St. Mary's invited Vi and her partner to a worship service, they came and the church people were "wonderfully welcoming to them," Willa said. Subsequently, Vi came to Willa for counsel.

If Vi arrived for a session angry, Willa would say, "You sit in that chair and behave yourself, Puddin'," and Vi obeyed. Willa still remembered how to discipline—she had learned from raising her children and foster children.

Willa could see that after Vi accepted the Lord, she fixed her heart steadfastly on Jesus. A group of church women accepted Vi as a friend and ministered to her. After some months, she wanted to look more feminine. Especially, she wanted her tattoos removed. Someone from St. Mary's paid for the lengthy, painful procedure.

Though Vi's ex-partner returned to a homosexual life, she never did. After she moved away from the neighborhood, she attended an Assemblies of God church nearer her new home, where she was accepted and loved until her death years later.

The desire to look more feminine is an important part of reorienting for many SSA women, especially those who previously dressed in a male or unisex way. Alan believes this is partly because of "the tremendous power and significance of symbols." Clothes, he said, "tend to be outward and visible signs of some reality, of some trait or characteristic that can be terribly important to us."[6]

For Harriet, even after months attending Regeneration, dressing like a woman required effort. When she finally surprised her friends and wore a skirt, they congratulated her so vigorously that they deeply embarrassed her. She vowed never again to wear a skirt or dress. The next week she was back to what she called "my shell-like blue jeans and flannel shirt."[7] Eventually, though, she relented and wore feminine clothes. She even began carrying a purse.

A man, Walter, came to Alan for counsel and became part of the ministry team along with Harriet. When Walter started showing interest in her, Harriet said to Willa, "I hate him! Why doesn't he leave me alone?"

Harriet went through a period of rejecting him. "Don't let me sit next to him at staff meetings," she would implore Willa, who responded by keeping them apart as much as she could. Then one evening, Willa was preparing refreshments in the kitchen to serve after the meeting. Harriet and Walter came into the kitchen, holding hands.

"Something's happened," Harriet said. "We're in love."

A little over six months later, and nearly eight years after Harriet's first Regeneration meeting, they married. Alan, Willa, and all the rest of Harriet and Walter's ministry and church friends were thrilled. "It was so beautiful," Willa said.

The couple celebrated their wedding with flowers, prayers, a beautiful liturgy and sermon, luscious food, and the greetings and gifts of many friends and family, all with hearts full of love. This was the first time in Regeneration history that two people from same-sex attracted backgrounds married. More than twenty-two years later, the marriage is still strong. Harriet and Walter are parents of four children. According to Willa, "Harriet is a wonderful mother."[8]

In her testimony, Harriet wrote, "I praise the Lord for the work He has done in my life. God *didn't* make a mistake. Through Him I can now not only accept, but rejoice in, my femininity."[9]

---

In a newsletter article written in the mid-eighties, "Healing—What Does It Mean for the Homosexual,"[10] Alan admitted that he was still learning how to minister to the people who came to him for help. SSA men and women differed, he said, in the problems they presented. Men usually came "with terrible stress over behavior they can't control or over powerful temptations that make life a constant struggle." Women, on the other hand, came sometimes with "emotional needs that are controlling their lives" or with sexual struggles or both. In other words, women were sometimes enmeshed in destructive emotional dependence apart from acting out sexually. This had been Harriet's problem.

Nevertheless, the means of change is roughly similar for both men and women, and Alan said he believed "the principles laid out here can apply to change from all life-dominating sins and lifestyles."[11] Change begins with a commitment to follow Jesus: "Seek ye first the Kingdom of God, and all these things shall be added unto you" (Matthew 6:33).

According to Alan, usually Jesus doesn't heal us instantly. Nor does He work according to some formula. He wants us to enjoy and cultivate fellowship with Him. "There is one thing that is even better than being healed from homosexuality," Alan wrote. "That is to be in a deep, loving relationship with our heavenly Father." One's commitment to daily time with the Lord, praying and studying His Word, will lead to knowledge of the truth, and especially, for SSA strugglers, the truth that God "created us male and female, in His image." They will learn to appreciate God's intention for creating the genders—that man and woman unite in marriage and bring forth children. "It follows that homosexuality is a distortion of God's plan, a form of brokenness, a result of sin in the world," Alan said.

Students of the Bible will then come to appreciate "who God is, who we are, what God has done for us, . . . that He loves us . . . [and] the power He has given us." Adding to this knowledge, students must use their will to obey God by forsaking SSA acts as well as scenes and people that promote temptation, and also by participating in acts all Christians are required to do: living in forgiveness, giving up self-pity, serving others, becoming active in a church, befriending other Christians, and establishing accountability with them. God will heal each individual in His own unique way, through healing prayer, gifts of the Holy Spirit, and other means. Finally, Alan said, overcomers must be open to growth through taking on responsibilities and relationships they might have avoided in the normal growing-up process.

At this time, Alan was meditating on the way many SSA men have opted out of normal boyish activities during their growing-up years. He discovered that maturity comes to them, and they leave homosexuality behind, only when they complete the growing up process by doing the things normal men do—competing, cooperating in physical tasks, etc. This is a key difference between SSA men and women as they heal, Alan discovered: men need to be affirmed by other men when they do manly deeds. In the normal growing-up process, this affirmation assures boys that they are becoming men.

With women, "their femininity is there, but it is encrusted with defensiveness and hatred of men, and also hatred of being women—that is, hatred of being vulnerable." Therefore affirmation from other women, though important, is less so than with men. Rather, forgiveness is key, for it opens them up to trust and to love.[12] "Lesbianism, put simply," Alan said, "is a defense against being hurt by men. Our women have rejected their femininity."[13]

More men than women over time came to Regeneration for help, eighty percent men to twenty percent women, Alan said after more than twenty years of ministry.[14] Abuse was present in about seventy-five percent of the women, a much higher percentage than in the men.

The healing journey for SSA women is more difficult than for men, Alan said.[15] This is because boys want to be men; therefore, when an SSA male understands that he can grow into full manhood, he wants to do it. He "is moving from weakness to strength."[16] However, the SSA woman "is moving from self-protection to vulnerability." Often she wants to be healed part-way to wholeness—enough to resist homosexual activity and dependent emotional relationships with other women and to live a life pleasing to God.

Most women succeed in this. But they quit Regeneration at this point. They remain outwardly strong and confident but "scared rabbits" inside, still needing the defense of staying in control emotionally in close relationships. Both Alan and Willa, in a co-written article, "Control: the Last Stronghold in Lesbianism," said that women tend to stop short of the goal, when "the feminine person within can dare to live without her shell and be vulnerable."[17]

In "Womanhood: Strength with Vulnerability," Alan explained that when a woman has shed her shell, she can "live out of her feminine strength." He defined this strength. "It is calm; it is wise; it knows in an intuitive sense. In the woman it is literally life-giving. It sustains life and it provides the glue—the center—that holds the family together.

It provides the place of security for the strongest man, where his strength can be renewed." To live like this, a woman must first "let go of her false masculine strength."[18]

The recovering woman must learn to find her "safe place" in Jesus. The Lord's plan is for man to physically protect woman, but since all men are sinful, they will therefore protect women imperfectly. Trusting Jesus, Alan believed, "is difficult for any of us, especially for any person who has been badly hurt in the past." However, when a woman can trust Jesus to care for her, she can allow herself to become vulnerable and fully feminine.

---

Over 400 full-time conferees came to Exodus XIV in July 1989, in Philadelphia. At the next to last evening meeting, an Exodus leader announced, "Willa Medinger needs a hairdresser; in fact, Willa needs all of the hairdressers she can get. If you are a hairdresser, meet her after tonight's session."[19]

Four men answered this call, and two women makeup specialists also volunteered to work with Willa. She was in charge of a special feature at this time—makeovers for women who wanted them. The four men cut, colored, and set the hair of fifty women, some, but not all, from lesbian backgrounds. The makeup artists applied the women's makeup. Willa invited one heterosexual lady to take part, knowing she was one who served others and seldom treated herself.

As her hairdresser worked, this woman told him how she and her husband, months earlier, had cared in their home for a man with AIDS until he died. She related how much they loved this man and how they had grieved at his death. The hairdresser "was almost in tears" hearing her story, because he too carried the HIV virus. He said he had believed nobody would care when he became sick and died, but now he had hope.

The conference ended with a banquet, followed by communion. Alan sat in the auditorium watching the conferees cross the stage to receive communion. Among them were the made-over women and the men who had fixed their hair. "I never saw a more radiant and beautiful group of women than those who had been 'made over,' and I never saw a more manly group of men than those who had served these women so lovingly," he said. "I saw the beautiful femininity of these women as something that had only been flickering within them. God not only did not quench it, but He caused it to flame up and shine forth."

CHAPTER 13:

# Defensive Detachment

*Homosexuality is essentially a state of incomplete development.*

~ Dr. Elizabeth Moberly

IRWIN MEDINGER DIED ON JUNE 30, 1986, when Alan was fifty. He wrote about his father's life and his own in an article, "The Chain Is Broken."[1] His father's chronic depression had robbed young Alan of a "God-given role model, the one from whom [I] should learn what it is to be a man," and Alan had made a decision "that I would meet all of my own needs and would meet them at any cost. This further insulated me from the kind of life-giving relationships that we all need." Thus he had begun his journey into a world of fantasy, his "secure retreat from the pain of life."[2] With these decisions, Alan had established in himself "the set up" for developing same-sex attractions. Even so, he said, "In no way did my father make me a homosexual." Rather "the brokenness in [my father's] life led to the sinful decisions that I was to make."

After his father's death, Alan tried to understand the reasons why Irwin had been depressed. Alan discovered problems in Irwin's childhood that might have "set him up, so to speak," for a life of depression, just as the problems in Alan's developing years could have set him up for homosexuality. These thoughts convinced Alan of an ongoing chain of sins passed down in families, illustrating the Bible truth that "he punishes the children and their children for the sin of the fathers to the third and fourth generation" (Exodus 34:7 NIV).

Nevertheless, Alan said, because of the cross of Jesus, this process is not inevitable. When Jesus came into Alan's life, He "shattered the chain that fastened me to my past and to the sins and hurts of the generations before me."[3] Alan saw that he did not have to pass his sins on to his own children. In fact, his father, too, had experienced freedom from his chains some time before death when he gave his life to Jesus and later responded to healing prayers for his depression.

---

Regeneration was growing. In November 1986, the seven-year-old ministry gave an appreciation dinner at a hotel for 85 supporters, some coming from as far away as Lancaster, Pennsylvania, and the Shenandoah Valley in Virginia. The planned budget for 1987, one-third larger than 1986, was $88,000, to allow Alan and Luanna to move to a larger office and hire another part-time person. In February 1987, the ministry served fifteen women in the wives' group, twelve parents in the parents' group, and 130 men and women in Regeneration's four main support groups. Correspondence counseling served 200 persons, and phone counseling more than 200.[4]

---

Dr. Elizabeth Moberly was the principal speaker at the 1987 Exodus in St. Paul, Minnesota. She was a British research psychologist and theologian with expertise on defensive detachment. Many considered her the originator of gender-affirmative therapy for SSA people. In 1983 she had published two relevant books, *Homosexuality: A New Christian Ethic* and *Psychogenesis: The Early Development of Gender Identity.*

A graduate of Oxford University with a theology major, Dr. Moberly studied psychoanalysts whose writings the American Psychiatric Association ignored when they delisted homosexuality from the 1973 *Diagnostic and Statistical Manual of Mental Disorders (DSM).* She had read the 1962 work by Irving Bieber and other authors, *Homosexuality: A Psychoanalytic Study.*

Their theories she accepted and contrasted to earlier work by Dr. Sigmund Freud, who asserted that SSA persons experienced disturbed relationships with opposite-gender parents, especially sons of domineering mothers. Instead, Moberly believed it was deficits in love needs involving same-gender parents that caused the condition. Her unemotional, scientific tone was calming and encouraging for persons accustomed to emotionally charged, guilt-inducing Christian writings. Both Alan and Willa found her teaching helpful.

The homosexual drive, Moberly said, is not sinful. It is a reparative drive to meet a lack of same-gender love that is necessary for normal development. Homosexuality, she said, "is essentially a state of incomplete development," and the desire to complete development, being entirely normal, is not contrary to God's intent for any person. What *is* contrary to God's intent is that normal love needs go unsatisfied. Since these are, for a boy, his needs for his father's love and affirmation, they can only legitimately be met through a loving friendship, in a nonsexual relationship, with a man.

For anyone to hate persons because they are same-sex attracted, she said, is illogical. Her argument was as follows: the perfect will of God for a child is that he or she has parents. So an orphaned child is not living in the perfect will of God. "Although being an orphan is in this sense 'against the will of God,' one does not therefore seek to punish an orphan for being an orphan," she said.[5] Similarly, an SSA man did not experience the perfect will of God for his life growing up with an unmet same-gender love need. But one should not censure him for this.

Moberly delineated a two-fold causation for homosexuality and therefore a two-fold process of healing it. First, the boy, perceiving lack of his father's love, detaches emotionally from his father to protect himself from this hurt. Second, he resists restoring the attachment, though he still needs that love. Moberly says this is the crux for healing: he suffers "same-sex ambivalence." She calls this "an avoidance-approach conflict."[6] If the defensive maneuver is paramount, the boy will have problems with authority. He will be rebellious. If the need for attachment predominates, he will have dependency problems.

After puberty, the boy's need for same-gender love becomes sexualized. He may seek to satisfy these needs in a sexual relationship, but this will never truly satisfy him, she says, because the problem is essentially a pre-sexual one. In fact, neither abstinence nor sexual activity will solve his problem. It is solved by two means. First, the defensive detachment must be resolved. A person does this by recognizing the vow or decision through which he detached emotionally from his parent, and he must repudiate that decision with the help of counseling, understanding, repentance, and prayer. Second, and just as important, the unmet same-gender love needs must be satisfied. This is done through nonsexual loving relationships with same-gender persons, and it takes longer.

Moberly believed it is wrong for an SSA person to believe "God made me this way," implying God wants him or her to be and remain homosexual. God *did* create a person's desire to complete same-gender love needs, she said, but He intends those needs to be satisfied nonsexually. Same-sex attraction should be a temporary condition one outgrows, "just as children normally outgrow their relationship of dependence on their parents."[7] It is not God's intention that anyone remain in a homosexual—i.e., immature—state, she said. Though healing may take time, "in principle healing is possible for all."[8] She taught that "love, both in prayer and in relationships, is the basic therapy." Similarly, Moberly believed that marriage between same-gender lovers is wrong, "because marriage is not right for a relationship analogous to that between parent and child."[9]

Both Willa and Alan, by 1987 when they were 50 and 51, were aware of their childhood deficits in parental love and of the vows they had both taken to cut themselves off emotionally from their parents. Though Willa did not experience same-sex attraction, she, like Alan, knew what it was to feel like a needy orphan. Moberly's calm analysis encouraged them both.[10]

---

The following March, Alan invited Dr. Moberly to host a seminar sponsored by Regeneration in cooperation with seven Washington, D.C., and Virginia churches. The event attracted 76 people. At this time, Moberly was Director of Psychosexual Education and Therapy at the Institute for Christian Counseling and Therapy in Philadelphia, Pennsylvania.

---

Willa was now enjoying her life—her children and marriage—fully. Her relationship with Laura had improved during the seven years since Laura's helpful Christian counseling. Beth was married and, to her mother's knowledge, happy and harboring no long-term wounds from her growing-up years.

Willa felt herself completely healed and was able to tell a wife whom she counseled through letters, "Jesus has done a real miracle in my own life in bringing me to a place of such inner peace, confidence, love of myself, and joy that I can function apart from any problems which my husband might or might not have."[11] By this, she did not mean to imply that Alan had problems. The wife whom she addressed believed her own husband had problems, and Willa wanted her "to attend to your own healing." She always prayed for and worked for the health and healing of wives, whether the husbands got better or not.

Alan was at a serene place emotionally too. He described much later, in his unpublished book, *God's Sexual Man,* how Willa's anger problem had taken a toll on their sexual life for many years, but as her anger abated, she became more able "to give herself to me sexually." Alan discovered that male sexuality "is one of God's great gifts . . . but by its fundamental nature [it] cannot be enjoyed by us alone as its recipient. . . . We must in turn give it away to another." Alan found that to "maximize the joy of sexual experience, the thing that more than any other will make [a man] a great lover is his heart's desire that his body and his manhood be a gift to his wife."[12]

This insight came, Alan said, after God led him to pray each time before he and Willa came together, "Oh Lord, let me bring joy and pleasure to her." This set him free from focusing on his own performance and enabled him "to experience the true abandon in which a husband and wife achieve true union."

---

Alan and Willa put Elizabeth Moberly's advice to work. If her theory was correct—that people grew up from a homosexual condition when their same-gender love needs were met non-sexually, then the Medingers wanted to encourage this. At annual Regeneration retreats held in Catonsville, Maryland, they provided a place for friendships to develop.

Alan said eighty to ninety percent of SSA males, to his knowledge, are inferior athletes growing up. The way to become a man, he believed, is to do what men do, and so he invited his men to compete in sports. He established a "softball ministry," because softball was a sport where individual failings are especially on display. Many of his clients had dreaded being chosen last for a team, dropping the ball in the outfield, or not being able to throw it far enough to make an out. Playing softball in their youth, they concluded that they didn't measure up, and that "I'm different from other men—less than them."

A softball team from Baltimore Regeneration played another from Washington/Northern Virginia Regeneration at a secluded place every week from April throughout the summer of 1987. No females were allowed, except Regeneration staff as referees. The field where they played was surrounded by a church and its parking lot, a riding stable, and some woods, so the only spectators were horses. Teams were not picked by captains but determined by the place where their group met, Baltimore or Washington, D.C. Everybody played, and they rotated positions. No one was allowed to sit out any inning, unless injured.

After his first experiment, Alan wrote an article, "Washington Stops Baltimore in 22-19 Slugfest." He said, "To the amazement of all who were there, what started out as a protected exercise in therapy evolved into a spirited . . . totally enjoyable, somewhat competitive softball game." The men had so much fun, they decided to do what jocks in beer commercials do—they went out after the game to celebrate.[13]

In this and subsequent years, the softball ministry thrived. Some men discovered they were athletes after all. They joined softball teams at their churches and found that playing ball with men who knew nothing of their sexual struggles proved to be a boon to their developing sense of manhood.

---

It was not until early June 1994, seven years after Alan's father died, that he realized something—the wounding in his relationship with his father went both ways: his father had injured him, but he also had injured his father. One morning during Alan's private devotions, he struggled to remember Irwin's birth date. He knew it was in early June, but he often confused it with Father's Day. Then he realized he had a habit of forgetting his father's birthday, though he was usually sharp with numbers and remembered the birth dates for his mother, brother, Willa, his children, and some close friends.

"I felt like a hot poker was being driven through my heart as truth after truth overwhelmed me faster than words could express them," Alan wrote soon after in an article, "Honor Thy Father."[14] He had hurt his father by withdrawing from him, by not honoring him. Suddenly, Alan saw a picture of his father different from his usual memory of a depressed, crying, pathetic man. He saw him in a different, also accurate way: good looking, kind to everyone, with a sense of humor, doing his best to help the handicapped people who were his clients. Alan saw his father fishing and enjoying it. He remembered his father offering to take him fishing. Usually, he had refused to go.

Another memory shamed him. Once when he was a teen, Alan accompanied his father to the basement, where Irwin demonstrated how to light the pilot light on the gas furnace in case it went out. He was preparing for a stay in a mental hospital and wanted to be sure Alan could cope as the man of the house in his absence, since Alan's older brother, Pete, had already grown up and moved out. Alan remembered thinking, "Thanks, Dad. This is all you have to show me. I'm already doing everything else that you should be doing in the family." He had held his father in utter contempt.

Though it was now too late for Alan to ask his father's forgiveness and develop a friendship with him, he did what he could. He prayed for the Lord's forgiveness, acknowledging that he had sinned against his father, and he let the lesson of the fifth commandment in Deuteronomy 5:16 sink into his soul. "Honor your father and your mother, as the Lord your God has commanded you, so that you may live long and that it may go well with you in the land the Lord your God is giving you" (NIV).

He wrote in *Regeneration News* that complete healing from homosexuality requires that "we . . . become sons." This starts "by repenting of having rejected our fathers. Repentance is almost always the key that opens the door to change and growth."[15] Alan said this means facing one's father, if he is living, and acknowledging to him one's sins against him, without justifying them, even if this is painful. If the father is already dead, as Alan's was, "then we seek to be the sons of another—our heavenly Father."

CHAPTER 14:

# Called According to His Purpose

*She helped us know that we would make it, even if our husbands didn't.*

~ Carol P., describing Willa's ministry

WILLA WAS PASSIONATE ABOUT HELPING women with problems, especially wives. "I will never, ever, as long as I have breath, stop helping wives," she said. "I yearn for God's glory to be shown in their marriages. I think He shows His glory in Alan and me. He loves to take an impossible situation and make it beautiful."[1]

Her call to the wives' ministry came at a difficult time for Alan—after Willa quit working for Regeneration in the winter of 1991/1992. He wanted her back. Without her, he felt less confident leading Regeneration, because, as he put it, "I'm an administrator, but she is a gifted minister."

Lack of time wasn't the problem for Willa in 1991. Steve was in tenth grade and the girls grown and gone from the house. Willa sensed the Lord saying she needed to step away from Regeneration completely because she was working in the ministry to earn Alan's approval, not because God had called her to it. Alan disagreed. He didn't think the idea of quitting was from God. He thought Willa was disobedient to God even to entertain such an idea. Nevertheless, for almost two years, Willa did step away. Eventually, they both agreed that Willa needed something to occupy her time. They talked about a job for her.

"What kind of job?" she asked him.

"Well, what do you really like to do?" Alan asked.

"Hang wallpaper."

So they started talking about buying a truck or van for her to use in her own wallpaper- hanging business. Willa ended the discussion. "This is foolish," she said. "We both know I'm going to end up working for Regeneration."

"Looking back," Alan said later, "picturing Willa driving her truck up to a job is about as ludicrous as anything we could have imagined. We laughed at it."[2]

Willa sensed a call from God developing during her sabbatical—a call to help wives of SSA men and wives of sexually addicted heterosexual men. It became "a burning passion." When she resumed ministry work, "What I did for wives was life to me," she said. No longer did she entertain any ambivalent feelings about the ministry and the way it had redirected her life.[3]

Back in the office, she worked as a paid employee counseling women, initially two days a week, eventually full-time. Contrary to what many people might expect—that most women want to leave husbands whom they discover are same-sex attracted—Willa said, "No! They want their marriages to work!" She based her faith on her own reaction to Alan's unfaithfulness. By 1992, she also understood something of the dynamic behind wives cleaving to their husbands and their marriages even in the face of shocking revelations. In many (but not all) of these marriages, as in Willa's own marriage years earlier, the women were emotionally codependent on their men. This condition, Willa said, is "a huge need to be needed. You place your own life on hold and become addicted to being loved by that person." That is, a woman measures her own worth by how much her husband loves her.

As Willa worked with wives, she discovered her primary ministry gift. "It is loving with the love of the Holy Spirit," she said. Her God-given love for each woman helped in the healing process. Carol P. clearly remembered her first meeting with "a short older lady" in a group of twenty-five wives. She said, "Willa's heart is bigger than her little body, and we all knew that she loved us and understood how we felt, because she had been down that road also."

Karen C. said she immediately felt loved by Willa, even before meeting her, because of her voice over the phone saying, "Awwww, Honey!" as Karen told her story. It "made me feel like I was being wrapped in the arms of my mother and grandmother at the same time."[4] She added, "All my apprehensions melted away, and she prayed with me right then and there. I always loved praying with Willa. Sometimes she would pause, and you'd think she was finished, but she'd go on. Her prayers were very healing for us."[5]

When Willa returned to Regeneration, at first she talked to wives in the office. Shelley C. came because someone in her husband's church recommended Regeneration for him, and after he came for counsel, they discovered Willa for her. Shelley's marriage was "pretty much in the graveyard." Her husband was overly controlling, and since Shelley was quiet and reserved and grew up with a controlling father, she was easy to intimidate.

"I felt I was in a deep, deep box, looking up," she said. "Every time I tried to do something, my husband would close the lid on me."[6] When her husband told her he was same-sex attracted, the news destroyed her remaining bit of self-esteem.

Willa gave Shelley hope. "She brought me out of the box!" Shelley said. At several early meetings, she described what was happening in her marriage, and Willa cried, while Shelley was dry-eyed.

"Why are you crying?" Shelley asked.

"Because you can't," Willa answered.

Shelley said, "Willa would pray with me a lot, which I liked." After some months of Willa's encouragement, Shelley went to a Regeneration retreat in Fairfax, Virginia, and heard Andrew Comiskey speak on "Things that Bind People." As he concluded, he invited participants to come forward to a big wooden cross, where they were asked to lay their problems at its foot. Shelley went forward with her marriage problems. After spiritually laying them down, she sat on the stage and discovered "I was actually able to cry." This was a breakthrough. She was so accustomed to repressing her emotions that before she attended the conference, she never cried. Earlier, she and her husband had gone to the movie "Shadowlands," about the marriage of C.S. Lewis and Joy Gresham, and Roger cried, but Shelley could not.

During the first months with Willa, Shelley was home-schooling her four children, ages seven to seventeen. The children were unruly and disobedient, and Shelley was frustrated, confined to her home, children, and husband nearly every hour of her life. Willa told her to send her children to school because they were putting too much strain on her. It was a difficult transition, but in the end, it worked. Slowly, Shelley became "my own person," which, she said, "has helped our marriage. I was more dependent on my husband than I was on the Lord, and Willa had to bring me out of that."

Shelley encouraged Willa to start a wives' group, and she did. "Wives Need Healing Too" was the title of Willa's testimony and a theme of the group, designed for wives of men in Regeneration groups. Sometimes wives of unrepentant men came to the group even after continued unfaithfulness by the husbands ended the marriages. "Whoever would benefit" was invited to the Medinger home in Towson, Maryland, to meet Monday evening once a month, which later changed to twice a month.[7] The group began in October 1997 and continued under Willa's leadership as long as she was able to lead (until June 2009) and it still continues under other leadership.

Willa always began the meetings with a hospitable welcome in her dining room, where she served coffee and cookies, creating a nurturing atmosphere. Often new women were reticent about sharing secrets with strangers. Sheri, for example, said that when she entered Willa's home for the first time, "my self-image was in the dumpster." Even though she found the women in the group "very sweet," she was "leery" about opening up to them. "I was desperate to save my marriage," she said, "but I would be an observer before trusting the input of anyone. I had been through too much and was guarding my heart like never before."[8]

As the meeting began, the women went around the table introducing themselves and telling a little about their situations. If a new woman said very little, the others, led by Willa, accepted that and didn't press her. They were careful to respect her space. They didn't hug her either (as they did each other sometimes), but held back, trying to discern what she needed. About a new woman, Sheri H. said, "You could see the weight she was carrying on her shoulders. Many of these women were trying to work, raise their children, serve in their churches, save their marriages, and maintain a presence and a life that hid the pain." Often, they were exhausted.

Sheri said Willa was "open, honest, and safe. She told funny stories. I loved her enthusiasm for life and her ability to laugh at herself." Looking like an affluent grandmother, Willa was gray haired and somewhat overweight. She took pride in her appearance and chose classy clothes. Sheri said, "I always felt so blessed to be with Willa. It was like being with an aunt or a good friend. She was a great role model of a womanly woman." She added, "Willa loved the dog, Luv, and animals in general. Even though the Medingers had a beautiful home, and she had a lot of class, she was a down home girl."

After a woman spent a meeting or two observing, she usually opened up because Willa made her feel safe. Sheri said after several meetings, "I knew there would be confidentiality and support from other women like me who wanted to walk with the Lord and do the right thing in their marriages."

When the new woman decided to share, "usually a lot came spilling out," Sheri said. Once in a while, a wife would spill out so much anger that the other women couldn't rally behind it. Sometimes if that was the case, she wouldn't come back. On the other hand, occasionally a wife would be passive and apologetic for her husband because she had taken on the role of mothering him. She didn't expect him to take responsibility—to be a man. In this case, the women encouraged her to name what he was doing wrong, even if it caused her to become angry.

Karen said Willa knew how to let women vent. She was very understanding, but she also knew when to lovingly confront them. Karen said, "She also had a way of seeing things through the spouse's eyes. She always hit a balance there, which was helpful. I don't think she said anything our husbands couldn't have heard."

In time, Shelley became a facilitator for Willa—that is, when Willa was out of town, Shelley unlocked Willa's house and fixed coffee and cookies, then greeted the women and welcomed them. Other women took over teaching when Willa was away.

After greetings, refreshments, and introductions, the normal format was for a leader to read and summarize highlights from the book the group was studying together. She would speak for about half an hour. Then the women were asked to share their thoughts on the book. This opened them up to sharing what was happening in their lives. Finally, the women prayed for each other. Meetings began at seven p.m. and were supposed to end by nine, but sometimes they went over—to ten or even later. All during the meetings Willa told stories, especially from her marriage, sharing her wisdom. Karen said Alan and Willa gave the women a picture of what a healed marriage looks like, how two people can grow in their love for each other.[9] Over the years, the wives group became a team effort, with Sheri and then Karen co-leading with Willa.

Some of Willa's stories—inspired, she believed, by the Holy Spirit—were effective in healing inner wounds. Karen remembers once when Willa told of a vision or dream she had had—she wasn't sure which it was. In it, "a good Willa" and "a bad Willa, throwing a temper tantrum" were together in a room. Jesus entered, paused, and looked around. Willa said, "I thought He would go up to the good Willa, but he didn't. He went to the bad Willa and put His arms around her."

At the time, Karen was learning about the Lord's unconditional love, and, she said, "This story made me cry."

Some women who marry the kind of men Regeneration serves are codependent before they marry, and some others become codependent after marriage, so books about this psychological problem were favorites with Willa. She used a book, *Stone Cold in a Warm Bed,* by Kathryn and Paul Wilson. When she found *The Avenue: Unintended Journey* by Susan Allen, she thought it expressed the problem best. After this book, she didn't want to use anything else. Now, with that book out of print, the group uses other books by Susan Allen, *The Healing Choice Guidebook I and II—The Journey Continues* as well as *The Healing Choice* coauthored by Susan Allen and Brenda Stoeker.[10]

Willa's goal was to help wives understand not just their husbands, but even more importantly, themselves. They needed to know "why I was attracted to someone like this." She encouraged them to work on healing what was wrong with themselves, with the help of the Lord. Sometimes they came from rough backgrounds and hadn't known the Lord until after they married. The first Allen book's chapter headings indicate the messages: "Emotions. Red Flags. Unhealthy Behaviors. Understanding Sexual Addictions. To Trust or Not to Trust. Prayer Moves Mountains. What Does His Recovery Look Like?"

Willa also recommended another book, *Someone I Love Is Gay: How Family & Friends Can Respond.*[11] The authors were Bob Davies and Willa's good friend, Anita Worthen. In June 1996, when the book was published, Willa reviewed it with glowing words in *Regeneration News*: "I would like to go up on a hill and shout, 'If you want answers on how to really help yourself and your "gay" loved one, this is the book.' It has the answers."

Sheri said about discussions in the wives group, "Willa could be quite blunt about the reality of sexual addiction. Women need to know how dark, dirty, and ugly it is." Sometimes a wife shared horrible things about her life, and Willa invited the other women to come forward, stand around the suffering woman as she sat in a chair, lay hands on her, and pray. This was, at first, hard for Shelley and some of the others from churches where laying on of hands wasn't done, but it always seemed to help the suffering woman.

According to Willa, her meetings prompted laughter as well as tears. One memorable night the men's and women's groups both met at the

Medingers' home. It was one of those nights when mostly "old-timers" (women who had already experienced much healing) were present. As the men shuffled down to the basement, their wives sensed they were thinking, "What will our wives say about us?"

For some reason, Sheri said, "we were just cracking up" the whole time. It wasn't planned; different situations just struck them as funny. Sheri added, "Laughter was such a key element of being free again for us . . . of looking at the lighter side of life." She also said that when the men came up from the basement that night, they didn't look amused.

The closeness of women in a group of old-timers was something precious. Karen said there is no other place for wives to speak about their problems except in a group like Willa's, where they know they can discuss anything and nobody will speak outside the group.

Sheri once said to Willa, "Now that I've been in this group, I don't feel I can relate to normal women. I can't be deep with them anymore." But Willa told her she needed to be around normal people, and as for herself, Willa made an effort to have friendships with women whose lives held no sexual traumas—to have balance in her life.

Willa's home group usually accomplished what she thought the Holy Spirit wanted in these marriages. Over seventy-five percent of the couples stayed together as the men overcame their sexual problems. Sometimes, the couples would separate. Karen said that in these situations, "the wives wanted to save their marriages, but the husbands refused to admit they had problems, or they continued to break the trust in major ways."[12] When this happened, Willa's desire was to help the women heal so they could move on to happier lives. She wanted them to experience what she had experienced: being set free to love.

Willa never said to a wife, "You should leave your husband," though sometimes the other women in the group suggested this. Willa left the decision to the woman. Shelley and her husband remained together, and today, many years later, they have a strong marriage, with all four children grown and two "really cute" grandchildren added to the family.

Sheri wasn't able to hold her marriage together, though she tried for more than four years. Her husband had become sexually addicted at age nine and was deceptive about it. He went to a few Regeneration meetings and then stopped going. Finally, Sheri moved back home to California. Her husband followed her, but after a week, he left her. Sheri said the chapter in Susan Allen's book "What Does His Recovery Look Like?" was important to her, because what her husband told her didn't match the chapter. He was deceptive about the recovery he claimed to experience.

Willa taught the women to find their identities in the Lord, not in their husbands. Even though her husband rejected her, Sheri was able to heal. She said, "Unfortunately, my marriage didn't make it because my husband chose to leave. But I must say that under Willa's ministry, going through the process of understanding sexual addiction and attempting to stay married, I learned more than words could express."[13] After her husband deserted her, Sheri decided to divorce him. When she called Willa for advice, Willa was okay with this. She said that Sheri's husband was one of the toughest cases she had ever seen because he never seemed to want healing.

Not long after the divorce, Sheri met and fell in love with a pastor in California. She phoned Willa for advice, and Willa said, "Yeah, Sheri, I think you're ready." Today they are happily married and serve the Lord together. Sherri was thrilled to be able to travel back to Maryland with her new husband sometime after their wedding and introduce him to Willa and Alan, who entertained them in their home for lunch and a long talk. Now Sheri desires to minister to women in devastating marriages like her previous one.

After Sheri moved to California, Karen and Willa led the wives' group together, and then Karen (in a restored marriage) led it alone, following Willa's pattern of leadership, her choice of books, and her empathetic, loving attitude. The group remained between six and eight women, about the same size as when Willa led it in 2009. In the late 1990s, it often numbered twenty to twenty-five.

---

Convinced of her calling to minister to wives, Willa started another very effective wives group at the annual Exodus conference. Carol P. attended the conference unwillingly her first time, in 1994, because she was still angry at her husband, who had asked her to go with him. He was being counseled at First Stone ministry in their hometown, Oklahoma City, Oklahoma. Carol only went after her counselor told her to ask the Lord if He wanted her to go, and, in case of a positive answer, if He would provide the money.

When the money came in, Carol traveled with her husband to Exodus, but she went with a bad attitude. She met Willa leading a group of twenty-five wives, and that attitude began to change. Willa emanated a certain confidence that said, "I know what you haven't discovered yet."[14] She helped Carol see "that there was a light at the end of the tunnel, and it wasn't a train, but the healing Holy Spirit of the God who loved us and our husbands enough to die for us and give us a hand up out of the sin and hurt we were experiencing." With this assurance, Carol began to hope for a restored marriage.

Every year after that first one, Carol and her husband attended Exodus if they could, he for the teaching and healing he knew he needed, she because of the friendship with other hurting wives "and the loving spirit and arms of a short little lady whose name was Willa. Oh, how she loved us, and we all knew it," Carol said. "She made us feel safe with each other and with God and helped us know that we would make it, even if our husbands didn't."

Carol's husband did make it. He is now free of the homosexual lifestyle, she says, and their children know his history, and they forgive and love him. Both Carol and her husband minister together in an ex-gay ministry, Love and Grace. Carol says, "My arms are open to the wives that come in our door. I only hope I can love them the way Willa loved me and show them where their hope and strength come from."

---

When on January 1, 2000, Willa left the Regeneration staff as a paid worker and reassumed a volunteer status, her work with the wives group continued. The ministry honored her at their annual Regeneration Anniversary dinner, where Alan presented her gifts from the staff and thanked her for her "mother's heart." A tribute in the newsletter mentions her ministry to same-sex attracted women, to wives, and to couples. She had offered many people inner-healing prayer, including other staff members. She had helped "in hundreds of ways" in the Regeneration office, and "in her home she has hosted ministry people for literally thousands of nights, and she has served them many thousands of meals."[15]

Alan said that even though he was an officer of Exodus for many years and its first executive director, at the annual Exodus conferences he was recognized as "Willa's husband."[16]

---

When Willa said, "I will never, ever, as long as I have breath, stop helping wives," this was a deeply-felt declaration. In June 2009, she suffered a massive stroke on the right side of her brain, which left her unable to use the left side of her body. Her family eventually took her home from the hospital and rehabilitation centers where medical people had worked to restore her. They hired a Christian woman, Cecilia ("Celi"), to help with her care each weekday morning, and Alan devoted himself to care for her the rest of the time, along with the couple's children, their spouses, the couple's grandchildren, and some friends.

Even confined to a special recliner wheelchair, lying almost supine most of the time, Willa never stopped ministering to wives. Celi and Willa developed an unusual rapport, talking during their hours together. One day Celi confided to Willa some problems in her own long-standing marriage. Willa advised her to "keep your focus on God and pray, and God will direct your path. Everything will work out."

Celi said, "And it *is* working out."[17]

CHAPTER 15:

# Counsel by Correspondence

*You are safe with me and can be transparent. I will not leave you or forsake you. . . . Jesus said this, and the Christ in me says this as well.*

~ Willa Medinger letter to Olivia F.

REGENERATION STAFF COMMUNICATED NOT ONLY in person, but also by phone and written correspondence. What did this form of ministry look like? Was it effective?

Olivia F. is one example of the wisdom of this kind of outreach. A good-looking blonde, she was thirty-one years old with no job skills and no means of support when her husband told her he was gay and wanted to move out to live with a man. She had thought that he was attracted to her and the marriage was sound. She begged him to stay with her in their home in Hampton, Virginia. The couple had a son, four; a daughter, two; and another son, eight months and still nursing. This was in the spring of 1988.

Olivia's best friend, Tammy, was one of the first to comfort her, and she came with more than prayer and sympathy. Tammy asked her friend Sy Rogers how to help both Olivia and her husband, Buzz. Sy said, "Tell her to call Alan and Willa Medinger." This proved to be vital advice.

Olivia did phone them. Alan spoke briefly to Buzz and advised him, "Support your family and stay with them!" But Buzz left for California anyway, leaving no address and no money. It was September 1988.

Olivia panicked. She had only a high school education and had not excelled even at that, having been a "C" student. How would she be able to live and care for their three children? It looked impossible. At first, Olivia's church helped her financially so she could stay in her apartment for several months while she set herself up for welfare checks and food stamps. But because Olivia's friends "had a hard time dealing with this," she needed emotional support and spiritual advice. Then Willa began her good work and became Olivia's "life line to sanity." All of Willa's counsel, for more than ten years, was by means of letters and a few phone calls. Olivia never met Willa, which she now deeply regrets. She's counting on a joy-filled meeting with her in heaven.

In the first letter Willa wrote to Olivia, she recommended two books on codependency, *Women Who Love Too Much* by Robin Norwood and *Codependent No More* by Melody Beattie. Olivia read both books and found them helpful because they made her angry when she understood the pattern she had assumed in her marriage—one of being a doormat to her husband.

Willa also sent her own written testimony and advice. "One of the hardest things wives have to do," she said, "is to let go and to let God, even when it seems our husbands will head right down into the pit of hell. It means letting God straighten him out, and that might be in a way that we would never choose and one that is terrifying to us."

This first letter began a correspondence in which Olivia said she "was always writing a letter to Willa." Many of these she never sent, and many she sent without hoping for an answer, knowing how busy Willa was. But writing them was therapeutic. Olivia also kept a journal in which she could vent, as Willa suggested.

Several months after Buzz left, Olivia's church friends helped her move into a new house that she and they had fixed up for her and the children. The first day, after her friends completed their work and left, Olivia felt utterly alone and unable to cope. All three children began screaming. Olivia retreated to the bedroom and closed the door. She prayed, "God, I cannot do this. I just can't do this."[1]

Then the phone rang. It was Willa. She had perceived that Olivia needed her. Olivia answered the phone, crying hard. Willa asked, "What is that sound?"

Olivia said, "I'm crying and my kids are crying."

Willa told Olivia to open the door. So she did and took the children onto her lap. They quieted. "Now, isn't that better?" Willa asked.

"I think someone else should raise these kids," Olivia said.

"No, you're fine." This intervention, just in time, gave Olivia the will to continue. Later she faced another decision. Buzz asked to come back into the marriage in April 1990. Willa then gave her difficult advice. She said Olivia should insist on Buzz paying all the support money he owed her and getting a steady job in one place for at least two years before she would consider taking him back. Willa knew a second betrayal from Buzz would crush Olivia.

In her letter, Willa counseled, "For the first time, you are dealing with reality, which is that your husband is an unrepentant sinner who has strayed from God and all that he knows is right and good. God has sent him into exile, which is where he must remain until he hurts so bad that he gives up and surrenders [to the Lord]."[2]

Though Willa always worked for restoration of marriages, she never did so at the expense of wives. "Thank God you've finally got enough love for yourself to be upset when people take advantage of you," she told Olivia. "You are in God's hands. I'm praying for you constantly and look forward to your letters. So keep on keeping on, little lady. May God bless you and keep you, always."[3]

When Olivia's younger boy began pre-school, she heard of an opportunity to attend school herself. She attributes what happened next as a gift from God and Willa, who was counseling and praying with her through this process. Somehow Olivia managed to be accepted at Thomas Nelson Community College in a program called "gender equity," which sought to educate women in traditionally male job skills, and men in women's job skills. She asked for training to become a secretary, a job included as gender neutral in the curriculum. After several phone calls, she was accepted, and the program paid her tuition.

Then for nearly five years, as she studied part-time, Olivia rose at 4 a.m., packed a picnic lunch, dressed, and spent time with the Lord before rousing her children, feeding them, and supervising their preparations for school. After they left for the day, she went to college, and after school, she picked them up and took them and the picnic to Buckroe Beach. They ate together, and then the children played while Olivia did her homework. To supplement her income, on weekends she bartered her time with other mothers. She cared for their children, and instead of money in return, she asked for items on a list of things she needed, like shampoo and toothpaste.

Next, Olivia was accepted in a volunteer program, "Students Helping Students." She became a mentor to other students. After two years, the college created an eight-hour job for Olivia in the registration office. She was "senior registration official." Later she ran the office of the man who headed the adult continuing education program, "Welfare to Work." Without realizing it, she was creating a fine resume. Olivia said working with these people for three years "changed my life."[4]

All this time, Willa cheered her on. Her letters came with Scriptures and comments like, "The Lord gave me this Scripture as a promise to you: 'And they shall come and shout for joy on the height of Zion, / And they shall be radiant over the bounty of the Lord . . . /and their life shall be like a watered garden, . . . /For I will turn their mourning into joy, / And will comfort them, and give them joy for their sorrow.'"[5]

Olivia said, "I lived for those letters for the longest time." She believes Willa realized how important her letters were. She encouraged total honesty from Olivia, the bad with the good, "not just the sweetness," because, as Willa put it, "I love and accept all of you. You are safe with me and can be transparent. I will not leave you or forsake you. . . . Jesus said this, and the Christ in me says this as well."[6]

Willa by now knew something of Olivia's childhood struggles. Both women had experienced the same pressures to be "good girls."

Willa understood what it is to be invisible—learning to work at keeping others happy at the expense of one's own happiness. This pattern had long ago, when Willa first understood it, produced in her intense anger. She told Olivia, "I have had to dump all over my family and my church." But, she said, "As the anger, bitterness, and resentment slowly released, God was able to fill that vacated place with the Holy Spirit. . . . With every release of anger and pain came a new place filled with the Holy Spirit. . . . I thought I had to suppress my angry side and control myself. Little did I know He would give me a new heart."[7]

But Willa told Olivia that anger would never go away if she denied it. Time would not heal it. "The only way out is through,"[8] Willa said. "We need to feel the pain of our past and allow Jesus to heal it. Only then can we go on to find the wholeness that Jesus died to give us."

Halfway through her college work, in September 1993 after Buzz had been gone more than five years, Olivia served divorce papers on him. She said, "Willa was the only one who said it didn't matter if the divorce happened or not."

Willa did not argue in favor of the divorce. She let Olivia figure it out.[9] After Olivia prayed about this and was certain it was the best decision, Willa agreed and sent a check for $75 to help begin the proceedings. The money gave Olivia confidence to hire the best divorce lawyer in the area. Olivia considers what followed a miracle: her lawyer never cashed the check or asked for a penny.

She graduated in the spring of 1996, *magna cum laude,* having done what seemed the impossible. But shortly before this, Willa helped her through another crisis. Olivia's oldest child, Ari, then twelve, remembered his father from when he was four and they had lived together. Ari wanted to restore a relationship with him. That same spring, Buzz had appeared on Olivia's doorstep, eight years after leaving her. He was very sweet to the children during his two-week visit, and when he left, Ari had a total breakdown and left a suicide note.

Hearing of this, Buzz returned to Olivia's house and said, "Let me have him for a couple of weeks." Olivia was sick with worry. One night, after Buzz said, "I'm taking him," she was on her knees begging God for wisdom. The phone rang, and it was Willa—the second phone call.

Willa said, "God just told me, 'Let him go.'" She thought the message was about Olivia letting Buzz go. When Olivia explained that the "him" who might go was Ari, Willa stayed firm. She said she knew this message was from the Lord.

That night, Olivia hugged her son and cried and cried. She said good-bye to him the next morning and went to work. All day she hated herself, and she prayed, "Okay, Lord, if he's there when I come home, I'll be so happy."

But he was gone. This turned out to be a blessing, Olivia said much later, because Ari got to know his dad and discovered a different person from the one he had imagined.

Buzz didn't return Ari to Olivia as promised, so when she graduated soon after, she sold everything she had and moved to San Diego, California, to be near her son. She wanted to see Ari and keep the three children together. Because of the excellent resume she had, based on her years at Thomas Nelson Community College, she found a job with a temp agency in California, followed by better jobs. Willa wrote her, "Your letters continue to enchant me, and I am overwhelmed by the act of restoration that Jesus has done for you. I am so happy that you've made it to the top and that you find people appreciating the person that you are."[10]

In a phone conversation on Thanksgiving Day 1996, Ari told his mother about a gay pride parade that Buzz had taken Ari to so they could march in it together. Olivia was amused to hear Ari say he enjoyed the parade because he held hands with his dad's partner's daughter through the whole event. He didn't notice anybody else. She thought this must be God's protection.[11]

As time and letters went by, Olivia noticed that she and Willa grew into a friendship of equals. Olivia cared about Willa and sometimes wrote to encourage her when stresses in Willa's life multiplied. Once

Willa complained about Alan not understanding her, even after more than thirty years of marriage.

Willa: "Alan doesn't get me at all!"

Olivia: "Yeah, God really healed him good. He's a real man now. [They really don't understand us.]"

Willa laughed and laughed at this.[12]

In December 1999, Olivia found an excellent job. Willa wrote, "Your new job sounds quite impressive and a place where you truly will be heard and have a voice." She promised, "One day we'll meet."[13]

In 2002, Olivia found an even better job at an outstanding medical center in San Diego County.

After Willa suffered a disabling stroke in June 2009, Olivia sent Alan an e-mail saying that Willa "will forever be one I hope to meet someday. Please tell her thank you for holding me in her heart thru the darkness. Sometimes, I felt like she was the only one who cared."

Alan responded that, when he read the letter to Willa, "one tear fell from her eye. Her memory is perfect, so she remembers you quite well, and she was greatly blessed by the letter."[14]

At this writing, Olivia still lives in California and works at her excellent job. The family, including Buzz, reunites for various gatherings like Thanksgiving and Christmas. Her children, now 30, 28, and 26, have turned out "uniquely incredible," she says. They "are able to love both mom and dad for the humans we be."[15] None of her children is same-sex attracted. They have given her four grandchildren to date. She spends lots of time with her children and grandchildren, and "they light up my life," she says.[16]

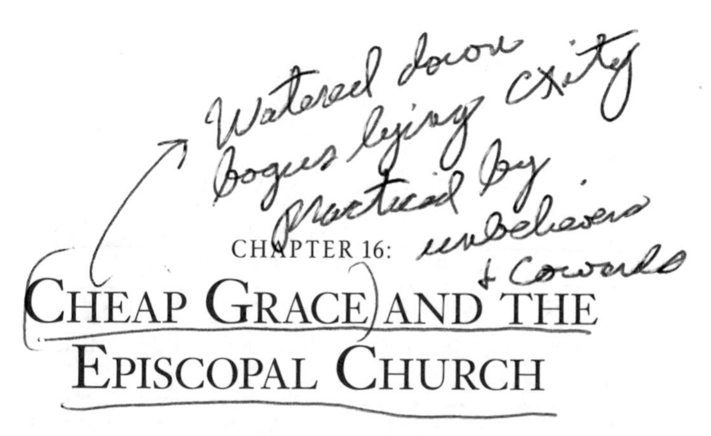


CHAPTER 16:

# Cheap Grace and the Episcopal Church

*Cheap grace is the preaching of forgiveness without requiring repentance. . . . Cheap grace is grace without discipleship, grace without the cross, grace without Jesus Christ, living and incarnate.*

~ Dietrich Bonhoeffer in *The Cost of Discipleship*

FOR MANY YEARS, ALAN SOUGHT to take his message of redemption for same-sex-attracted people to his denomination, the Episcopal Church United States of America (ECUSA). Is his message one that any church should make a top priority? Alan believed it is. He quoted in *Regeneration News* a letter from a practicing psychiatrist who was also a bishop in the Mennonite Church: "This issue touches all the most central issues of the Christian faith and Christian life: the nature of man, the nature of sin, what it means to be saved, what Christ brings to a person, the nature of the church, the place of Scriptures in the Christian community, and how we interpret them."

Dr. Enos D. Martin had concluded, and Alan agreed: "This issue is not peripheral; it is central to our identity as a people."[1]

Two denominations, Episcopalians and Presbyterians, supported Regeneration financially in the early years. Alan believed something about those two denominations made them, at that time, open to his kind of ministry. They were churches that were "essentially conservative"—that is, they were faithful to "the historic faith and to Scripture," but they were also liberal in the sense that they were open to reaching hurting people. Theirs was "an openness to new ways to minister, an openness to unlovely people, an openness to things like healing."[2]

However, in the 1980s and 1990s, as Alan learned more about the opinions of leaders in the Episcopal Church, he grew disillusioned. In 1985 he went, for the first time, to an Episcopal Church General Convention (this one in Anaheim, California) with Willa and his staff member, Luanna Hutchison. At this triennial convention, delegates make decisions for the church's future guidance.

Alan, Willa, and Luanna set up a booth to explain the work of Exodus International, and in particular, Regeneration Ministry. From gay men Alan had expected hostility to the message that Jesus brings redemption and healing to SSA people. But the numerous gays at the convention opposed the message only in a "limited and tempered" manner, he said. It was militant feminists who verbally attacked the Regeneration people "vociferously."[3] Women priests and other feminists accused Alan and Regeneration of homophobia. They showed no interest in Alan's message of healing. On the contrary, they accused him of being responsible for "causing gay people to commit suicide."[4]

---

In the same year, 1985, Kathleen Boatwright attended All Saints' Episcopal Church in Pasadena, California, and took part in the Eucharist alongside her lesbian lover, happy to have found a spiritual home. "We held hands and wept," she said. "We could go forward because in the Anglican tradition, the Eucharist is open for everyone. God extends Himself. There are no outcasts in the Episcopal Church."[5] She found strength, with this connection, to leave her Assemblies of God church, her husband and four children, and start a new life with her lover.

---

In 1988, Alan and Luanna again attended the Episcopal Church General Convention, this one in Detroit. Here he met Louie Crew, the founder of "Integrity," a pro-gay Episcopal group that calls itself a "healing community." It had begun in 1974 when Crew launched a publication by the same name, *Integrity,* after he encountered difficulty finding fellowship for himself and his gay lover in San Francisco's Grace Cathedral, which he called "the most liberal of all Anglican houses."[6]

Alan said of Louie Crew, "He is a likeable and very shrewd guy."[7]

At the convention, more than 500 resolutions were put to a vote, some of them contradictory. For instance, one resolution barred "discrimination based on sexual orientation" for those beginning the ordination process leading to priesthood, while another affirmed "traditional sexual morality." Two of the voting bodies, bishops and priests, agreed, on the first resolution, that sexual orientation should not be a factor in choosing future priests, but laypeople voted to retain the church's position against ordaining gays. However, all three bodies agreed to delete a sentence in the traditional morality resolution that said sexual activity must be limited to heterosexual relations in marriage.[8]

Nevertheless, Alan was encouraged by the mostly cordial reception from many people who stopped by the booth "Episcopalians for Biblical Sexuality" that he, Luanna, Carrie Wingfield, and Robbie Kenney staffed. Whereas in Anaheim, Integrity members had been hostile, in Detroit, they were "extremely cordial." Alan suspected that Louie Crew advised pro-gay Episcopalians to behave "more kindly" toward Alan and Regeneration because hostile behavior would not benefit them or their cause.[9]

Bishop John Shelby Spong, Episcopal bishop of Newark, New Jersey, published a book in 1988, *Living in Sin? A Bishop Rethinks Human Sexuality,* which commanded attention in the church and the wider public because of his pro-gay beliefs. He explained later, when interviewed about his part in the gay rights struggle, "We have to bless gay unions because I think these relationships are holy, and what a blessing does is announce publicly that this is a holy relationship."[10]

Spong also authored a platform for church change: "Twelve theses: Call for a New Reformation." In it, he said "theism is dead," and therefore to understand Jesus as the incarnation of God is "nonsensical." The

Virgin Birth "is impossible," the miracles Christ is said to have performed never happened, the cross as a sacrifice for sins is "a barbarian idea," and Jesus was never resurrected bodily. He also said, "There is no external, objective, revealed standard writ in Scripture or on tablets of stone that will govern our ethical behavior for all time." (That is, moral values are relative.) He believed it was futile to expect "a theistic deity to act in human history in a particular way in response to prayer."

Spong's books and speeches to publicize them made him one of the best known and most controversial persons in the Episcopal Church. Though his statements are outside orthodox Christian faith, he retained his bishop's position in the church hierarchy.

Episcopal Bishop William Frey, President of Trinity School for Ministry in Ambridge, Pennsylvania, said in a *Time* magazine interview about Bishop Spong, "The [Episcopal] House of Bishops has shown itself to be impotent in the face of challenges to the core beliefs of the church. We've been paralyzed by our politeness."[11]

In July 1989, four years after leaving her husband and children, Kathleen Boatwright was a gay activist and a member of Integrity. Eric Marcus interviewed her for his book on gay rights history as she sat on a park bench outside San Francisco's Grace Cathedral. She was waiting for Bishop Spong to address the four hundred Integrity workers who had come to hear his encouraging words.[12]

"Integrity gives me a forum for the things I want to say both as a lesbian woman and as a committed Christian," she told Marcus. "Because of my background and experience, I can speak to the church I love on a variety of issues that others cannot. I can say, 'I call you into accountability. . . . The church needs to change.'"[13]

Even though his own local Episcopal church, St. Mary's, stood solidly behind the work of Regeneration, Alan slowly lost hope that the current Episcopal Church leadership would protect biblical sexuality. In July 1991, however, he spoke to the Episcopal convention in Phoenix,

Arizona, on the issue. He lamented that the church seemed not to know what Scripture said about homosexuality, even though until "quite recently" it had been clear that God's "plan for our sexuality was one man, one woman in a lifetime commitment. 'For this reason a man shall leave his father and mother and be joined to his wife, and the two shall become one flesh.'"

This, Alan said, was the Bible provision for sex in Genesis, in the words of Jesus, and in the words of Paul. "Fornication, adultery, homosexual activity were outside God's plan. Every reference to homosexuality in Scripture was negative," he said. "I believe God [gave] us a plan, and . . . His plan is not arbitrary, but is for our benefit and blessing. . . . Homosexuality is outside of God's original intent, and therefore, brings the potential for great suffering."[14]

In June 1995, fifty years after the conclusion of World War II in Europe, Alan reminded his *Regeneration News* readers of a related occasion—the fiftieth anniversary of Dietrich Bonhoeffer's execution by the Nazis. In his best-known book, *The Cost of Discipleship*, Bonhoeffer described "cheap grace," which is, he said, preaching a God of "love and little else" [in Alan's words]. From SSA strugglers, Alan had often heard a church doctrine similar to cheap grace that sounds like the gospel but is really a seductive half-truth—"God accepts me and blesses me just as I am." Because this idea is close to the truth, Alan said, it has power to persuade.

He reminded his readers of its effect on his former foster son, Bobby. At an Episcopal Church retreat, leaders had told him, "God loves you and accepts you just as you are; there is no reason for you to give up your homosexuality. We are freed from such legalism." After the retreat, he dropped out of Regeneration and returned to a gay life. The day before Alan wrote about Bonhoeffer, he had gone to see Bobby, who had just signed papers ordering that his body be cremated. He was dying of AIDS.[15]

Alan urged his readers to seek "costly grace," in Bonhoeffer's words, "the call of Jesus Christ at which the disciple leaves his net and follows Him. It is costly because it costs a man his life, and it is grace because it gives man the true life."[16] A person is not to surrender to "warm, fuzzy Christianity" that demands nothing, Alan said. He or she is not to call the church to accountability if it teaches Bible truth. Rather that person must accept the love of Christ who asks that we follow Him, repent of sin, and be accountable to Him.

In 1994 and 1997, Alan and Willa attended two more Episcopal Church General Conventions, in Indianapolis, Indiana, and Philadelphia, Pennsylvania. By the last conference Alan had concluded that current Episcopal Church leaders were beyond hope of returning to biblical orthodoxy. He wrote an article explaining "How the Battle over Homosexuality in the Episcopal Church was lost—and How It Could Have Been Won."[17] "The decline of scriptural authority," he said, is the first of seven factors that led to a pro-gay-agenda church. Scriptural authority is the fundamental issue on which the others hang. As more than nineteen centuries of Bible teaching on sexuality was questioned in Episcopal Church dialogue, the battle was lost. "By just agreeing to talk, we undermined two of our own primary sources of authority—Scripture and tradition. Besides, we were lied to; the leadership of the church never intended for this to be a true dialogue."[18]

By this he meant the leaders didn't consult people in the church—people like Alan—who held answers to how to love same-sex-attracted people while at the same time encouraging them to take the road to sanctification that all Christians are required to take.

He traced the weakness of Episcopal Church leaders back to the 1960s, when they tolerated the teachings of Bishop James Pike, who, like Bishop Spong, had questioned bedrock Christian doctrines—the virginity of Mary, the doctrines of hell and of the Trinity. While at Grace Cathedral in San Francisco, Bishop Pike had promoted gay issues. Heresy procedures were begun against him four times, but in the end, the church backed down from convicting him, though his fellow bishops did censure him in 1966, which led to his resignation. Alan believed this was "an abdication of the Episcopal Church's authority over its teaching and beliefs."[19] When Bishop Spong introduced his heretical beliefs two decades later, the church tolerated them.

---

In 1996 Alan observed another lapse in church discipline. Bishop Walter Righter, assistant bishop of Newark, New Jersey, ordained an openly gay man, Barry Stopfel, as a deacon, a step toward priesthood. Ten bishops asked that the church try Righter for "teaching false doctrine," but a group of thirty-six bishops responded in his defense, saying, "Should he be found guilty, we are guilty."

The question was—did he break the 1979 Episcopal Church resolution that described the ordination of non-celibate homosexuals as "not appropriate"? After consideration, the church court of nine bishops said Righter was not guilty, because the church "has no clear doctrine" on this issue, and therefore he did not violate any "core doctrine." In effect, Alan said, the case was thrown out because one couldn't violate the church's sexual ethics, there being none.

Alan observed that Righter had previously left his wife, divorced her, married his secretary, then divorced her, and married a third wife. The conservative bishops who wanted Righter disciplined had never said anything about this because, Alan said, "even conservatives were not taking positions or giving sermons on sexual fidelity within marriage."

After the Righter case, Alan felt the Lord tell him, "The church is gone. You don't have to stay in it anymore."[20]

In October 1997, Alan and Willa announced their decision to leave the Episcopal Church after 37 years' membership for Willa and 61 for Alan. They said, "Our decision was made after long, agonizing deliberation and much prayer." The reason they felt this move necessary was their belief that "the Episcopal Church as a national denomination has moved beyond the margins of historic Christianity and . . . there is almost no hope for reform within that institution in the foreseeable future." Alan continued to believe that the Episcopal Church's openness to mystery and to the Holy Spirit made it potentially one of the best denominations for redemptive ministry to all kinds of broken people, SSA people included. But he felt any hope of reform lay with future generations of leaders.

The Episcopal bishop of Central Florida, John W. Howe, wrote to Alan and Willa when he heard they were leaving the denomination. As rector of Truro Episcopal Church in Fairfax, Virginia, he and his church had been early backers of Regeneration. His belief in the Medingers' ministry continued. He wrote, "I am profoundly saddened by . . . your decision to leave the Episcopal Church. Your witness and ministry has been one of the most heartening things going in a confused and apostate church. . . . It is an appalling loss, and you will be sorely missed. I pray God will continue to anoint the ministry of Regeneration with his Holy Spirit. . . . My love and deepest admiration for you accompanies this note."

In response, Alan urged his readers in a brief article to pray for those who "stay and battle" within the church.[21]

Alan and Willa hoped their positive relationships with individuals and churches within ECUSA would continue after they left the denomination. In September 1997 they began attending Christ the King Church in Towson, part of the Charismatic Episcopal Church.[22] This change meant Alan would no longer fight within ECUSA in hopes of influencing leaders to teach and/or follow biblical sexuality.

They left St. Mary's Episcopal Church with deep regrets. Under the leadership of Father Richard Lipka, it had always been a Bible-believing and loving church as well as a loyal supporter of Regeneration. In April 1988, Fr. Lipka had become Regeneration's board president. But a year later, in June 1989, he left Regeneration and St. Mary's after seventeen years as its pastor, accepting a call from St. Mary's Church in Honolulu, Hawaii.

Membership in St. Mary's declined after Father Lipka left. The bishop sent an interim priest who was a "super-liberal, feminist, pro-gay" woman, in Willa's words. She persuaded some women to return to active lesbian lives. Under her leadership, the liturgy changed from "Father, Son, and Holy Ghost" to "Creator, Savior, and Sustainer." Feminist language snuck into her prayers. Families began leaving the church.

Next came a priest who was a Bible believer, but he was "a terrible preacher and administrator," again in Willa's words. More people left. On December 31, 1999, St. Mary's closed its doors for the last time.

Like Father Lipka, Father Ed Meeks, the rector of Christ the King Church, supported Regeneration. He joined its board in September 1998.

Nearly six years after Alan and Willa left the Episcopal Church, its leaders ordained as bishop Gene Robinson, a man who had divorced his wife and left his children in favor of a gay lover. Alan observed the event as an outsider and remarked, "I think it was good that they finally started to do openly what they had been doing secretly all along. It was the final evidence many believing priests and other leaders needed to realize that the Episcopal Church was no longer a valid Christian church."[23]

amen!!

CHAPTER 17:

# CHALLENGES

*We argue that, for all practical purposes, gays should be considered to have been* born *gay.*

~ Marshall Kirk and Hunter Madsen, Ph.D., gay activists

ONLY TWO DECADES AFTER THE gay revolution began with the Stonewall riot in 1969, it had made little progress and, indeed, was losing ground due to the public's fear of AIDS and ignorance about how the disease spread. Then two bright Harvard graduates, gay activists skilled in advertising, published a book, *After the Ball: How America Will Conquer Its Fear and Hatred of Gays in the '90s*. They drew up an aggressive agenda to change public opinion.

The techniques they propose are, in the words of authors Marshall Kirk and Hunter Madsen, Ph.D., "unabashed propaganda, firmly grounded in long-established principles of psychology and advertising."[2] The authors call for an inundation of media, especially TV, featuring gays pictured in such a way that "straights" would think they are "just like us . . . wholesome and admirable . . . conventional young people, middle-aged women, and older folks of all races." SSA persons are to be seen as victims of circumstance who "no more chose their sexual orientation than they did, say, their height, skin color, talents, or limitations."

Kirk and Madsen pushed the "born gay" idea: "We argue that, for all practical purposes, gays should be considered to have been *born gay*." (Italics are by the authors.)[3]

However, they clearly state in the book, written for a gay audience, that they believed "born gay" is not true. They said, "Sexual orientation, for most humans, seems to be the product of a complex interaction between innate predispositions and environmental factors during childhood and early adolescence. . . . To suggest in public that homosexuality might be *chosen* is to open the can of worms labeled 'moral choice and sin' and give the religious intransigents a stick to beat us with. Straights must be taught that it is as natural for some persons to be homosexual as it is for others to be heterosexual: wickedness and seduction have nothing to do with it. *And since no choice is involved, gayness can be no more blameworthy than straightness.*" (Italics are by the authors.)

Activists sought to indoctrinate the public with the idea that SSA persons, "born that way," are minority groups similar to blacks and women, covered by the Civil Rights Act of 1964, which applies to classes of people who have suffered discrimination. If people are not born same-sex attracted, and they can potentially change, the Civil Rights Act does not apply to them. If the Civil Rights Act does not give them special status, then their rights as individuals are the same as all other Americans.

---

The greatest challenge to Regeneration in the 1990s was the growing acceptance of homosexuality in the mainstream culture following the publication of *After the Ball*. Some people came to the ministry hoping to change their sexual attractions and orientation by means of a quick fix. After they learned that a long process of discipleship lay ahead, they melted back into the gay culture. Their consoling thought was that the culture was right—homosexuality was normal and unchangeable.

Establishing a new branch of ministry—Regeneration Books—was a big achievement, but it proved a challenge too. In the late 1980s, as formerly homosexual people published their stories of redeemed lives, Alan realized that many of his clients couldn't find these books, because secular bookstores didn't carry anything about Christianity, and Christian stores didn't carry anything about sex. He decided to make these helpful books available through an ambitious new outreach.

*Regeneration News* had published reviews of books related to its ministry off and on almost from its beginning. In August 1988, when Alan reviewed *You Don't Have to be Gay* by Jeff Konrad, he believed the book so helpful that he ordered a number of copies and allowed Regeneration to sell them. This might be called the beginning of Regeneration Books.

Reviewing the Konrad book, Alan acknowledged that "an enormous wall exists between many homosexual [persons] and conservative Christians. . . . To many gays, we are the enemy, the one group that stands between them and the acceptance they long for. This book is sensitive to that reality."[4]

The hope in July 1989, when Regeneration Books officially began, was that this outreach would "meet an important need in the body of Christ," supplying hard-to-find books, and that it would also "help support Regeneration financially."[5]

In January 1990, Alan announced the book ministry was "generating regular income"[6] to help support the wider ministry. Regenbooks grew, selling books and tapes at a total value of $119,000 in 2000.[7] For many years the book ministry thrived, furnishing hard-to-get materials to people seeking to understand same-sex attraction. In the ministry's most successful year, it sold more than 12,000 books, grossing about $180,000.[8] Lani Bersch, the book ministry director, said, "We know that hundreds of lives were changed because of Regeneration Books."

However, the book ministry didn't pay for itself as Alan originally hoped, and it required many hours of labor. In March 2006, he closed Regenbooks after more than sixteen years. In the 2000s, Amazon.com and some bookstores carried books on homosexuality, making it easier for the public to buy them.

---

Alan and Willa endured many personal challenges too in the 1990s. In September 1993, Alan developed heart problems. *Regeneration News* requested prayers for "quick and complete healing for Alan and peace and comfort for the rest of the family."[9]

Willa wrote her good friend Olivia on September 20 to say, "My dear, precious Alan was taken into the hospital on Saturday afternoon." Alan had waited through ten days of irregular heartbeats before telling Willa that morning that he was having trouble breathing. She rushed him to the emergency room. They admitted him "for atrial fibrillation and an irregular heartbeat."

Doctors were divided on how to treat him. Willa wrote, "My security has been blown to kingdom come—because Alan was going to live forever and be indestructible and take good care of me when I went senile. . . . I feel very vulnerable and frightened."

In December, Alan and Willa went on sabbatical. Both needed rest to recover from the shock and weakness occasioned by Alan's heart problems. Willa experienced "severe major depression" for several months. Not until May of 1994 were they able to return to ministry. Even then, Willa was not totally better. She wrote Olivia, "I'm BACK!!!! I don't know how well I'm back, but I'm here."[10] She asked Olivia to pray that Willa would discover that "all of this pain has a purpose and reason. Please pray . . . not that God would take this away, but that I would remain where I need to remain that He might accomplish His purpose in me."

Both Willa and Alan enjoyed the 1995 Exodus conference in San Diego and a fun week after it, vacationing with Frank and Anita Worthen. This was the first of many vacations the two couples spent together. Anita said the two women were "a bit apprehensive" at first about whether they would get along for a whole week, since they were "so much alike."

Afterwards, Willa wrote Olivia, "Anita is just like me, and Frank and Alan are two peas in a pod." They went to the zoo, to some international restaurants, and to Tijuana, Mexico, shopping and sightseeing.[11]

Both Alan and Willa had a wonderful time. Each year after that, the couples vacationed together for a week after the Exodus conference. They traveled to many places in North America, Europe, and Australia. Willa especially liked Hawaii and Puerto Vallarta, Mexico.[12]

However, Alan's heart problems continued. He was tired and mildly depressed because of them. May 18, 1996 was Alan's sixtieth birthday. Willa decided to celebrate with a big party (160 came) because she feared he would not live to see seventy. Those who came were "the gang" of friends from Alan's college years, neighbors, church friends, family, Regeneration staff, and many who had benefited from Alan's ministry, some from nearby states.

Held in the backyard of the Medingers' Towson, Maryland, home, the party featured a Willa-type feast: hamburgers, hotdogs, potato salad, fried chicken, deviled eggs, iced tea, lemonade, soda, beer, wine, and birthday cake. A podium set up in the side yard provided a stage where people could give testimonies.

"I'm married. I have children. I'm alive today—thanks to this ministry!" This was a theme voiced by many. Laura Medinger said this was the first time the three grown Medinger children realized how many were impacted by Regeneration.

The event blessed Alan as Willa had hoped, but Sue and Jack O'Neill, long-time family friends, saw how pale and sick he looked. Jack took him aside and suggested he have his heart checked again. He did, shortly after.[13]

The last day of May, Willa wrote to Olivia, "Things at Regeneration have been an absolute disaster—funds, interpersonal struggles, and sickness like you wouldn't believe. Mostly the person so sick has been Alan." He had been fighting an off-and-on fever for two months that caused shivering spells and night sweats. Willa said, "He seems to be turning yellow more and more. Before this, he was an awful gray, and the yellow actually makes him look healthier."

In June, Alan was hospitalized for twelve days and given "heavy duty antibiotic treatment," then released. But on July 17 he returned to the hospital. An infection had attacked a damaged heart valve, causing further damage, and he needed emergency surgery.[14] However, Alan's kidneys shut down, and his very urgent surgery had to be postponed for twelve days. He nearly died.

Willa earnestly appealed for prayers around the world from everyone she knew. In some cases her appeals were unnecessary, for the Lord Himself communicated Alan's need. One such person who sensed Alan's need was Sonia Balcer of California. She wrote Alan later, in December, describing her intense sense that he had needed prayer. It started at the June Exodus conference, which Alan missed because he was unwell. Sonia didn't know what was wrong, but praying for him, she "kept seeing a mass of a whitish substance on what I assumed to be heart valve tissue, and I prayed against its advance."

Despite encouraging reports on Alan, Sonia's "sense of uneasiness grew into an intense anxiety." The image became more vivid until she "felt the most intense urgency about your state and [I] began checking my e-mail every few hours." Then at last, on the night of July 17/18, feeling "especially troubled," she received news that Alan had been hospitalized with mitral valve infection. She checked the internet and saw a color picture "that made my blood run cold—here for the first time was a precise view of the image I had seen repeatedly in prayer!" The accompanying description said that people so infected usually died, but Sonia did not stop praying. Rather, she enlisted the emergency prayer chain at her church, and they prayed for Alan fervently. Sonia wrote Alan, "At no moment did I doubt that [the Lord] intended to heal you." She had a "strong conviction that it was not your time to die—that there was much He had yet for you to do in this life—many articles full of honest, clear, holy searchings to write on behalf of His kingdom and all those who were likewise searching." Sonia said she was "deeply grateful for the privilege of being enlisted in this great work of healing."[15]

She was not alone in this prayer work. Alan said on July 27 he "was given a sense of those prayers being like a mighty river lifting me up into the very presence of God, where He touched me and my healing began." The day after this revelation, Alan's kidneys began to function, and the infection abated. The operation proceeded on July 29 and was "a great success."[16]

During this difficult time, other calamities occurred as well. Alan's brother, Pete, and his wife, Wilberta, traveled to Europe in late June for the "trip of her dreams." Willy was a meticulous planner, and she had thought through and orchestrated every detail of this once-in-a-lifetime trip. But at breakfast in Italy one morning, she died without warning of a heart attack. This nightmare ending of the dream trip was compounded by all the difficulties Pete, helped by his stateside family, encountered trying to bring Willy's body home for burial.

At Regeneration, a sudden resignation left the staff badly understaffed, with Alan unable to work because of his illness. Billie Baldwin, who had been with the ministry less than a year, did the work of three full-time persons for a while. Then Mike, an important volunteer leader, was severely injured and crippled for some months by an automobile accident, and Hurricane Bertha tore off part of the roof of the Medingers' vacation home, Pelican Palace, and removed half of the sand dune that protected it. Willa took care of repairs.

In September, Alan returned to the hospital with more heart symptoms from fluid build-up around his heart. Willa drove straight from the hospital (after they admitted Alan) to Pelican Palace in North Carolina (an eight-hour trip), leaving the hospital at midnight. She checked on damage from Hurricane Fran, which had struck Topsail Island two nights before and severely damaged forty percent of the houses on the island, thirty percent beyond repair. With help from her daughter Laura, Laura's husband, and a Regeneration friend, they ordered about $25,000 of repairs to the beach house, all of it covered by insurance, they discovered later. Willa said in a letter to Olivia, "I don't know how I did what I did, but I did it."[17]

Alan remained very sick for ten days, but he got better after doctors removed the fluid around his heart. By the end of the month, he was able to work at home, and the doctors cleared him to drive so he could work some in the office too. At this time Willa wrote to Olivia, "I fell apart when Alan got all well."

But by October, both Alan and Willa were well enough to travel to Hawaii for a two-week vacation with Anita and Frank Worthen. Willa told Olivia, "We get along so beautifully and are like kids together. GOD IS SOOOOOOOO GOOD." Even with this respite, it was May 5 before Willa returned to work, having spent March and April at the vacation house, recovering from the trauma of the previous year. By then, she said, "Alan has had a miracle recovery. He looks better than he's looked for ten years. He's gotten all his strength back."[18]

Alan had, in fact, gained back the fifty pounds he lost during his illness, and he said, "With a heart that really works now, I actually have more energy and feel stronger than I have felt in years."[19] He had wondered during the first twenty-two years of his Christian life how he would react to hardship. Now he could say from experience, at age sixty, that he never lost faith for a minute in the reality or goodness of God, and he was never tempted to go back and comfort himself in the old ways of his youth.

---

Willa, throughout their marriage, entertained family and friends with her offbeat sense of humor, and Alan played along with it. For many years, Willa proclaimed her love for pigs. Once, during Lent, Alan located a local farmer who agreed to rent out two piglets. Willa knew nothing about this until Easter morning, when Alan crept into their bedroom with the animals. Willa woke up to find two pink baby pigs in bed with her. She was delighted. It was a special Easter for Willa, though the pigs had to return to their farm home after a day or two.[20]

CHAPTER 18:

# MATURITY

*Now Alan saw himself "as an elder in ex-gay ministry, a man of trust and maturity, a symbol of stability on whom other leaders can draw."*

~ Alan Medinger from *Regeneration News*

RETURNING TO MINISTRY IN THE spring of 1997 with a restored heart and fresh energy, Alan entered a satisfying mature stage of his ministry. Convinced that Regeneration's early years were solidly founded, he reiterated what he had always believed: "The most important thing you can do to overcome homosexuality is to spend time with God." This advice he scrupulously followed, getting up very early five or six days a week and communicating with the Lord through prayer, Bible reading, and meditation for about an hour and a half. He said his time with the Lord was the primary source of all his good ideas for writing and ministry.

Alan described exactly how to develop a relationship with Jesus. Beginners should spend at least half an hour a day in private devotions, working up to longer times. They should find a quiet, private place large enough to kneel and sit to read. He suggested starting by focusing on the Lord with praise, spoken or sung, even if this seems awkward at first. Next are thanksgiving and confession, acknowledging that we need forgiveness every day. Intercession follows, preferably on a schedule, for instance, pray for family and close friends every day, but also pray on Monday for "the church around the world," on Tuesday "for our country," etc. Scripture reading, followed by prayer and reflection are essential, he said, and should be implemented by a good Bible study guide.

He promised the ones who followed his advice, "You will be with the only One who can meet your every need, and you will start to become who He wants you to be."

In his mature years, Alan addressed difficult themes in his newsletters. He had not avoided controversy before, but after recovering from heart surgery, Alan wrote bold articles more often. He was finally able to define healing from homosexuality, which was difficult to state in a simple formula. Ministry participants had found a 1981 article helpful, "Healing for the Homosexual: What Does It Mean?" In it he had described the stages of recovery one could expect. After changes in behavior would come changes in identity and attractions. But this was not a straightforward definition.

In June 1997, he wrote, "You are healed when you are ready to marry."[2] As marriage is God's intention for most men untroubled by same-sex attractions, so it is also for those who recover from them. He added that this readiness to marry is not equivalent to actually getting married. For that, one must find a suitable mate, and not everyone does this.

Alan adopted 1 Corinthians 16:13-14 (ESV) as a favorite verse: "Be watchful, stand firm in faith, act like men, be strong. Let all you do be done in love."[3] In this light, he began speaking more strongly against the effects of homosexual sin. He called on his readers to hate what homosexual acts do to participants: "When a man engages in homosexual behavior or when he dwells in the fantasies of submitting himself sexually to another man [or experiencing another man submitting to him], he desecrates that which God created in His image."[4]

Alan explained that God created the masculine to embody "strength, initiation, prevailing, conquering, authority, protecting." But male homosexuality, he said, often "embodies response, submission, obeying, being controlled or protected," and those who experience these feelings see themselves as "one who is less than a man."

For the first time, Alan asked his readers to confront false and harmful gay rights propaganda. "We must actively oppose acceptance of homosexuality," he said. Exodus ministries had previously avoided getting involved in political issues, because they feared this would distract from their primary mission of healing, but after consulting the Regeneration board and praying, he now believed the direction of the culture toward normalizing homosexuality could not be ignored without damaging ministry clients.

"Every gay rights ordinance, every affirmation of same-sex marriage, every recognition of domestic partnerships declares that homosexuality is worthy of protection and even encouragement," Alan said. The normalization of homosexuality that followed after the APA delisted the condition from its manual of mental disorders caused many to accept rather than resist same-sex attractions, and so, he said, it encouraged homosexual behavior.

The argument that homosexuality is normal and good is based on four premises, Alan said. All are false. None is supported by scientific evidence:

> Homosexuality is determined before birth.
>
> Therefore, homosexual [persons] cannot change.
>
> The problems they face are caused by other people's attitudes toward them (gay people are victims), and
>
> There is nothing wrong with homosexuality; it is just different.[5]

Alan wrote about the attempt by gay activists to persuade the culture that SSA people are "born that way." After surveying "the most widely known authorities in the field of human sexual behavior," he had concluded, "the overwhelming consensus from experts in the field is that homosexuality is primarily learned behavior, and if there is any genetic element, it is almost certainly a minor contributor. . . . If homosexuality is, indeed, learned behavior, then there is the strong possibility that it can be unlearned."[6]

Alan reported on a twins study at Northwestern University by J. Michael Bailey and Richard Pillard. They compared 56 sets of identical twins in which one of each pair was same-sex attracted. They sought to know--if one twin is homosexual, will the other be homosexual too? In 52% of the cases, he was. Alan said, "the study seems to rule out the possibility that homosexuality is caused entirely by genetic causes," since the fact that identical twins always carry identical genes means homosexuality would occur in 100% of twin pairs, if one were homosexual.[7]

Another twins study published in the *British Journal of Psychiatry* by Dr. Michael King and Elizabeth McDonald is even more conclusive. Among 20 identical twin sets with one twin homosexual, only 2 reported a homosexual twin and 3 reported a bi-sexual twin, for a combined concurrence rate of 25%. The authors concluded that "genetic factors are insufficient explanation of the development of sexual orientation."

Alan carefully reviewed all the scientific data and said no study proves that homosexuality is inborn. He said, "If there were conclusive evidence from any source that homosexuality is inborn, we would want to know as much as anyone. We have no interest in ministering to people on a false premise."[8]

---

For many years, Alan did not effectively communicate his love to his daughters. Their own problems and struggles were mysteries to him. Either he did not observe their lives closely, or he blocked out what he saw. This problem, unacknowledged by him, impeded Alan's full growth into mature manhood. On the surface, both young women seemed to be doing all right in 1997. Laura was 34, married, and the mother of two children. Beth, 33, was also married, the mother of three children, the youngest two years old.

But in January 1998, Beth's husband left her. Beth remembers her father's reaction, because it was atypical and surprised her. She couldn't remember Alan crying much during her life, but when Larry left, Alan cried and said, "This is the worst thing that has happened to our family." He lovingly offered to help Beth in any way he could.

During the difficult childhood years for Laura and Beth, Alan had been especially close to Laura, resulting in a deep, hurtful sense of neglect in Beth. But in her marriage crisis, Beth saw Alan's love for her. She knew his heart was broken. It became a turning point in their relationship. In time, Beth recommitted her life to the Lord and recovered emotionally and spiritually. Some years after her divorce, she met a Christian man, married him, and with him had two more children. Both Alan and Willa loved this new member of the family with all their hearts, just as they loved Laura's husband.[9]

---

As early as November 1998, Alan and Willa began planning for the big Regeneration twentieth anniversary celebration, still almost a year off. They sent out in the newsletter a request for testimonies, asking former clients to pray about providing their stories as encouragement to others. "One of the great hindrances to the growth and acceptance of ministries like Regeneration," Alan wrote, "is . . . that so few people who have experienced victory over homosexuality are willing to give testimony to that fact."[10] They want to blend into the culture instead, and live normal lives.

The celebration occurred in two parts, a dinner in Baltimore and a dessert in Fairfax, Virginia. In 1999, on Friday evening October 29—the exact day the first group of three men had met in Alan's living room twenty years earlier to begin the ministry—150 people gathered to honor Alan and Willa at Timonium Presbyterian Church in Timonium, Maryland, near Baltimore.

Many people gave testimonies, and then Alan spoke. "I want to tell you about a man who couldn't be here today," he said. "That man is me, if God had not saved me."

Alan described what might have happened. In the days before Alan's conversion, the four Medingers tended to split into two groups. Whenever tensions grew, Laura sided with her dad, Beth with her mom. Alan said, "Without the Lord, I would have separated from Willa, and Laura would have chosen to come with me, leaving Beth with Willa. But then I would have contracted AIDS and died, leaving Laura completely abandoned, because Willa would never have taken her back after she chose to leave. And Stephen would never have been born."

When Laura heard Alan's words, their truth struck her. She experienced "an absolute revelation that God had spared me and the rest of the family."[11] She realized Alan's miracle had always been intended to bless many more than just Alan—the whole family as well as others.

After the speeches, Jeff Johnston, Baltimore Regeneration director, presented Alan a gift he had carefully put together: three bound volumes of all the *Regeneration News* issues to date, plus the first letters Alan wrote to Frank Worthen and Bob Davies in 1977 and 1979 and their responses. This gift was a treasure to Alan. For Willa, Jeff had another gift, almost as precious. He presented her a large framed print of an Andrew Wyeth drawing, a pink pig. Everybody knew this would delight Willa.

The second anniversary event occurred a week later, a dessert at Church of the Apostles in Fairfax, Virginia. Individuals helped by Regeneration again shared powerful stories of healing. Josh Glaser said later, "The testimonies were really amazing." About 100 people came to this event.

About the celebrations Alan wrote, "How does God bless us? One anecdote speaks volumes. A person attending was heard to say, 'When I came in, I had decided what I was going to contribute. After the first testimony I doubled it, and after the second I doubled it again.'"[12]

His vision of himself changed during the years he led Regeneration. In the beginning Alan saw himself as "a strong leader of a vital local ministry," which, he said, was a big vision at the time. Twenty years later, his vision had grown. Now he saw himself "as an elder in ex-gay ministry, a man of trust and maturity, a symbol of stability on whom other leaders can draw."[13] This vision, too, challenged and energized him.

---

Alan enjoyed rewards of his ministry labors over the years. Many of his former advisees experienced restored lives and became friends. For instance, Alan and Willa met Mario Bergner at a weekend conference at College Hill Presbyterian Church in Cincinnati in the spring of 1984. After hearing Alan's testimony and meeting Willa, Mario hoped, for the first time, that he too "would find an understanding, godly wife" and have a family. Mario came to the 1984 Baltimore Exodus at Willa's invitation, and he said he "encountered the presence of God the Father" there after Dr. Robert Frost prayed for those wounded by fathers. This was a "life-changing healing" for him. He attended every Exodus from 1984 through 1991, until events in his life prevented him from attending.

Alan reviewed Mario's 1995 book, *Setting Love in Order,* with positive words: "This book uses one man's testimony to illustrate the principles of healing as perhaps no book has before. . . . He has a wonderful way with words; the capacity to express deep truths very simply."[14]

Several years later, when Mario married, Alan and Willa rejoiced. Over time they were gratified to see him become a devoted father of five, as well as an Anglican priest, associate rector of a church in Massachusetts, and leader of a very effective ministry in Boston, Redeemed Lives.[15]

Another leader (and past president of Exodus International) whose career Alan and Willa watched and encouraged was Joe Dallas, now an author and director of a biblical counseling practice in Tustin, California. They came to an Exodus meeting when Joe spoke for the first time. He was intimidated, but he clearly remembered them "nodding, smiling, and giving me encouraging looks as I taught, then graciously coming up to me afterwards to encourage me and urge me to continue. You can't imagine how much that meant to a green newcomer."

He said that Willa "was a woman of great humor, a fitting and complementary match for Alan's seriousness. Some of my happiest memories of them involve staying in their home when asked to speak at their conferences, laughing late into the night as we exchanged war stories and mutual teasing."[16] Alan, as well as Joe, enjoyed their rich fellowship as they co-labored.

Many individuals who had no homosexual pasts, but who believed as Alan Medinger did, became his friends over the years. One was the Reverend Ronald Scates, now senior pastor of Highland Park

Presbyterian Church in Dallas, Texas. During the eleven years Pastor Scates served as senior pastor of the Central Presbyterian Church of Baltimore (1989–2000), he and Alan enjoyed one another's companionship and wisdom. Pastor Scates served on the Regeneration Board of Trustees, the last three years serving as its president.

"Both Alan and Willa shaped my life and ministry," He said. He learned from Alan that no one can truly be called a "homosexual," since God only makes males and females whom he intends to be heterosexual. Alan also taught him to understand that all of us are "broken somewhere along the spectrum of urges and lifestyles," and that, therefore, a pastor's role is to love SSA people just as he loves other people and to offer them the best that God has for them—salvation and healing.

Pastor Scates said that "Central Presbyterian was a better, more faithful congregation because of its close association with Alan, Willa, and Regeneration." The church people became more compassionate toward those infected with AIDS and bolder in standing against the "cultural captivity of the mainstream church." He added, "I'm a far better pastor and follower of Christ than if I had never met and known Alan and Willa."[17]

---

Anthony B. is one whom Alan helped during the late nineties. Anthony remembers the day he heard a radio ad for Regeneration: "Are you struggling with homosexuality and looking for a way out?"

Being "desperate for help," as he put it, Anthony phoned the ministry and spoke to Alan, then met him and joined the weekly men's program. Anthony says he fit two profiles Regeneration was eager to serve: he was black, and, more important, he was struggling with same-sex attractions and "wanted to walk more in line with how God had designed me."

After Anthony married, both he and his wife met with Alan and Willa repeatedly for advice. Several years ago, Anthony sang at a Regeneration banquet. The words in the song were meant especially for Alan: "If I can help somebody as I pass along—if I can cheer somebody through a word or song—if I can show somebody they are traveling wrong—then my living shall not be in vain." This, he says, is what Alan did for him.[18]

Another man whom Alan helped, beginning in 1995, was Dennis O., who lives in Pennsylvania, far from Regeneration. He was encouraged by only a few personal meetings with Alan. Dennis read Alan's newsletters and said, "I fully believe that his letters were the cause of a third of my healing—profound words bearing the love of Jesus!" After some years, Dennis was able to attend several Regeneration conferences, where he met Alan and Willa and also many who "struggled with sexual brokenness." With all this help, he overcame his feelings of hopelessness and thoughts of suicide, experienced healing of his same-sex attractions and a restored relationship with his wife. He is even an accountability partner with several pastors now.[19]

Dave E.'s relationship with Alan began as that of a prodigal son and godly father. They met in 1988, after Dave read about Regeneration and contacted Alan. Dave became a small group leader in northern Virginia under Bob Ragan's leadership, dated a girl named Karen, and developed a "fantastic" relationship with the Lord. But he slipped into a deep depression and lost his job, his girlfriend, and his peace with God. Alan and Willa took Dave into their home for a month and paid his bills to keep him out of a psychiatric hospital. They treated him like a son. Dave said that though his own father left his mother before he was born and never returned, and his step-father was an abusive alcoholic, "God fathered me through people like Alan."

Nevertheless, after living with the Medingers, Dave returned to homosexuality for seven years. Aware that God was displeased, he turned back at last to Regeneration in 2000, feeling himself "a wreck," in his words. He offered to give back to Alan the money the Medingers had spent on him, but Alan refused to take it back. Instead, Alan mentored Dave. They had been in touch by phone several times a week since 1996. "He would get on me about my sin," Dave says, "but he was never superior. He was always humble. And he was always for me."

Since 2002, Dave has been active in his church's healing ministry that deals with sexual brokenness, as well as leader in the men's group there. He works with international poverty and justice ministries. In 2007, Alan asked Dave to be his own accountability partner, making their accountability mutual. Theirs became a friendship of equals.

---

For Willa, becoming mature meant, in part, becoming more free to express the *joie de vivre* she had always brought to those around her. Her daughters said, "She had a taste for the unusual."[20] Her nephew Pete Medinger said, "She invented ideas of what would give herself joy, and then she went out and did them."[21] He mentioned "her Indian curry phase, her cloth flowers phase, her fireworks phase, and her Beanie Baby phase."

Her grandchildren gave her joy, and she taught them many things. For instance, sitting on the edge of her front porch, she taught the children by example how to spit watermelon seeds for distance, a skill she did well.

Over time, Willa enlarged her pig collection—ceramic figures, stuffed animals in pig form, pig hats, pig slippers. Then she and Alan wrote a clause in their will, leaving the entire collection to Laura's husband, Charles, whom they loved. ("I used to say she loved Charles more than me," Laura said, laughing.)[22]

Willa planned to stuff the family dog, Luv, after it died, and place it in front of her fireplace, but she never did.[23] She was fond of stuffed animals. One Mother's Day Willa persuaded Alan to give her gifts from a taxidermist's auction. He bought her a stuffed squirrel, a stuffed fox, and a stuffed adult black bear. The bear stayed with the Medingers as long as they lived on Hart Road (until 2007), and he came to many of their parties, dressed like the other guests. At Halloween, Willa placed him in front of the house to make children laugh.

CHAPTER 19:

# HELPING MEN GROW INTO MANHOOD

*God does not heal our immaturity. He wants us to grow out of it.*

~ Alan Medinger

AT THE TURN OF THE millennium, scores of good books had already been published on overcoming homosexuality—books for SSA men and women, for churches, for counselors, and for family members. But nobody had published the book Alan believed needed to be written, one explaining to men the steps they had to take to assume full manhood. Recovering men, like women, experienced the essential steps for healing—understanding, praying, and forgiving. In addition, many men required another step. Growing up, they had dropped out of the rough and tumble of the male adolescent competitive world to become mere watchers. They never found their place in the world of peer masculinity. Alan said they needed to complete the last step of growing up. Thinking and praying themselves into manhood wouldn't work. They could only grow up by doing the things men do.

To assist these men, in July 2000 Alan published his book, *Growth into Manhood [Resuming the Journey]*. He had completed the growth process in his own life and watched many of his Regeneration participants do it too. He believed that "male homosexuality is, at its core, a matter of undeveloped manhood."[1] Something went wrong in the development of SSA males—himself and others. They grew into men physically without achieving a secure sense of manhood, which is developed in heterosexual men through their interactions, testing and affirming one another. The normal process for a boy is that first with his father, and then with other boys, he models masculine behavior and is affirmed in it. The early "Big Boy!" affirmations change and continue through the years. It is always males who must impart masculinity into a boy's life, Alan said. You have to have it to give it. A woman's affirmation doesn't carry the same effect.

After years of repeated testing and affirmation, most adolescent boys develop a secure sense that they are male. But the typical SSA man was not affirmed sufficiently either by his father (or father substitute) or his male peers. He feared failure in the competition, usually athletic, with other adolescents, and he withdrew from the boys' world. He remained immature, and Alan said, "God does not heal our immaturity. He wants us to grow out of it."[2]

In his book, Alan laid out the recovery program in practical steps, including how to live comfortably in the world of heterosexual men. For instance, Alan had introduced softball to his Regeneration clients, and some discovered they were able athletes. Those men sometimes then joined their church softball teams, playing with heterosexual men who knew nothing of their SSA problems. When they were affirmed for good play by these men, their sense of manhood grew. Alan counseled his clients to seek groups of men and join them in activities involving physical work or play.

Another step he suggested was for a man to examine whether he is living out of his "little boy" or "wounded child." He must give that being to the Lord and then desire and purpose to grow into manhood. Alan added that narcissistic SSA men might find this step difficult.

When all is done, he said, the SSA man will become adult in every way, not just physically. Alan defined "complete manhood" as "being able to do all of the things that a man does—being a husband, father, provider, citizen, and Christian—and doing them well."[3] (It was the readiness to do these things that he stressed; for some, complete manhood would not involve marriage or parenting.)

Alan did not say that the recovered homosexual will never again experience illicit attraction to persons of his or her own gender. Though after his miraculous healing Alan went many years with no same-sex attractions, temptation did return to him in later life when he was under severe stress. At first, he was surprised and displeased. But he soon identified it as a warning from God that he should slow down and handle stress better—perhaps get some rest or some help. With this perspective, He thanked God for the warning and heeded it.[4]

Alan wrote, "Where wrongful patterns of sexual attraction and response have taken root in us, they may not go away easily. But in the longer run, one of the great promises of the New Testament is freedom. We know that this means freedom from the power of sin, but it must also mean freedom from life-dominating temptations. Our new life is to be experienced here, not just in heaven. God may allow our temptations to continue in order to bring us to deeper levels of repentance or healing, but His ultimate goal for us is freedom."

An SSA man who has grown into maturity will begin to relate to women in a healthy way. Again, with practical advice, Alan explained how this happens. One "grows out of buddy relationships with women"[5] and begins to see them as "the other," that is, persons imaging God in a way different from men.

Alan offered an important discovery about how heterosexual desire comes to a recovering SSA man. He may expect that when he recovers he will experience lust for women like a heterosexual man, lust fed by visual attraction. But this doesn't happen. God doesn't exchange homosexual lust for heterosexual lust. In the average fallen man, Alan said, wholeness of mind, body, and spirit is shattered because of sin. He experiences his sexuality "broken off from the rest of him." This is to say, most worldly men experience a kind of "free-floating" sexuality that allows them to enjoy sex without emotional or spiritual bonding to the woman. But this was not the Lord's original intent, Alan said.

The healed SSA man is able to experience sex the way God planned it. He first meets "that one special woman."[6] He likes her and appreciates the womanly qualities that make her different. He begins to know her better and to desire to be with her. Finally, these feelings blossom into romantic love. Only then does he want to "be close to her, to hold her, and finally . . . to be totally one with her—in mind, spirit, and body," Alan wrote. "[His] desire for union with her has flowed naturally and beautifully out of loving her." (After the Lord healed Alan in 1974, he had experienced sexual desire for Willa in this manner.)

"We are actually in a better place than most men," Alan said. "We are closer to God's original intent for our sexuality."[7] The "overwhelming majority of our [Regeneration] marriages" are successful sexually, he reported. This is in part due to wise ministry support and counsel to men and women when they marry.

In full recovery, a man comes to the point where he leaves behind his adolescent narcissism and discovers that "manhood is something we give away."[8] A complete man, Alan said, is outer directed. "His face is toward the world, toward others, toward God. For him the world is a joyous challenge, something to both overcome and be delighted in. His lack of self-consciousness draws people to him."

---

*Growth into Manhood* was mostly well received. One Amazon.com reviewer, giving the book five stars, said, "This book is like a gift from a warm, wise and perceptive uncle." Reviewers noted that Alan's advice was pertinent to any immature man, whether he was same-sex attracted or not. Not surprisingly, gay readers reviewed the book with fewer stars. A reviewer who gave the book only two stars complained that "This book shows complete ignorance of what an untroubled, healthy gay man is like."

By year's end, *Growth into Manhood* sold out of the first printing. It was reprinted and continues to sell through Amazon.com and the online Barnes & Noble store, BN.com.

Leaders of ex-gay ministries lauded the book. Dr. Joseph Nicolosi called it the work of "one of the true sages of the Christian ex-gay movement [whose] life has been blessed by a hard-earned wisdom." Bob Davies, then executive director of Exodus, said the book "goes beyond any other books I've seen for the former homosexual in painting a clear picture of what mature and godly manhood really looks like and how it can be attained." Andrew Comiskey praised the book for being a "practical but never simplistic guide" that "tackles hard issues with sensitivity, forthrightness, and a peaceful authority."

At first, Alan helped his publisher, Random House, sell the book by engaging in radio interviews. Then over the years he spoke on it many times, in churches and at Exodus events, including workshops at the annual conference. After four years, the book was translated into Polish, sold out the first printing, and was reprinted. In September 2006 Alan accepted an invitation to travel with Willa to Poland to conduct workshops in several cities for Christians who had read the book and wanted help applying it. Less than two years later, Alan's assistants, Rev. Bob Ragan and Josh Glaser, returned to Warsaw, Poland, to train psychologists, therapists, pastors, and other leaders in how to help SSA men. Bob and Josh also spoke in the host protestant church and met with individuals. They addressed audiences on Christian radio and also spoke on a late-night TV show.[9] An overwhelming number of individuals contacted the church for help following the TV interview.

Alan wrote his book because, as he aged, he desired to pass along wisdom he had learned from life experiences and daily communication with the Lord. For years, writing articles for *Regeneration News* gave him pleasure, and eventually he sensed that God had endowed him with a second gift—writing—in addition to his administrative skills (the "Ministry of Chairs"). "When I write," he said, "I can feel the Lord."[10]

---

The year 2000 was notable for a reason other than the publication of Alan's book. Both he and Frank Worthen received diagnoses of cancer. Frank's was a rare and fast-growing skin cancer. Alan's was cancer of the prostate. The two couples had planned an autumn vacation in Mexico, and they went, though both men were awaiting surgery.

Alan was determined to enjoy every minute. With his cancer in mind, Alan decided, "in case I should die," to go parasailing. To do this, Alan stood on the beach fastened to a motorboat, a parachute on his back. The boat accelerated, and Alan was thrust forward as the parachute inflated. He floated over the water. Frank, Anita, and Willa stood on shore, watching Alan fly.

The couples also prayed together in Mexico. Anita said she and Willa could always talk about anything and pray about anything, even on the phone, as the men also did. All four of them, on this occasion, prayed for healing from cancer. After they returned home, Frank and Alan had surgery and both recovered.[11]

---

One of the manly qualities, Alan believed, was leadership. Desiring to expand his ministry, he developed a satellite, Regeneration of Northern Virginia, led by a man he considered a capable leader, Bob Ragan. Alan encouraged and trained Bob, who came to the Baltimore ministry for help in 1988, served as a support group leader, and in January 1993 opened the northern Virginia office and became director there.[12] Bob led a rapidly growing Living Waters program. In ten years he helped change Regeneration NoVA from a few people meeting around a table to a ministry with a leadership team of over 20, serving more than 100 participants a year.

Alan often drove three hours round trip to the Fairfax, Virginia, office to mentor Bob because he admired his protégé's counseling abilities. "Bob is ten times better than me at counseling and leading groups," he said.[13] Therefore, Alan handled the administrative and financial responsibilities for the satellite ministry and released Bob from those duties so he could use his ministry gifts fully.

"Alan handed me the ministry on a silver platter," Bob said. "He so released me to do ministry that he gave me total freedom. He . . . allowed me to respond to the Lord's directions."

Bob sought to follow the Lord, and Willa, as well as Alan, helped him learn to do this. She was Bob's first teacher on healing prayer, coming alongside him, teaching and praying with him. "Healing prayer," Bob said, "is still a significant component of the programs and support we offer through Regeneration NoVA."

---

For many years Alan wrote against the view that homosexuality "is a normal variant in the human condition . . . determined before birth, and homosexual behavior is natural for those so oriented." He considered this idea false and destructive. Therefore, he was elated to discover that Dr. Robert Spitzer published a study supporting the idea that SSA people can change. Rev. Bob Ragan was part of that study.

Back in 1973, Dr. Spitzer had been the man who led the American Psychiatric Association to delist homosexuality from its manual of mental disorders. But in May 2001, he called himself a person who "oppose[s] the prevailing orthodoxy." This time he found himself "challenging a new orthodoxy" that said change in sexual orientation is impossible.

In a *Wall Street Journal* article Spitzer said, "Many professionals go so far as to hold that it is unethical for a mental health professional, if requested, to attempt [change] psychotherapy."[14] This, he said, is wrong and violates a fundamental tenet of mental health workers—that they must respect "client autonomy and self-determination."

Spitzer presented a paper, "Can Some Gay Men and Lesbians Change Their Sexual Orientation?" at the 2001 APA annual meeting. He had studied 200 volunteers over a 16-month period after they completed, at least five years earlier, work to minimize their homosexual and maximize their heterosexual attractions and behavior. He found that the majority of participants reported change from a "predominantly homosexual orientation" before therapy to a "predominantly or exclusively heterosexual orientation" following therapy. Of Spitzer's subjects, 97% were Christians. These people had received help from Exodus ministries and other therapy sources, such as psychiatrists in the National Association for Research & Therapy of Homosexuality (NARTH).

Alan commented in the June 2001 *Regeneration News*, "We thank God that the truth about this issue is being spoken."[15]

Two years later, in October 2003, Spitzer published his study in the *Archives of Sexual Behavior.* It met an onslaught of negative peer reviews. He said, "Many of my colleagues were outraged." In the gay community, he said, "there was initially tremendous anger and a feeling that I had betrayed them." Later, asked if he planned a follow-up study, Spitzer said "no" because he felt "a little battle fatigue."[16]

Under this fierce criticism, Spitzer came to regret his paper, and in May 2012 he published a retraction, saying that his belief that the participants' reports were "credible and not self-deception or out-right lying" had been incorrect and that he now believed "there was no way to determine if [their] accounts of change were valid."[17]

This scruple had not occurred to him in 1973 when he accepted the testimony of gay people that they were mentally healthy.

A more thorough study than Spitzer's appeared as a book in 2007: *Ex-gays? A Longitudinal Study of Religiously Mediated Change in Sexual Orientation* by Professor Stanton L. Jones, Ph.D. and Professor Mark A. Yarhouse, Psy.D. Its conclusions back up the belief in sexual orientation change that Alan had held for over thirty years—that is, since he experienced it himself.[18]

The Jones and Yarhouse research sought to verify or falsify the claim 'that sexual orientation, homosexual orientation in particular, cannot be changed, that it is immutable."[19] They said their research proved the thesis false. They also examined the claim that "attempts to change sexual orientation are harmful" and concluded that this claim is also false.

---

After hiring Jeff Johnston in March 1997 to direct the Baltimore Regeneration, Alan contemplated retirement, for he felt the men in charge of his two Regenerations, Jeff and Bob Ragan, were competent to lead. He officially retired January 1, 2001, shortly before his prostate cancer surgery, but he continued to write the lead article in *Regeneration News*. Now he did this without pay. He also served as Exodus Regional Representative for the Mid-Atlantic Region of eighteen ministries. During his retirement, Alan did not plan "to smell the roses." He wanted to write the books he believed the Lord had put upon his heart.

In September 2004, Alan came out of retirement to again serve as executive director of Regeneration because Jeff Johnston left to work for Focus on the Family in Colorado Springs, Colorado. Regeneration celebrated 25 years of existence on November 6 that year. They held a conference and banquet for 200, featuring a talk by Joe Dallas, who "shared powerfully," according to Alan, on "The Church—God's Army, God's Hospital."[20]

On June 30, 2006, Alan was happy when Josh Glaser took over as Regeneration's executive director. Josh wrote an article, "Alan Medinger Retiring—Again."

"Alan would never say it himself," Josh wrote, "but those who know him know that he is the epitome of selflessness in ministry to those struggling with homosexuality. He is perhaps one of the few men who knows his calling and pursues it no matter what."[21]

After this, Alan continued as a member of the Regeneration Board and newsletter article writer. *Theology of the Body* by the late Pope John Paul II, a book he reviewed in *Regeneration News,* stimulated ideas for his book on male sexuality. The pope's book focuses positively on the goodness and purposes of God's gift of sexuality, not negatively on sex problems. Alan recommended it to his readers, saying, "I believe it could be the most important teaching on human sexuality in our time."[22]

In his retirement years Alan also continued, with Willa, hosting early autumn retreats for ministry directors at Pelican Palace until the last one in 2008. Jeanie Smith remembers walking the beach to the pier and back one evening with Alan that year. They talked meditatively of conflict at that summer's Exodus conference. Alan asked, "Jeanie, what would you do differently if Exodus closed tomorrow?"

She was surprised and took awhile to respond, then said, "Well, nothing."

"Exactly," Alan said. "The truth is that those who've been called will continue to do what God called them to do."

Quietly, Jeanie said, "I would miss the conferences."

Alan responded, "You would find a way to have fellowship."

Much later, Jeanie said, "Alan was wise, and he had clarity. He believed that obedience to God is unconditional, and God will provide, so don't get yourself worked into a froth." Still, knowing how much Alan had poured into Exodus, she found it remarkable that he could give it up (theoretically) so easily.

"Alan was prophetic," she said. He was also right. The mid-Atlantic directors' retreats at Pelican Palace continue six years after Alan and Jeanie talked. And other networks, Restored Hope on the west coast, and Hope for Wholeness on the east coast, are replacing Exodus International, which shut down in June 2013.

In the spring of 2007, Alan and Willa moved into a wing of their son's home, a place designed to give them privacy and space as well as access to Steve, his wife, and their children. The move came at a good time, for Alan received a diagnosis of leukemia the same year, though he was told it was a "fairly non-aggressive" type, and he "would probably die with it, not from it." He and Willa continued to live life fully.

In the autumn of 2008, Alan found himself with severe double vision from Graves' disease, but after prayer in his North Carolina (vacation) church, he was healed of it. Then his leukemia worsened, and he received chemotherapy. Three weeks later, he developed pneumonia and a blood infection. His kidneys failed, he bled internally, and he was hospitalized for 28 days. But Alan insisted on going home from the hospital for his bishop's upcoming visit to Christ the King Church. On Saturday, he was bleeding. He received communion at church the next day and prayed, "Lord, I am not worthy to receive You, but only say the word and I shall be healed." The bleeding stopped. Half a year later, his white cell count, the marker for leukemia, had improved.[23]

Even with the sicknesses, these retirement years were happy ones for Alan and Willa. They were content in their marriage and found great joy in their family. Of their ten grandchildren, seven lived within walking distance, and the other three were frequent visitors. Holidays like Thanksgiving, Christmas, and Easter were fun-filled, with delicious food at family dinners and much singing, accompanied by Willa on the piano.

The Medingers' good friend Bruce McKutcheon said of their early ministry years, "They had to struggle through a lot of things, and they did." During the three years after Alan's retirement, however, "they were completely at peace with each other."[24]

In 2009, after recovering from his various physical setbacks, Alan wrote, "I want to live. I have the most wonderful life any man my age could have."[25] He mentioned his recent 73rd birthday party, with all eighteen members of his immediate family together celebrating. "Willa's and my marriage is wonderful," he said. "We are in a wonderful church. I have a purpose and challenge in life, writing. I could go on and on about how God is blessing me."[26]

Looking back on their lives together, Willa said they could see that "God has had His hand on us from the beginning. He put this marriage together and gave us exactly what each needed in a mate."[27]

CHAPTER 20:

# In Sickness and In Health

*A quiet joy . . . in serving his one, his only, his Willa . . . overtook any self-pity or regret. This was the culmination of his commitment to true masculinity.*

~ Andrew Comiskey, ministry leader and friend

CLIMBING THE STAIRS TO REGENERATION'S office, Karen K. heard a soft incoherent mumbling. She had arrived early on Monday evening, June 15, 2009, to assist Willa with the weekly wives group. But she found Willa lying on the floor face up, her body neatly tucked between the computer desk and the wall. Like a large malfunctioning talking doll, eyes open, she was trying to say something.

Just ten minutes earlier, Alan had dropped Willa at the office and waited in his car until the lights went on. She seemed perfectly normal on the forty-minute drive from their home in Churchville, Maryland. Satisfied that she was safe, Alan drove on to their nearby church, Christ the King, to take a class on a subject he enjoyed, the teachings of Thomas Aquinas.

Karen called 911 at once and directed the paramedics, who sped to the scene in an ambulance. When they arrived, they carried Willa away on a stretcher.[1] Karen also phoned Alan, interrupting his class, and he rushed to the hospital, shocked to see Willa's altered condition.

No more than forty-five minutes elapsed between the first symptoms of Willa's stroke and her arrival at the hospital emergency room, where doctors did a CAT scan and discovered the blood clot that had caused the problem. They gave her a "clot-buster" drug within the short time when it could do the most good—the first three hours. Alan saw this as "God's hand in how and when things happened."[2] He also thanked God that Willa's hospital, St. Joseph's Medical Center, specialized in stroke disorders, unlike the hospital near their home where she would have been taken if the event had happened there.

Willa's diagnosis was a massive stroke on the right side of her brain and a very small stroke on the left. She could speak only a few hard-to-understand words but move nothing on her left side, except her toes. At first, doctors were unsure about her potential for recovery, but the family was hopeful. They set up a "care pages" blog to alert family and friends of Willa's situation and to ask for prayer. At first, besides "total recovery," Alan wanted friends to pray for "an end to her headaches," "a quick return of her ability to swallow," and "God to work in her family as we are blessed to care for our beloved Willa."

By Friday, four days later, Willa's neurologist told their daughter Beth he believed Willa would regain her ability to speak. He was unsure whether she would grow strong enough to walk.

That afternoon, after Alan returned to Willa's room from a short break working in the hospital computer room on her blog, Willa said, "I." Their daughter Laura coached, "love," and Willa said "love you."

Then she responded to Alan's, "I love you!" with the sentence, "I love you too."

This simple exchange filled Alan with joy. It confirmed the wholeness of their love, and he had doubted his own, from time to time. Several years before, working with Josh Glaser on the manuscript of his new book, he had resolved never to write anything he didn't know was true from his own experience. The topic of *God's Sexual Man* was marriage and male sexuality. When Alan wrote, "Men, speak words of love to your wives," he had felt he couldn't continue writing, because he himself didn't speak words of love to Willa except during sex. He was telling men how to be "great lovers," but did he himself qualify as one?

Several things happened after that. Josh became too busy to continue co-writing. (He was working overtime as Regeneration's executive director, and he and his wife had four babies in five years, so he was also working full-time as a husband and father.) In addition, Alan was diagnosed with chronic lymphocytic leukemia, and he was often unwell and unable to write. He had welcomed this pause in the book. During it, he began speaking words of love to Willa more often, but the question of whether he loved her enough to instruct other husbands continued to bother him.

Then, the night of Willa's stroke, he found his answer. Sitting in the emergency waiting room with his children and his pastor, Alan experienced shock and fear. He thought of what the future might be for Willa and him. He imagined himself feeding her, dressing her, and even changing her diaper, and he wrote later in the unpublished manuscript, "to my utter amazement, I *wanted* to do these things. With all of my heart I wanted to take care of her. The old selfish, irritable, wanting-his-own-way Alan never entered the picture at all. This was Christ living in me."[3] (Alan acknowledged that later this Christ-like love was sometimes interrupted by the old "me first" Alan, when he was overtired or unwell, but the Christ-like love nevertheless continued most of the time.)

By the first Sunday, Father's Day, Willa was talking better. She greeted her youngest grandchild, Chase, age three, with words easy to understand, "Hi, Chasey-Boy. I love you, Chasey-Boy." Later that day, when the whole family gathered for a party in the ICU (with Willa-type food of fried chicken, deviled eggs, strawberry shortcake, cookies, cake, and pie), she was trying to make everyone laugh.

Ten days after her stroke, Willa left the hospital by ambulance for one of the top rehabilitation facilities in the area, Good Samaritan Hospital. The family, sobered by doctors' reports, still believed, in Beth's words, "God wants her to still be here. . . . If God wants her here, He must have a purpose planned for her, so she needs to get better and get busy!"

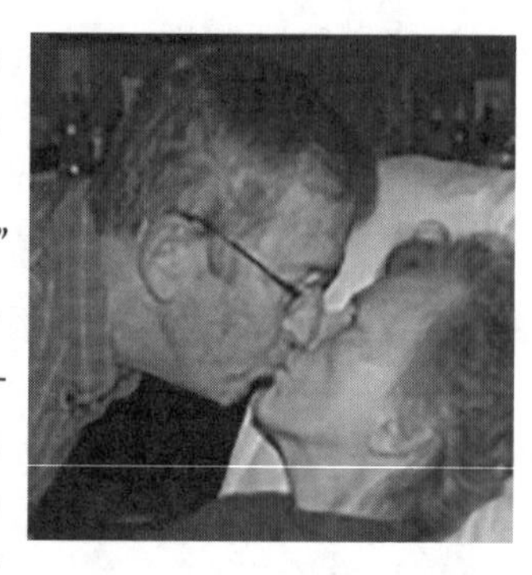

They looked for signs of hope. Three days later, Willa cracked her first joke. Alan said to her, "Tell me something smart."

After a short pause, she said, "Willa!"

As days went by, she healed enough to swallow pudding-like foods, and this increased her energy. However, her medical prognosis was not good. Since two-thirds of her right brain was "dead," doctors at Good Sam considered Willa unable to benefit from the intense work that is their specialty there. This was crushing news, but the family found another rehab place, Bel Air Health and Rehab Center, closer to home, and she moved there four weeks after the stroke.

They looked for God's goodness to them on this difficult path. One blessing noticed by many who read the "Willa's Walk" blog (176 bloggers at this point) was the devotion she received from her family. Her niece wrote after a visit with Willa, "She chatted with me the whole hour, eyes wide open! . . . Your whole family is so attentive to your mother. It is so beautiful. . . . It is so very sweet to see how she and Uncle Alan dote on each other."[4]

Alan observed that Willa's illness "has certainly brought Willa and me into a deeper level in our marriage."[5]

By the beginning of August, Willa had gained so much strength that she made her own peanut butter and jelly sandwich and managed to eat a quarter of it. Alan took her some Rainier cherries, her favorites, and she took them into her mouth, spit out the seeds, and ate them. And she had "driving lessons" in her wheelchair, which she managed to move with her right hand and leg. Alan said, "I wouldn't issue her a license yet," but she was starting to move down the hall on her own.

However, Alan's health deteriorated. On September 3 he had outpatient surgery. Two days later, Beth's husband Bill drove him to the Johns Hopkins Bayview Hospital emergency room because of significant bleeding. He was taking the blood thinner Coumadin, as he had done since his heart valve operation in 1996, so controlling the bleeding posed difficulties. He stayed in ICU for some days.

Willa in early September was doing much better. She was cooking simple dishes aided by an occupational therapist in Bel Air and walking with the aid of an air splint and support from Carrie, her therapist, in preparation for returning home. The family hoped that event would take place October first. A nurse told Laura that Willa had given her some advice for a friend in an abusive relationship. "That just warmed my heart that she could still witness and help those around her," Laura said.[6]

So with Willa doing well and Alan hospitalized, Laura, Beth, and Steve decided to set up a reunion in the Johns Hopkins ICU. Laura wrote that "throughout the course of Mom's recovery, their love has grown and blossomed. Dad has even shared that he can't stop thinking about Mom when he is away, so they had been really missing each other."[7] On September 10, the hair stylist at Bel Air gave Willa a haircut and curled her hair. Beth applied her makeup, and Devon and Laura dressed her in attractive clothes from home. Transporting her was easier than they expected. Steve picked her up like a baby and put her in his van.

At the hospital, Beth told Alan they had a surprise for him, and then they wheeled in Willa. "Tears of joy began to flow," Laura said. "The Scripture for the day was 'Love . . . bears all things, believes all things, hopes all things, endures all things'" (1 Corinthians 13:7, NASV), and Laura added, "There was no doubt in theirs or our minds that with God's help, they will continue to demonstrate that truth to the world."

The next day, doctors started Alan on chemotherapy. Willa was improving. She swallowed chopped foods and was able to kick with her left leg, even while wearing a weight on her left ankle. Four days later Alan returned home, feeling much better. He began planning for Willa's return home in three weeks. Steve built a handicap ramp at the house, and the family hired Cecilia Brown to help with Willa's care, happy that Cecilia was "a woman of God."

On October 6, Willa was well enough to come home. She mentioned often that first day how wonderful it was to be there. But a week later, depressed, she stopped talking, and her muscles stiffened. Steve's wife thought Willa suffered in her old surroundings, realizing how little of her former activities she could now do. She could still eat some spaghetti but had difficulty swallowing. Then she suffered a very brief seizure and left by ambulance for the hospital. The family's emotional roller coaster headed sharply down.

By then, Alan was exhausted from caring for her. Several weeks later (on October 27), he was taken to Hopkins Bayview emergency room again, this time with fever and breathing difficulties—pneumonia. By November 4 his condition was "critical." He had pneumonia in both lungs, an irregular heartbeat, and kidney and liver damage that looked irreversible. The Medinger children began making plans for what had been unthinkable—Alan dying before Willa.

On November 8, his doctors diagnosed Alan with H1N1 flu and said this had caused the pneumonia. Jeanie Smith phoned him in the hospital and didn't expect him to pick up the phone, but he did. He told her he had asked his doctors to lift his quarantine restrictions because "I respond to healing prayer better than medicine."

Alan's doctors doubled his anti-viral drug, because chemo for his leukemia had compromised his immune system. He remained in critical condition. Willa's health deteriorated too, and she struggled with an inability to swallow as well as pain that caused her to cry out.

Alan and the others believed it was prayer, in addition to medicines, that healed him enough to leave the hospital for Beth's house on November 15. He was weak but otherwise felt well, continuing on two antibiotics, one of them "unbelievably expensive." Alan's oncologist informed him that he was one of three people in the U.S. to have "documented Tami-Flu Resistant H1N1."

Willa by now had regressed to a state where she cried out every ten to twenty seconds, and the family could find no way of quieting her. Then she became confused and was difficult to wake, so they called an ambulance, and at the hospital, tests showed a "significant urinary tract infection" as well as elevated thyroid levels. Willa returned to Bel Air Rehab for two weeks.

Alan was recovering his strength. He returned to their Churchville home from Beth's house before Thanksgiving and enjoyed the feast with his family and Willa, who came home for four hours and managed to enjoy some delicious pumpkin pie that her daughter-in-law made, following Willa's mother's recipe. The day after Thanksgiving, Alan was well enough to attend an 80th birthday party for Willa's sister, Janice Benson Paulsen. Several days later he watched the Baltimore Ravens (his team) beat the Pittsburgh Steelers.

Christmas was difficult for the Medingers, because Willa, now home again, continued calling out often during her waking time, and though the family tried everything, they couldn't calm her except through drugs that fogged her mind. They (and she) preferred not using them. The best holiday experience for Willa seemed to be visiting her beloved Christ the King Church for their Christmas Eve service. Willa said, "Can't we all just stand up for Jesus?" She tried to stand up during the worship, and Laura helped her do so twice.[8]

In mid-January, Frank and Anita Worthen flew to Maryland for a week's visit that Anita said "was mixed with joy and sorrow."[9] In California, Frank had said to Anita, "We need to go see Willa." They felt "God said just go and we did." They were able to enjoy long talks with Alan, but Willa basically couldn't talk anymore. She cried out a lot, which was disturbing. Still, she managed to let Frank and Anita know she recognized them and was deeply glad they came.

In early March, Andrew Comiskey flew from Kansas City to Baltimore to visit, which touched Alan. Andrew noted that Alan "was intent on serving his one, his only, his Willa. He was honestly grateful for a chance to serve her, to manifest practically his love for her. A quiet joy in such service overtook any self-pity or regret. . . . This was the culmination of his commitment to true masculinity. He wanted to end his days sacrificing for his wife the way Jesus laid down his life for the Church."[10]

At this point, the family had given up hope of Willa recovering physically, but they hoped she would improve mentally, and from time to time, she did.

One afternoon, Willa said to her daughter-in-law, "I want a new husband."

"Who do you have in mind?"

"Frank Worthen."

Alan said Willa was being funny and knew it.

He had to go to Surf City, North Carolina, in late March to prepare their beach house for renters, assisted by his good friend Bruce McKutcheon. For the five-day week he was gone, Willa stayed in a nursing home. She was unhappy there and worried that the family would forget where she was.[11]

On Friday Willa returned home, and Beth cared for her overnight. When Alan returned on Saturday, Willa suddenly stopped her habit of crying out. He and Beth saw "a real peace coming over her." She seemed to understand the world around her better and to be aware of the Lord's presence. On Sunday, Alan and Willa enjoyed a long talk, which he said was "the most wonderful and meaningful conversation I had had with her since the stroke." She told him "with utter sincerity how God had blessed her life." They expressed their love for one another, in what Alan said were "words of love for each other that were deeper and more profound than any that had been spoken in our almost fifty years of marriage." He called this conversation "one of the most joyful times of my life!"[12]

Willa, in great peace, could converse on Monday too. But she slowly lost her ability to communicate fluently. Hospice workers warned that she might be "preparing to go home." Alan took Willa back to Christ the King Church on Easter Sunday, her first visit since Christmas Eve. And a week later Alan reported that Willa, who "has always been a bit unpredictable" was stronger again, was talking and enjoying watching the Baltimore Orioles on TV and commenting on the news programs they watched together.

A week after Easter, I (the author) drove to Churchville because Willa had asked to see me to tell me some things for the book. Alan wanted me to come too because "your visit would give you a first-hand view of the state of our marriage after the momentous year we have experienced."[13]

I found Willa in her living room, attended by her doctor. She sat in a special wheelchair (a Barton chair), her left arm held rigid in a brace that stretched her fingers so they wouldn't curl up into a claw. She looked very small, having lost over thirty pounds from the healthy 140 she weighed in June, before the stroke. Her face was remarkably pretty, her skin smooth and luminous. Between the left-arm brace and her body, she held a pink stuffed pig.

Alan was his usual self while I was there, energetic, caring, and intelligent. The Medingers' house was littered with Willa's pigs. In her bedroom were a pig hat and pig slippers, in the living room small ceramic pigs on bookshelves, and on a main wall Jeff Johnston's gift, the large framed print of an Andrew Wyeth pig. Willa's baby grand piano sat in a music room wing of the living room, and framed photos of the family were everywhere. Especially prominent was the large family portrait that hung over the fireplace of Alan and Willa, their three children with their three spouses, and ten grandchildren.

Mostly, Willa wanted to talk about Alan. "I love Alan so much. He's been the greatest thing in my life. I love men now because of Alan. It's amazing."

Alan said, "It's surprised me too. We had the most hopeless marriage, and God has redeemed it. He has given us deeper love."

Willa: "How sustaining is the love of Alan Medinger for me—that someone would love me when I have nothing to add to his life."

Alan: "But you do!"

Willa said she had heard recently from a woman whose marriage was saved because of her influence. "I told her to stay in the marriage no matter how much he hurt her." They had three children and were thinking of divorcing. Now they have four children and are happy together. "There's so much we don't see," Willa said. "Terrible things are happening to the family. Forgiveness is the most important thing."

Alan and I talked deep into the evening after Willa went to bed. He believed God is working good from this experience of illness. Willa seems, at last, to have experienced inner healing of the mild depression she suffered for years, he said. She had covered it up so she could shine light and joy into the lives of others. Perhaps the love poured out on her during her illness helped heal her. Perhaps the Lord alone did it. "She is coming to understand that she is loved for who she is, not for what she does," he said.[14]

About troubled marriages, Alan said, "It's never too late. God will keep improving our marriages as long as we live."

He didn't speak about what took place in his own soul during the difficult months of Willa's illness. But his friend Bruce McKutcheon told me that Alan, as well as Willa, was edified by all the love showered on them both during that year. Alan felt deep appreciation, sometimes expressed in tears, for the kindnesses he received from his children, sons-in-law, daughter-in-law, and many close friends. Like Willa, he received love he hadn't experienced before, Bruce said. It was his "final sanctification—a real gift of God."[15]

---

On Friday May 28, Alan and Willa quietly celebrated fifty years of marriage by exchanging gifts. She gave him a watch engraved "I love you forever." He gave her a silver bracelet monogrammed "WB." Their children and grandchildren celebrated with them their "abundant lives, full of the things that really matter." On "Willaswalk" the children described the event to 236 followers, many of whom responded with notes thanking the couple for profoundly affecting their own marriages. Willa was so weak she didn't want to leave her bed. She only wanted "to be hugged and kissed and held." Alan and her children and grandchildren obliged her.

CHAPTER 21:

# Thoughts on the Future

*Truth has a way of winning out, even over mass stupidity.*

~ Alan Medinger[1]

LIKE JOHN MILTON, ALAN HAD supreme faith that truth will eventually triumph in the marketplace, even the secular marketplace. As he put it, "I think truth wins out. We're in a society that is so fickle. But truth has a way of winning out, even over mass stupidity."

On the occasion of Regeneration's 25th anniversary in 2004, instead of looking back at the ministry's history, Alan wrote "A Newsletter from the Future" to tell his supporters—his "little army . . . fighting for truth"—what he thought might lay ahead. First would come a worsening of the culture wars, with homosexuality continuing to be "a prime battlefield." After extreme left-wing politicians took power in Congress and the Presidency, he predicted, freedom of speech for ex-gays would be curtailed. The push for same-sex marriage would succeed, and a broadly worded hate crimes bill would threaten Christians faithfully teaching the Bible. Exodus leaders might even be jailed and fined for continuing to say that homosexuality is a harmful and curable condition. Ministries like Regeneration might see their tax-exempt status taken away, but this would not shake them. Christian supporters would continue and even increase their giving. And jailed ministry leaders would bring healing through Christ to prisoners "in bondage to sexual sin."

As political correctness, enforced by thought police, became more and more suffocating, Alan said, "absurd contradictions of post-modernism [would become] harder and harder for intelligent people to deny." At last a counter revolution would begin as people saw the results of the secular left agenda: families falling apart, fatherless boys becoming the norm, women waking up to how the sexual revolution brought them "exploitation, disease, and single motherhood."

Christians would draw closer together, and many in the mainstream churches would realize their "complicity in the sexual and relational depravity of our culture." Therefore they would fast, confess, and repent, seeking the Lord's help to change their ways so that churches might please God by becoming the havens and hospitals He wishes them to be for those caught in sexual sin. Christian families would grow stronger, causing nonbelievers to look at Christians and find their own lives inferior by contrast. Worldly people would lose faith in their own thought systems and would "no longer have the heart to sustain beliefs that seemed to have nothing to back them up but their own wishful thinking."

The final reckoning for the post-modern thinkers, Alan predicted, would be the total discrediting of Darwinism. In one scientific field after another—logic, microbiology [genomics], mathematics, statistics, geology, and the fossil record itself—it would become clear that the best explanation of phenomena was intelligent design. People would see that this means a designer is the best explanation of how the natural world came into being, and if a designer, then, by another name, a creator. More people would come to believe in the Creator.

With this shift in popular thinking, people would reevaluate their ideas on sexuality. No longer would they see people as merely higher forms of animals, with sex drives that demanded to be satisfied—how and with whom unimportant. People would begin to see that sex is best experienced in a setting of love and commitment that is "truly manifested only in the glorious complementarity of one man and one woman in marriage."

Alan did not predict that homosexuality would go away, but the culture would see it for what it is—"an unfortunate condition in which a person has to deal with same-sex attractions, a condition that most any rational person would want to overcome if he or she could."

No longer would the gay rights movement have any power, since people would understand that homosexual persons do not belong to an unchangeable class—that they are entitled to the rights all Americans enjoy, not to special rights. Those who wish to pursue homosexual lives would give up hope of having their manner of living affirmed by the general public.

Alan concluded his 25th anniversary wrap-up by answering a question people often asked him—"What works? What were your keys to success?"

"I don't know," was his honest answer. Sometimes he would work and pray with someone for years, and he or she would go back to a same-sex relationship. Then another time, someone would hear just a bit of his testimony and tell him later that it changed his life forever. Alan said that it is always God who does the healing, and He allows each person to choose the path for his or her own life. "The main thing I did was show up and try to point to Jesus."

He had always wanted to speak the truth in love, and the truth part was not difficult for him, but the love part was done best by Willa. "As for Willa and me," he said, "our lives have been blessed beyond anything we could have ever imagined—or deserved."[2]

Describing Alan and Willa and what they gave to Regeneration, the ministry's executive director, Josh Glaser, said, "Most would agree Alan was better with Willa. The two of them seemed simultaneously an odd pair and a perfect fit—in many ways a model of the complementary nature of man and woman. And over the years, hundreds of men and women came to feel Alan and Willa were like a surrogate father and mother to them."

He added, "For Alan, Regeneration remained an expression of wanting for others the life-changing love and power of Jesus."[3]

EPILOGUE

# Until Death Do Us Part

ONE NIGHT IN 2008 AS he walked the beach near Pelican Palace with Jeanie Smith, Alan said, "Jeanie, when I go home to be with the Lord, I want to just go to bed at night and wake up with Him."

And that's what happened. On the morning of Monday, June 28, 2010, he died of complications from chemotherapy/leukemia. Instead of waking in his bedroom for his private time with Jesus, like any other day, he woke in the presence of the Lord.

Alan had enjoyed his last week. On Wednesday, he went to a Baltimore Orioles baseball game with three of his favorite people—his son Steve and his two sons-in-law, Charles and Bill. On his last full day, Sunday, he drove to the church he loved, Christ the King, to worship and receive communion. Then he spent the day with his family and Willa. His last wakeful moments were spent with her. They prayed together, he kissed her good night, went to bed, to sleep, and to heaven.

He had hoped for at least three more years and the chance to write and publish three more books. He had planned to care for Willa until the day she died. Instead, the family rallied round her and cared for her at home for almost another three months—until September 16, when Willa joined Alan. During his last year, Alan reaped the harvest of his years of growing into a godly man and father—his children repaid him and Willa as they could for the way their gradually healing parents had nurtured them to live as whole, loving people.

Alan and Willa's departure left a void on earth. But they established a legacy—their loving Christian family of sixteen people (three married couples and ten grandchildren), a vital Regeneration ministry, and an impact for the Kingdom of God upon thousands of men and women around the world.

# Where Do We Go from Here?

WHAT CAN YOU AND I do if we believe God would have us live differently from today's gay-affirming culture? We could try thinking along the lines suggested by Andy Crouch in his book *Culture Making: Recovering Our Creative Calling*. He explains how to change culture. It isn't by criticizing what is. And it certainly isn't by doing nothing.

Crouch illustrates the change process with the personal story that follows, which is not an analogy of the church and gay culture but simply an illustration of how culture changes, no matter what the culture.

His children dislike the chili he cooks for them and his wife every Tuesday, his night to cook. But he and his wife dearly love that dish, and he knows how to make it, and so the children keep on eating chili. They could refuse to eat it. Or they could continually carp about how horrible tomatoes are when cooked together with beans and spices. But this would do no good. The only effective option for them, he says, when they have grown old enough to handle knives, is to surprise him, go into the kitchen before he comes home on a Tuesday, and cook a substitute meal of equal or better tastiness and creativity. This would delight him, and, supposing the children kept on doing this, the Crouch family culture would change.[1]

The lesson: we change culture by creating new culture. If the church were to understand this and also understand that Alan Medinger speaks truth, we could do much more than ineffectually sit on the sidelines and complain while gay activists take over what people believe and do. We need people who will shine their lights in communities and churches to show what Jesus' power to save and heal means. They could create an overcoming culture. Some suggestions on how to do this follow, based on what a few people have already done:

> A church woman might befriend a woman struggling with SSA and encourage her on her road to mature womanhood. She might then share the experience (write about it);
>
> Many pastors could become famous for their pep talks on marriage—and on single blessedness;
>
> Churches could establish a special day each year for testimonies from many types of overcomers—recovering alcoholics, gamblers, shopaholics, workaholics, and the sexually addicted, including those with porn addictions and homosexual addictions;
>
> A big church could offer a games-and-sports program to help male strugglers grow into manhood. Nobody would mention anyone's sexual orientation. The program could become so popular that people in the community would join in and never ask or care about orientations;
>
> Youth groups might befriend and help HIV and AIDS victims here and elsewhere (maybe Africa) and write about it;
>
> Pastors, aware of how gay jokes drive away sensitive, confused young people trying to make sense of conflicting sexual desires, could teach on becoming aware of the power of our words, even when we're having fun;
>
> Leaders of young adults might pay special attention to shy attendees who come to church services and quickly duck out afterwards. Some of these people are possibly SSA, but whether they are or not, they need special encouragement for fellowship. Leaders

might take them out for lunch and slowly welcome them into church groups;

Churches could stock their libraries with materials about local and national ministries to SSA strugglers as well as books telling stories of people who have overcome same-sex attractions. Scores of good books on this topic are available.

People could think of ways to make homes and churches safe places to practice Christ-centered prayer and healing.

In other words, we church people could stop pretending that we're all living in perfect contentment, and we could own up to our own problems and tout their solutions.

You have probably thought of many more ideas as you traveled with Alan and Willa through their years of discovery. I invite you to use the Study Question section to help you think of more solutions and then send them to me, care of my publisher. I'd like to start a blog, using stories of people celebrating lives lived according to their God-given gender, people who might have chosen another way to live.

These solutions might seem very small, but who knows what can result from small beginnings?

# Study Questions

## Chapter 1:

1. Do you believe it's possible for God to deliver someone from same-sex attractions? Why or why not?

2. Have you or anyone you know ever had an experience with ex-gay ministry?

3. Something to consider as you read this book:

In June 2013, Alan Chambers, president of Exodus International, closed down the organization because, he said, many gay people had told him over the years that they were frustrated by Exodus' insistence on change of sexual orientation as its goal. They said they didn't experience complete change to heterosexuality and, since they believed the Exodus leaders who counseled them were completely changed, they felt shamed in comparison. Then, when they discovered that some of those leaders still experienced residual same-sex attractions, they were angry. In his farewell speech, Chambers said that Exodus had become "a religious institution of rules and regulations focused on behavior, sin management, and short on grace" and that it was hurting rather than helping people.

No doubt he described the network accurately as he saw it, but many leaders disagreed and didn't want it shut down. Alan Medinger and his good friend Frank Worthen had worked during the 1980s and 1990s to build Exodus as a Christian umbrella organization over ministries, providing conferences and accountability. First created in 1976, the network at one time consisted of about 200 ministries. In *By God's Design,* you can see the optimism, love, and wisdom that animated Exodus in its early years and that, hopefully, will animate the networks that are replacing it, Restored Hope on the West Coast and Hope for Wholeness on the East Coast.

As you read this book, please ask yourself the following questions (some of these answers are deep into the book):

1. Did Alan Medinger teach that change of sexual orientation was the goal of ex-gay ministry?

2. How did he handle his own residual attractions?

3. What is the scientific evidence that these ministries either hurt people or do not hurt them?

4. Did Exodus in the 1980s and 1990s seem to be "a religious institution of rules and regulations focused on behavior, sin management, and short on grace"?

5. Do you believe that Christian ex-gay ministries serve a useful purpose?

## CHAPTER 2:

1. How do you think today's cultural acceptance of homosexuality affects adolescent people who discover they are same-sex attracted?

2. Think about how different the cultural attitudes were in 1960. Many today believe that people who express disapproval of non-biblical expressions of sexuality, like same-sex activity, harm

people who practice them. In what way can this disapproval be helpful, according to Alan?

3. What is the argument that favors SSA people "coming out"—that is, telling others of their attractions?

4. Have you known someone who was a "prayer warrior"? If so, share some details of his or her prayer life.

5. What experiences with "the new birth" can you relate from your own experience or that of your friends?

6. With Willa, no other Christian was there to help her and lead her in prayer. Can you see the elements of conversion in her experience on the piano bench?

## Chapter 3:

1. How was Alan's conversion typical of the new birth experience? In what ways atypical?

2. Do you understand the defensive wall of protection that Alan created? Can you imagine what experiences might have led to this?

3. Can you understand Willa's fear of intimacy?

4. Do you know other examples of persons who, after encountering Christ, are enabled to love as they never did before?

5. Do you think Willa's anger at Alan was more extreme than a normal response would be? What do you think might have caused her anger in addition to Alan's words and acts?

## Chapter 4:

1. Gay activists in the 1970s believed that behavioral psychiatrists were abusive in their methods toward SSA patients. Make a case for this argument.

2. Today some people believe any attempt by a psychiatrist to help a patient change his sexual orientation, even if the patient wants this change, is abusive. Discuss this idea.

3. Do you consider homosexuality "normal"? In what sense?

4. Is it part of God's plan for human sexuality? Why do you think it is or isn't?

5. Was delisting homosexuality a scientific decision in your opinion?

6. Define what you mean by *science*.

7. What criteria do you use to decide if a behavior is mentally disordered or not?

## Chapter 5:

1. What are the implications of Alan's belief that "If being healed could happen to me, it could happen to anyone"?

2. Do you agree with the Exodus International mission statement? Why or why not? (It is that "God's standard of righteousness and holiness . . . declares that homosexuality is sin and affirms His love and redemptive power to recreate the individual.")

3. Discuss the difference between sin and mental illness.

4. How could sermons and other church messages lead "to further estrangement from anyone personally affected by homosexuality"?

5. Why did the Exodus V conferees conclude that God's call to personal holiness meant they should no longer minister with the narrow view that lifelong celibacy and an acceptance of one's same-sex attractions was the goal of ex-gay ministry? Do you agree?

6. Are you familiar with the teaching in 2 Corinthians 10:4 that we must tear down strongholds? Have you dealt with strongholds of false thinking in your own life, or do you know others who have done this?

7. Do you think Larry Dietrich's counseling method—prayer, plus allowing Willa to vent—is an effective one in her situation? When might it be less effective?

## Chapter 6:

1. Can you understand both points of view in the anger problems of Alan and Willa at Exodus V?

2. What does Willa mean when she says "Anger is a secondary emotion; the primary one is fear"? Explain this.

3. Have you heard about the problem of childhood vows? In what context?

4. In your own experience, how does forgiveness solve anger problems? (Define "forgiveness.")

5. Can you see how misleading and potentially fatal a simple teaching of "God loves you no matter what" can be? Is a loving father indifferent to the harmful acts of his children?

6. What does "love" mean in Jesus' explanation of the great commandment, "You shall love the Lord your God with all your heart, with all your soul, and with all your mind . . .and. . .you shall love your neighbor as yourself" (Matthew 22: 37, 39).

7. According to 1 John 5:2–3, what part does obedience to God play in loving God and our neighbor?

## Chapter 7:

1. Leanne Payne's books are used by people who practice healing prayer. Can you understand this kind of prayer?

2. Do you think healing prayer is applicable for everyone who needs prayer? If not, for whom would it be valuable?

3. How would you define "masculine" and "feminine"?

4. How would the secular culture define these terms?

5. How does the Bible define them?

6. Do you know of churches that reach out to SSA persons? If so, has this outreach helped or hurt the churches?

## Chapter 8:

1. Are you familiar with spiritual warfare? How would you define it? What are the weapons we are to use in this kind of battle? (See Ephesians 6:11–17.)

2. Discuss why you think it was difficult for Exodus ministries to resolve the question of what it means to be healed of homosexuality.

3. *Healed* is commonly used to describe change from same-sex attraction to other-sex attraction. What does this word imply? What other words might be used as effectively?

4. Do you think Alan's boss fired him because Alan announced publicly that he used to be homosexual or because he was now claiming to have changed? In our society, which situation would cause the greater reaction?

5. What other ministries do you know that might be called "fairly radical faith ministries," because they operate with no means of financial support apart from God's provision?

## Chapter 9:

1. Do you believe God created the genders to be different and complementary? Why or why not?

2. What difference would it make in the way we live if everyone believed the genders were supposed to be complementary?

3. Where do you see genders complementing each other in real life?

4. What are the implications if one believes the two genders are the same and interchangeable?

5. Since Alan wrote and taught these ideas in August 1985, our society has moved closer to a unisex idea of human personality—that anything a man can do, a woman can do and some women should do, and vice versa. Do you think that people who do what used to be the other gender's jobs are making progress for society? Why or why not?

## Chapter 10:

1. In the late 1980s, AIDS, a frightening new disease, was much in the news. It is less frequently mentioned now, even though it has not gone away. Why do you think this is?

2. The early reaction of gay activists to the AIDS disease seems irrational if one assumes people naturally want to live and not die. How would you explain it?

3. It takes a stretch of the imagination to think of Mike as "innocent," as Alan says he is. Can you understand the change process as it is described? Can you accept this description of

how Jesus creates a new and innocent soul in those who follow Him wholeheartedly?

4. Do you know any gay person who needs prayer for salvation? Can you think of a way to witness to him or her?

5. Do you think church people find it difficult to witness to SSA people? If so, why is this, in your opinion?

## Chapter 11:

1. Do leaders and teachers usually work by means of "watching"? Can you imagine how this is helpful in some situations?

2. What sort of situations would be best for leading by "watching"?

3. Alan's healing experience in 1974 came at a charismatic prayer meeting led by the Lamb of God Community. What evidence do you see in this chapter that Alan continued to seek to be led by the Holy Spirit?

4. From the world of business or the church, can you think of examples of leaders other than Alan who train others, "seeing the benefit of working himself out of a job"?

## Chapter 12:

1. Discuss the idea of clothing as "outward and visible signs of some reality."

2. What reality is suggested by the typical clothing of most young men and women today?

3. When Harriet came to Regeneration she was no longer acting out sexually, but she was "enmeshed in destructive emotional dependences." What does this mean? Why would it be difficult to change?

4. Discuss Alan's view that change from homosexuality follows the same path as change from any life-dominating sin.

5. What are the special difficulties of healing for same-sex attracted women?

6. Do you understand what Alan meant when he said many SSA women do not complete the process? Why does this matter? How would they then live?

## Chapter 13:

1. Can you think of situations where a boy might perceive that his father doesn't love him, but he would be wrong?

2. Do you know examples of the sins of the fathers being "visited upon" the children?

3. Do you know examples of this pattern broken with God's help?

4. What does Dr. Elizabeth Moberly mean by "a reparative drive"?

5. Why does she say being attracted to someone of the same sex is not a sin?

6. Why is abstinence alone not a solution to homosexuality, according to Dr. Moberly?

7. What does Alan mean when he says his male clients must become sons in order to be healed?

## Chapter 14:

1. Do you believe that God gives gifts to persons in ministry to help them do the work He has called them to do? What are some of these callings and some of these gifts, judging from people you know?

2. Name some ministries and gifts God calls people to in the Bible. (See especially 1 Corinthians, chapter 12.)

3. Why would being able to cry be important to Shelley? Explain.

4. In 1 Corinthians 13, Paul talks about a certain kind of love, called *agape* in the Greek. Please use a Bible dictionary to define this word.

5. Do you think this is the ministry gift Willa felt she was given when she began working with wives? How would such a gift, working through Willa, help heal the women?

6. Do you know anyone who is expert in *agape*? Please tell about him or her.

## Chapter 15:

1. What do you think are Willa's and Olivia's personality and character traits—or other factors—that allowed Olivia to benefit so greatly from Willa's counsel, even though they never met?

2. What strength of character does Olivia show throughout her ordeal?

3. How do you see the Holy Spirit working through Willa to bring healing? Please be specific.

4. Have you ever known anyone who received important counseling help solely by means of letters and phone calls?

5. How does this story point to God as the real Healer?

## Chapter 16:

1. How central to a church's mission do you believe the message of redemption from same-sex attractions should be? Explain your answer.

2. How would you suggest that a church implement such a mission?

3. How would you define "traditional sexual morality"?

4. Do you agree with the votes taken during the 1988 Episcopal Church's General Convention? Why or why not?

5. What philosophical and theological ideas result from Bishop Spong's statement that "theism is dead"?

6. Do you agree with Kathleen Boatwright that gay people enjoy a perspective that gives them special ability to criticize the church and suggest that it change? Why or why not?

7. Can you think of examples of "cheap grace" and "costly grace" from your reading or from your own experience?

## Chapter 17:

1. Do you see any evidence that the advice given by Marshall Kirk and Hunter Madsen in their book was followed and has borne fruit?

2. Have you shopped for books on homosexuality in bookstores, secular or Christian, or on Amazon.com or BN.com recently? Did you find them?

3. Have you ever experienced or witnessed unusual healing as a result of prayer?

4. Have you experienced the testing of your faith that sickness brings?

## Chapter 18:

1. Please discuss Alan's definition of healing from homosexuality: "You are healed when you are ready to marry." What qualities would a person have to have to meet this standard?

2. Alan's belief that homosexual sex degrades those who participate in it is very different from the claim of gay activists that these sex acts are normal and good. Which do you believe is true?

3. What does it mean to believe one is created in God's image? How would this belief affect a person's sexual beliefs and activities?

4. Pastor Ronald Scates said Alan taught him that a pastor should "love same-sex- attracted people just as he loves other people and . . . offer them the best that God has for them—salvation and healing." Does your pastor believe this as well? Do you?

5. Willa taught the women she ministered to that laughter and enjoying life are indications of overcoming problems. Do you agree? Is this true of you or anyone you know?

## Chapter 19:

1. Explain Alan's assertion that "God does not heal our immaturity. He wants us to grow out of it."

2. Can you think of examples of how boys affirm maleness in other boys?

3. What examples can you think of where men seek relationships with each other by means of doing physical things? Do the women you know relate to each other the same way? If not, how do they relate? Be specific.

4. Discuss Alan's description of how sexual attraction to the opposite sex occurs for recovering SSA men. Can you understand Alan's point that "We [formerly SSA men] are actually in a better place than most men"?

5. Do you consider being able to lead a quality of manhood? Note: a positive answer does not mean that women should never lead.

## Chapter 20:

1. Some people might find it hard to believe the often-repeated assertions that Alan and Willa's love deepened during the difficult year of her stroke. Can you believe what they said?

2. Have you known an older couple who experienced, in difficult times, an enrichment of their love for one another?

3. The Medinger family kept looking for God's blessings in the events they encountered. Do you do this too? If so, do you find these blessings?

## Chapter 21:

1. Have any of Alan's predictions from 2004 come true?

2. Can you name some of the "absurd contradictions of post-modernism" that Alan believed would eventually become evident to intelligent people and cause a counter revolution of thought?

3. Are you aware that Darwinism is discredited by some at the present time? (See recent discoveries about genomes and what used to be called "junk DNA.")

4. If the gay rights movement lost power, would this be a good thing or a bad thing for SSA people? Explain.

# Endnotes

## Chapter 1:

1. C. S. Lewis's comments are from his 1945 introduction to a new translation of St. Athanasius's fourth century treatise, *On the Incarnation* [Kindle edition].

2. *"Christ took away his same-sex attractions"* means that Alan's attractions to men disappeared; however, his unformed masculine identity, which underlay his SSA, remained to be healed slowly later. For years Alan experienced no same-sex attractions. To his surprise, they did return in later life to some degree, though never in the impossible-to-resist addictive form he experienced in his thirties. The return of his attractions is discussed in chapter 19.

## Chapter 2:

1. Personal information about Alan and Willa Medinger is from interviews with the author in their Surf City, North Carolina, vacation home on March 14-15, 2007 and March 5-6, 2009, as well as two days in their Churchville, Maryland, home on April 13-14, 2010.

2. Information about the Medinger daughters, Laura and Beth, is from an e-mail message from both women to the author, January 18, 2011; Beth Medinger telephone conversations with author, August 25, 2010, and February 17, 2011; and Laura Medinger telephone conversation with author, February 19, 2011.

3. The true names of Alan and Willa's foster children have been changed to "Jane" and "Bobby" in order to protect their identities.

4. Alan Medinger, *Growth into Manhood [Resuming the Journey]* (Colorado Springs, Colorado: Harold Shaw Waterbrook, 2000), 236-7.

5. Willa's prayer insights are from a workshop she conducted at the Hope for Wholeness Conference with Truth Ministry at First Baptist North Spartanburg Church, Spartanburg, South Carolina, February 22, 2003.

## Chapter 3:

1. Alan's conversion experience is from his article "A Testimony," November 25, 1979, (letter to Bob Davies), Volume 1, *Regeneration News* as well as from his book, *Growth into Manhood*, pages 237-238, and personal interviews.

2. About Alan's daily quiet times with the Lord, *Regeneration News*, October 1999, 1.

3. Quotes from Medinger, *Growth into Manhood*, 238-239.

## Chapter 4:

1. Alan Medinger e-mail to author, August 1, 2007.

2. Frank Kameny interview in *Making Gay History: The Half-Century Fight for Lesbian and Gay Equal Rights*, Eric Marcus, ed. (New York: Harper Collins, 2002), 81.

3. Kameny, *Making Gay History*, 83.

4. About the Bayer book: Ronald Bayer was associate for policy studies at the Hastings Center, Institute of Society, Ethics and the Life Sciences when he wrote *Homosexuality and American Psychiatry, the Politics of Diagnosis* (New York: Basic Books, Inc., 1981). This book is out of print, but Bayer published another book by the same name with a new "Afterword on AIDS and Homosexuality" (Princeton, New Jersey: Princeton University press by arrangement with Basic Books, 1987). Quotes are from the 1981 book.

5. Bayer, 103. Events at the APA conventions from 1970 through 1973 are carefully described and footnoted in the Bayer book.

6. Information from Bayer, 106 to 145.

7. Ronald Bayer, *Homosexuality and American Psychiatry: The Politics of Diagnosis* (New York: Basic Books, Inc., 1981), 126,127.

8. Barbara Gittings interview, *Making Gay History,* 179. Twenty million is a bogus number, a guess based on Kinsey's 1948 book that stated 10% of the population is gay. The real number is closer to 3%.

9. "The Dictionary of Disorder," Alix Spiegel, *The New Yorker* 80.41, January 3, 2005, 58.

10. Bayer, 127.

11. *Over 75 years of psychoanalytic knowledge . . . was disregarded*: Sy Rogers and Alan Medinger, "Homosexuality and the Truth," pamphlet by Exodus International, San Rafael, California, 1990.

12. Alan Medinger letter to author, August 1, 2007.

13. Information on the recent *DSMs* is from *DSM-IV-TR* and *DSM-5* by the American Psychiatric Association (Arlington, Virginia, published by the American Psychiatric Association, 2000 and 2013) and from *The Book of Woe: the DSM and the Unmaking of Psychiatry* by Gary Greenberg (New York: Blue Rider Press, 2013).

## Chapter 5:

1. *Growth into Manhood,* 238.

2. *Regeneration News,* November 1989, 4.

3. *Regeneration News,* August 1986, 3.

4. *Regeneration News,* November 1998, 2.

5. Alan Medinger letter of August 30, 1977 to Love in Action ministry, Volume I, *Regeneration News.*

6. Frank Worthen letter October 19, 1977 in Volume I, *Regeneration News.*

7. Frank Worthen's story is from his autobiography, *Destiny Bridge: A Journey Out of Homosexuality* (Winnipeg, Canada: Forever Books, 2011).

8. "The Exodus Story: The Growth of Ex-gay Ministry" by Bob Davies, in *The Crisis of Homosexuality,* edited by J. Isamu Yamamoto, (Wheaton, Illinois: Victor Books, A Division of Scripture Press Publications, Inc., 1990), 50.

9. Bob Davies e-mail to author May 31, 2009.

10. Alan Medinger letter to Bob Davies, November 25, 1979, Volume 1, *Regeneration News.*

11. Alan Medinger, "After Twenty years: Some Sure Signs of God's Hand on Our Ministries," *Regeneration News,* September 1999, 3.

12. Alan and Willa Medinger interview with author, March 14, 2007.

13. Alan Chambers, *Exodus International Newsletter,* July 2006, 1.

14. Roberta Kenney e-mail to author, February 8, 2007.

15. Davies, "The Exodus Story," 55, 56.

16. *Regeneration News,* November 1996, 1, 2.

17. Frank Worthen interview with author, May 18, 2009.

18. Frank Worthen interview with author, January 17, 2007.

## Chapter 6:

1. Frank Worthen interview with author, May 18, 2009.

2. Barbara Johnson, *Where Does A Mother Go to Resign?* (Minneapolis, Minnesota: Bethany House Publishers, 1979), 143.

3. Ibid., 80.

4. *Regeneration News*, October 1989, 7.

5. Willa Medinger letter to Olivia F-, April 23, 1991 from Olivia's private collection of Willa's letters.

6. About Meriam's brother, Bill Seipel, e-mail to author from Janice Benson Paulsen, September 26, 2010.

7. Alan commented in *Regeneration News* on Bobby's death, January 1996, 4.

## Chapter 7:

1. "Interview with The Rev. Richard W. Lipka" by Luanna Hutchison, *Regeneration News*, December 1986, in unnumbered supplement, "Teachings & Testimonies."

2. Leanne Payne, *The Broken Image: Restoring Personal Wholeness Through Healing Prayer* (Grand Rapids, Michigan: Baker Books, 1981), 9. About Matthew, 56, 57.

3. Listening prayer is explained fully in Payne's book, *Listening Prayer: Learning to Hear God's Voice and Keep a Prayer Journal* (Grand Rapids, Michigan: Baker Books, 1994).

4. Ibid., 39.

5. *Regeneration News*, December 1997, 2.

6. *Broken Image*, 51.

7. *Regeneration News*, December 1997, 2.

8. Alan Medinger, *Growth into Manhood*, 233.

9. Alan Medinger interview March 14, 2007.

10. *Growth into Manhood*, 234.

11. *Heaven's Calling: A Memoir of One Soul's Steep Ascent* (Grand Rapids, Michigan: Baker Books, 2008), 288, 289.

12. Laura Medinger phone interview with author, February 19, 2011.

13. Frank Worthen interview May 18, 2009.

14. Sy Rogers speech at Exodus XXVI conference in Asheville, North Carolina, August 7, 2001.

15. Sy Rogers at Exodus XXVI, August 8, 2001.

16. *Regeneration News*, October 1989, 2, and *Regeneration News*, December 1986, 3.

17. *Regeneration News*, December 1986, 2.

18. Ibid., 3.

19. *Regeneration News*, October 1989, 2.

20. *Regeneration News*, December 1986, 3.

21. Luanna Hutchison, "Interview with The Rev. Richard W. Lipka," supplement to *Regeneration News*, December 1986.

22. Alan Medinger, June 15, 1989 letter that served in lieu of the June *Regeneration News* that year.

## Chapter 8:

1. Davies, "The Exodus Story," 56.

2. *Regeneration News*, October 1989, 7.

3. 1983 Exodus board decisions are from Bob Davies e-mail to author, July 26, 2010.

4. Frank Worthen interview May 18, 2009.

5. Meriam Benson's struggles with cancer from Gloria Benson (Willa's sister-in-law) e-mail to author, November 11, 2010.

6. Meriam Benson's recovery, *Regeneration News*, November 1989, 4.

7. *Regeneration News*, October 1989, 3.

8. Bob Davies e-mail May 31, 2009.

9. Alan Medinger interview, March 13, 2007.

10. Mario Bergner, *Setting Love in Order* (Grand Rapids, Michigan: Baker Books, 1995) 129.

11. from Gene Chase e-mail to author May 4, 2010.

12. Katherine Allen's description of the Baltimore Exodus conference, e-mail from her to author July 26, 2010.

13. Beth Spring's report on the Baltimore Exodus conference, from Davies, "The Exodus Story," 56.

14. *Regeneration News*, May 1992, 1.

15. from Sue O'Neill phone interview with author, August 26, 2010.

16. *Regeneration News*, October 1989, 4.

17. *Regeneration News*, July 1985, 3

18. Ibid., 2.

19. Ibid., 4.

20. Alan and Willa Medinger Interview, March 15, 2007.

21. *Regeneration News*, October 1989, 4.

22. Ibid., 6.

## Chapter 9:

1. Frank Worthen, *Destiny Bridge*, 241.

2. Anita and Frank Worthen interview with author, January 17, 2007 when Frank was nearly 77 and Anita was 62.

3. Alan's comments on "the perennial question" are from "Homosexual Christians?" in *Regeneration News*, August 1985, 3.

4. The tenth Exodus International conference in San Francisco, Ibid., 1.

5. Anita Worthen interview, May 18, 2009.

6. *Regeneration News*, August 1985, 4.

7. *Regeneration News*, August 1985, 1.

8. Alan Medinger, "Masculinity," reprinted unnumbered in August 1985, *Regeneration News*. All of Alan's comments in this chapter about masculinity and femininity are from this teaching lesson.

9. Andrew Comiskey e-mail to author, July 26, 2010.

10. Josh Glaser e-mail to author May 3, 2010.

11. Frank Worthen interview with author, May 19, 2009.

12. Bill Karcher story from Alan Medinger interview with author, March 14, 2007.

## Chapter 10:

1. Jeffrey Satinover, M.D., *Homosexuality and the Politics of Truth,* (Grand Rapids, Michigan: Baker Books, 1996), 9, 11.

2. Ibid., 15.

3. Alan Medinger letter to author, August 1, 2007.

4. *Regeneration News*, September 1985, 2.

5. Alan Medinger letter to author, August 1, 2007.

6. *Regeneration News*, September 1985, 2.

7. *Regeneration News*, August 1986, 4.

8. *Regeneration News*, October 1986, 2.

9. Davies, "The Exodus Story," 57.

10. *Regeneration News*, September 1988, 1.

11. *Regeneration News*, October 1989, 5.

12. *Regeneration News*, August 1987, 2.

13. *Regeneration News*, November 1987, 3, 5.

14. *Regeneration News*, May 1993, 1, 3.

15. *Regeneration News*, October 1993, 1, 2.

16. Alan Medinger letter to author, August 1, 2007.

17. Alan Medinger interview with author, March, 15, 2007.

## Chapter 11:

1. *Regeneration News*, February 1986, 2.

2. Alan Medinger interview with author, March 14, 2007.

3. Medinger, *Regeneration News*, February 1986, 2.

4. Gene Chase phone interview with author, June 18, 2010.

5. Carrie Wingfield, e-mail to author, June 23, 2011.

6. *Regeneration News*, November 1985, 2.

7. *Regeneration News*, June 1987, 1 and 3.

8. Ibid., 1.

9. Penny Dalton, e-mail to author, May 20, 2010.

10. Ibid.

11. *Regeneration News*, October 1989, 6.

12. Katherine Allen phone interview with author, July 15, 2010.

13. Jeanie Smith phone interviews with author, October 19, 2010 and March 3, 2014.

14. Jani and Paul D- e-mail to author, March 20, 2011.

15. Elaine Silodor Berk e-mail to author, June 19, 2010.

16. Description of JONAH after eleven years, Elaine Silodor Berk e-mail to author, May 6, 2010, and letter June 19, 2010; Arthur Goldberg e-mail to author, May 6, 2010, and from the JONAH website.

17. Arthur Goldberg e-mail to author, May 6, 2010.

18. McKrae Game e-mail to author, May 6, 2010 and phone interview March 5, 2014.

19. Ragan phone conversation with author, January 10, 2014.

20. Gene Chase e-mail to author, May 4, 2010.

## CHAPTER 12:

1. *Regeneration News*, December 1988, 1.

2. Willa Medinger interview with author, March 5, 2009.

3. Harriet's testimony, "God Didn't Make a Mistake," *Regeneration News*, July 1985, 5.

4. Willa Medinger interview, March 5, 2009.

5. Alan and Willa Medinger interview, March 6, 2009.

6. *Regeneration News*, December l988, 2.

7. *Regeneration News*, July 1985, 5.

8. Willa Medinger interview March 5, 2009.

9. *Regeneration News*, July 1985, 5.

10. *Regeneration News*, November 1985, unnumbered article following the regular issue.

11. *Regeneration News,* "Change: Finding the Way," unnumbered article following August 1986 newsletter.

12. Alan Medinger interview with author after his workshop on *Growth into Manhood* at the August 2001 Exodus conference in Asheville, North Carolina.

13. Alan Medinger speech, "2000 Years of Ex-Gay Ministry," at Hope for Wholeness Conference by Truth Ministry, First Baptist Church of North Spartanburg, South Carolina, February 22, 2003.

14. Alan Medinger, speech at pastors' breakfast preceding Hope for Wholeness Conference, February 21, 2003.

15. *Regeneration News,* August 1993, 4.

16. Ibid.

17. *Regeneration News,* February 1991, 1.

18. *Regeneration News,* August 1993, 1.

19. "A Broken Reed," Alan Medinger, *Regeneration News,* July 1989, 2.

## Chapter 13:

1. *Regeneration News,* August 1986, "From the Director/The Chain is Broken," 2.

2. Alan Medinger, *Growth into Manhood,* 234.

3. *Regeneration News,* August 1986, 3.

4. *Regeneration News,* February 1987, 3.

5. Elizabeth Moberly, *Homosexuality: A New Christian Ethic* (Cambridge, England: James Clarke & Co., Ltd., 1983), 35, 36.

6. Moberly, 6.

7. Moberly, 37.

8. Moberly, 51.

9. Moberly, 37.

10. *Regeneration News*, April 1988, 1.

11. Willa Medinger letter to Olivia F., August 10, 1988.

12. Alan's comments on Willa's anger problem in his unpublished book, "God's Sexual Man," copyright 2010, 130, 131, 135.

13. *Regeneration News*, May 1987, 1, 2, 3.

14. "Honor Thy Father," *Regeneration News*, October 1994, 1.

15. Ibid., 3.

## Chapter 14:

1. Willa Medinger interview with author, April 13, 2007.

2. Alan Medinger e-mail to author, June 1, 2010.

3. Alan Medinger e-mail to author, June 1, 2010.

4. Karen C. remarks at Willa's funeral, September 20, 2010.

5. Karen C. phone interview, May 24, 2010.

6. Shelley C. phone interview with author, April 22, 2010.

7. *Regeneration News*, November 1997, 4.

8. Sheri H- e-mail to author, May 8, 2010.

9. Karen phone interview, May 24, 2010.

10. Karen, Ibid.

11. Anita Worthen and Bob Davies, *Someone I Love Is Gay: How Family and Friends Can Respond* (Downers Grove, Illinois: InterVarsity Press, 1996).

12. Karen e-mail to author, June 14, 2010.

13. Sheri e-mail to author, May 8, 2010.

14. Carol e-mail essay to author, "God Used Willa Medinger to Touch My Battered Heart," May 14, 2010.

15. *Regeneration News,* December 1999, 1.

16. *Regeneration News,* Ibid., 3.

17. Cecilia interview with author April 14, 2010.

## Chapter 15:

1. Olivia F. phone interview with author, December 12, 2010.

2. Willa Medinger letter to Olivia, April 10, 1990, in Olivia's private collection.

3. Ibid.

4. Olivia phone interview with author, December 12, 2010.

5. Willa letter to Olivia, January 6, 1991.

6. Willa letter to Olivia, March 19, 1991.

7. Willa letter to Olivia, April 2, 1991.

8. Olivia e-mail to author, January 14, 2011.

9. Willa letter to Olivia, September 20, 1993.

10. Willa letter to Olivia, May 31, 1996.

11. Olivia phone interview with author, December 12, 2010.

12. Ibid.

13. Willa letter to Olivia, December 29, 1999.

14. Alan Medinger e-mail to Olivia, April 8, 2010.

15. Olivia e-mail to author, January 14, 2011.

16. Olivia phone interview with author, December 12, 2010.

## Chapter 16:

1. *Regeneration News*, June 1995, 4.

2. *Regeneration News*, October 1989, 6.

3. Alan Medinger interview with author, March 14, 2007.

4. Ibid. and also *Regeneration News*, May 2001, 1.

5. Kathleen Boatwright interview in *Making Gay History, the Half-Century Fight for Lesbian and Gay Equal Rights,* edited by Eric Marcus, 286.

6. The Founding of Integrity," (http://www.Integrity.org/History/founding.htm).

7. Alan Medinger e-mail to author, August 1, 2007.

8. *Regeneration News*, August 1988, 1.

9. Alan Medinger interview with author, March 14, 2007.

10. John Shelby Spong interview in Marcus, ed., 296-7.

11. *Regeneration News*, February 1991, 4.

12. Kathleen Boatwright interview in Marcus, ed., 323.

13. Ibid., 324.

14. Alan's address to the Episcopal Convention in Phoenix, *Regeneration News*, August 1991, 3.

15. *Regeneration News*, June 1995, 2.

16. Ibid., 3.

17. *Regeneration News*, September 1997, 3.

18. Ibid.

19. Ibid.

20. Alan Medinger interview with author, March 5, 2009.

21. Alan Medinger, "Further Thoughts on Leaving the Episcopal Church," *Regeneration News*, December 1997, 3.

22. *Regeneration News*, October 1997, 4.

23. Alan Medinger letter to author August 1, 2007.

## Chapter 17:

1. Marshall Kirk and Hunter Madsen, Ph.D., *After the Ball: How America Will Conquer Its Fear and Hatred of Gays in the '90s* (New York: Doubleday, 1989).

2. Ibid., xxvi.

3. Ibid., 184.

4. Jeff Konrad, *You Don't Have to be Gay*, (first published by a private group, Pacific Publishing House in Hilo, Hawaii, 1987), mentioned in *Regeneration News*, August 1988, 3.

5. *Regeneration News*, July 1989, 1.

6. *Regeneration News*," January 1990, 1.

7. *Regeneration News*, June 2001, 2.

8. Lani Bersch e-mail to author, February 15, 2011.

9. *Regeneration News*, September 1993, 2.

10. Willa Medinger letter to Olivia, May 10, 1994.

11. Willa letter to Olivia, July 31, 1995.

12. Anita Worthen e-mail to author, February 12, 2011.

13. Sue O'Neill e-mail to author, February 15, 2011.

14. *Regeneration News*, July 1996, 3.

15. Sonia Balcer sent the author a copy of the letter she wrote to Alan Medinger on December 27, 1996, describing her experience interceding in prayer for him.

16. *Regeneration News*, December 1996/January 1997, 3.

17. Willa letter, May 5, 1997.

18. Willa letter to Olivia, May 5, 1997.

19. *Regeneration News*, December 1996/January 1997, 3, 4.

20. Beth Medinger phone conversation with author, February 17, 2011.

## Chapter 18:

1. *Regeneration News*, October 1999, 1, 2.

2. *Regeneration News*, June 1997, 1.

3. Josh Glaser's funeral eulogy for Alan, July 3, 2011 in Christ the King Church, Towson, Maryland.

4. *Regeneration News*, February 1998, 2.

5. *Regeneration News*, April 1997, 2.

6. *Regeneration News*, January 1988, 1 and 4.

7. *Regeneration News*, "Study of Twins Has Important Implications," June 1992, 1 and 3.

8. *Regeneration News*, September 1995, 4.

9. Beth Medinger phone conversation with author, February 17, 2011.

10. *Regeneration News,* November 1998, 4.

11. Laura Medinger phone conversation with author, February 19, 2011.

12. *Regeneration News,* December 1999, 4.

13. *Regeneration News,* June 1999, 2, 3.

14. *Regeneration News,* March 1995, 3.

15. Mario Bergner comments about Alan and Willa from "Genuine Prophets: Alan and Willa Medinger," an essay he wrote and e-mailed to the author on October 14, 2010, as well as from a message he posted April 5, 2010, on the "Willa's Walk" blog, created during her illness.

16. Joe Dallas e-mail to author February 9, 2012.

17. Pastor Ronald Scates e-mail to author, March 22, 2011.

18. Anthony B. e-mail to author, March 7, 2011.

19. Dennis O., "My Story for Alan Medinger's Tribute," e-mail to author, March 24, 2011.

20. Beth and Laura Medinger, e-mail to author, January 18, 2011.

21. Pete Medinger, at Willa Medinger's funeral in Christ the King Church, Towson, Maryland, September 20, 2010.

22. Laura Medinger phone interview with author, February 17, 2011.

23. Beth and Laura Medinger e-mail to author, January 18, 2011.

## Chapter 19:

1. Alan Medinger, *Growth into Manhood,* xii.

2. Ibid., 52.

3. Ibid., 25.

4. Alan Medinger, interview with author April 14, 2010.

5. *Growth into Manhood*, 200.

6. *Growth into Manhood*, 204.

7. Ibid., 205.

8. Ibid., 223.

9. *Regeneration News*, May 2008, 4, and also from a phone conversation between Bob Ragan and the author on January 10, 2014.

10. Alan Medinger interview with author March 15, 2007.

11. Frank Worthen interview with author May 18, 2009.

12. *Regeneration News*, May 2003, 1, as well as Bob Ragan phone interview with author, January 10, 2014.

13. Alan Medinger interview with author March 15, 2007, and Bob Ragan phone interview with author, January 10, 2014.

14. "Commentary: Psychiatry and Homosexuality" by Robert L. Spitzer, in *Wall Street Journal*, May 23, 2001.

15. *Regeneration News*, June 2001, 2.

16. *Wikipedia*, en.wikipedia.org/wiki/Robert_Spitzer_(psychiatrist).

17. Spitzer's article recanting his 2001 article is described by Gary Greenberg in *The Book of Woe: the DSM and the Unmaking of Psychiatry* (New York, Blue Rider Press, 2013), 42, 43.

18. Professor Stanton L. Jones, Ph.D., and Professor Mark A. Yarhouse, Psy.D., *Ex-gays? A Longitudinal Study of Religiously Mediated Change in Sexual Orientation* (Downers Grove, Illinois: InterVarsity Press, 2007).

19. Jones and Yarhouse, Ibid., 17.

20. *Regeneration News*, January/February 2005, 2.

21. *Regeneration News*, July 2006, 4.

22. *Regeneration News,* May 2006, 1.

23. *Regeneration News,* September/October 2008, 3.

24. Bruce McKutcheon quote from phone conversation with author June 6, 2011.

25. *Regeneration News,* July/August 2009, 3.

26. *Regeneration News,* July/August 2009, 3, and follow-up online article at www.RegenerationMinistries.org.

27. Willa Medinger interview with author March 4, 2009.

## Chapter 20:

1. Karen K. phone interview with author, May 24, 2010.

2. Alan Medinger, e-mail to author, June 18, 2009.

3. Alan Medinger, "God's Sexual Man," 132.

4. Willaswalk Care Pages, July 18, 2009.

5. Alan e-mail July 30, 2009.

6. Willaswalk, September 9, 2009.

7. Willaswalk, September 13, 2009.

8. Willaswalk, March 23, 2010.

9. Anita Worthen e-mail to author, February 12, 2010.

10. Andrew Comiskey e-mail to author about his remarks at Alan Medinger's funeral, July 3, 2010.

11. Willaswalk, March 23, 2010.

12. Willaswalk, April 3, 2010.

13. e-mail from Alan to author, April 6, 2010.

14. Alan Medinger interview with author, April 13, 2010.

15. Bruce McCutcheon phone conversation with author, June 6, 2011.

## Chapter 21:

1. Alan Medinger interview with author, March 15, 2007.

2. *Regeneration News,* September/October 2004, 3.

3. *Regeneration News,* September 2010, 2.

## Where Do We Go from Here?

1. Andy Crouch, *Culture Making: Recovering Our Creative Calling* (Downers Grove, Illinois: InterVarsity Press, 2008).

# Bibliography

Bayer, Ronald. *Homosexuality and American Psychiatry, the Politics of Diagnosis.* New York: Basic Books, Inc., 1981.

Bergner, Mario. *Setting Love in Order.* Grand Rapids, Michigan: Baker Books, 1999.

Davies, Bob. "The Exodus Story: The Growth of Ex-gay Ministry." In *The Crisis of Homosexuality.* Edited by J. Isamu Yamamoto. Wheaton, Illinois: Victor Books, A Division of Scripture Press Publications, Inc., 1990.

Greenberg, Gary. *The Book of Woe: the DSM and the Unmaking of Psychiatry.* New York: Blue Rider Press, 2013.

Johnson, Barbara. *Where Does A Mother Go To Resign?* Minneapolis, Minnesota: Bethany House Publishers, 1979.

Jones, Professor Stanton L., Ph.D., and Professor Mark A. Yarhouse, Psy.D. *Ex-gays? A Longitudinal Study of Religiously Mediated Change in Sexual Orientation.* Downers Grove, Illinois: InterVarsity Press, 2007.

Kirk, Marshall and Hunter Madsen, Ph.D. *After the Ball: How America Will Conquer Its Fear and Hatred of Gays in the '90s.* New York: Doubleday, 1989.

Lewis, C.S. Introduction to a translation of St. Athanasius's fourth century treatise, *On the Incarnation,* 1945 [Kindle edition].

Marcus, Eric, editor. *Making Gay History: The Half-Century Fight for Lesbian and Gay Equal Rights.* New York: Harper Collins, 2002.

Medinger, Alan. "God's Sexual Man." Unpublished manuscript, last modified June 2010.

_____. *Growth into Manhood [Resuming the Journey].* Colorado Springs, Colorado: Harold Shaw Waterbrook, 2000.

_____. *Regeneration News,* Volumes I, II, III from 1980 – 1999, plus unbound copies 1999 – 2010.

Moberly, Elizabeth. *Homosexuality: A New Christian Ethic.* Cambridge, England: James Clarke & Co., Ltd., 1983.

Payne, Leanne. *The Broken Image: Restoring Personal Wholeness Through Healing Prayer.* Grand Rapids, Michigan: Baker Books, 1981.

_____. *Heaven's Calling: A Memoir of One Soul's Steep Ascent.* Grand Rapids, Michigan: Baker Books, 2008.

Rogers, Sy and Alan Medinger. "Homosexuality and the Truth." Pamphlet by Exodus International, San Rafael, California, 1990.

Satinover, Jeffrey, M.D. *Homosexuality and the Politics of Truth.* Grand Rapids, Michigan: Baker Books, 1996.

Spiegel, Alix. "The Dictionary of Disorder." In *The New Yorker* 80.41, January 3, 2005.

Spitzer, Robert L., Dr. "Commentary: Psychiatry and Homosexuality." In *The Wall Street Journal,* May 23, 2001.

Worthen, Anita and Bob Davies. *Someone I Love Is Gay: How Family and Friends Can Respond.* Downers Grove, Illinois: InterVarsity Press, 1996.

Worthen, Frank. *Destiny Bridge: A Journey Out of Homosexuality.* Winnipeg, Canada: Forever Books, 2011.

# Additional Resources

Many ministries offer redemptive support for people who struggle with unwanted same-sex attractions.

Regeneration in Baltimore, Maryland, and northern Virginia continues to do Alan and Willa Medinger's good work. (Website is www.regenerationministries.org). They provide "safe and sacred communities where men and women grow in intimacy with Jesus, so those caught in cycles of sexual or relational sin find freedom, and those who have been wounded by the sin of others experience healing" as well as programs of coaching and support for pastors, leaders, parents, spouses, and loved ones of those who struggle.

A number of ministries from the former Exodus International network now make up the Hope for Wholeness network, established by Hope for Wholeness Ministry, in Spartanburg, South Carolina. (Website is www.hopeforwholeness.org). They say "Our desire is to shed light on the complicated issues of sexual and relational brokenness with a special expertise on homosexuality. We hope you find comfort and guidance through this ministry by a personal relationship with Jesus Christ and through godly love demonstrated by God's people. We have experienced freedom in Christ from homosexuality and other forms of bondage and share from this place."

Others have joined the Restored Hope Network, which is "an interdenominational membership-governed network dedicated to restoring hope to those broken by sexual and relational sin, especially those impacted by homosexuality." They "proclaim that Jesus Christ has life-changing power for all who submit to Christ as Lord" and they also "seek to equip His church to impart that transformation." (Website is www.restoredhopenetwork.com).

Exodus Global Alliance remains active, unaffected by the shutdown of Exodus International. They work around the globe, with ministries in Australia, Brazil, and Mexico and an office in Canada. (Website is www.exodusglobalalliance.org). Their work is "proclaiming that a transformed life is possible for the homosexual through the transforming power of Jesus Christ, equipping Christians and churches to uphold the biblical view of sexuality but respond with compassion and grace to those affected by homosexuality, and serving people affected by homosexuality through Christian fellowship, discipleship, counseling, support groups and other services."

Courage is "an international apostolate of the Catholic Church, which ministers to persons with same-sex attractions and their family and friends." (Website is www.couragerc.net).

Desert Stream Ministries, Andrew Comiskey's ministry, (Website is www.desertstream.org) teaches the need for local church support and lists church-based services in more than forty states. They are the creators of the Living Waters program, used by many ministries worldwide. Their mission statement is: "Based on the biblical foundation of compassion, integrity, and dependence on God, [the ministry] proclaims to the world the transforming power of Jesus Christ."

Leanne Payne's Pastoral Care Ministries is now, since her retirement, called Ministries of Pastoral Care, under the leadership of Dr. Gino Vaccaro, assisted by his wife, Cesli, and Dr. Sarah Groen-Colyn. Their mission is "Restoring souls through union with Christ." (Website is www.ministriesofpastoralcare.com).

Redeemed Lives, Mario Bergner's ministry, is located in Ipswich, Massachusetts. They offer pastoral courses, conferences, seminars, and newsletters from an Anglican perspective. (Website is: www.redeemedlives.org).

JONAH, Jews Offering New Alternatives to Homosexuality, located in Jersey City, New Jersey, offers small groups and an online library. (Website is www.jonahweb.org).

# INDEX

# Acknowledgements

MY GREATEST DEBT IS TO Alan and Willa Medinger themselves and their three children as well as their friends and family for granting me interviews and access to information, including all of Alan's newsletters from 1985 to 2010 as well as three chapters from his unpublished second book. Many people at Regeneration generously helped, especially Josh Glaser and Reverend Bob Ragan. Other ministry leaders offered their stories, in particular Katherine Allen, Sonia Balcer, Elaine Silodor Berk, Mario Bergner, Gene Chase, Andrew Comiskey, Joe Dallas, Penny Dalton, Bob Davies, McKrae Game, Arthur Goldberg, Roberta Kenney, Jeanie Smith, Carrie Wingfield, and Frank and Anita Worthen. Pastor Ronald Scates, Bruce McCutcheon, and Lani Bersch kindly helped me, as did many former clients of Regeneration, whose identity I have not disclosed, especially Olivia F. My writer friends Ray Blackston and Sarah Efird offered helpful comments, as did my friend Janet Yusi and my son, Andrew Hartzell. Father Charlie Carlberg (my pastor) of All Saints Anglican Church led a small critique group of Christian friends who gave me helpful insights on the manuscript. Jeanie Smith donated her editing skills as well as the wisdom from her years of friendship with Alan and Willa and her experience leading Set Free Ministry; she read the entire manuscript at least twice, and offered many invaluable improvements. Without encouragement and suggestions from my husband, Thomas Hartzell, and dear friend, Sally Berk, I might have given up the job.

The constant encouragement of my Christian writers group, headed by Nancy Parker, was indispensable. "I didn't know that!" and "This is an important book, Judy!" and all their other comments sharpened and strengthened me.

Thanks go to Tony Moore for taking the author's photo. I'm grateful to Samuel and Tim Lowry, my publishers, for believing in this book.

All mistakes in the book are my own, needless to say. I used to laugh at a professor who used that phrase, but sometimes one must say the needless-to-say things.

For more information about
Judith Hartzell
&
*By God's Design: Overcoming Same-Sex Attractions -A True Story-*
please visit:

www.judithhartzell.com
@JudithHartzell1
www.facebook.com/JudithHartzell

For more information about
AMBASSADOR INTERNATIONAL
please visit:

www.ambassador-international.com
@AmbassadorIntl
www.facebook.com/AmbassadorIntl